THOMAS SOWELL has degrees in economics from Harvard, Columbia, and The University of Chicago and is now a professor of economics at the University of California, Los Angeles. He has been an economist for the U.S. Department of Labor, a project director for the Urban Institute in Washington, and has taught economics at Brandeis, Cornell, Howard, and Rutgers.

He is the author of *Black Education: Myths and Tragedies, Classical Economics Reconsidered, Economics: Analysis and Issues,* and *Say's Law: An Historical Analysis.*

RACE and

ECONOMICS

Also by Thomas Sowell

Black Education: Myths and Tragedies
Classical Economics Reconsidered
Economics: Analysis and Issues
Say's Law: An Historical Analysis

RACE and

THOMAS SOWELL

David McKay Company, Inc.
New York

ECONOMICS

Introduction

Race makes a difference, in economic transactions as in other areas of life. There has been a tendency to pass over this unpleasant fact, or else to deal with it in purely moral terms. It needs to be dealt with in *cause-and-effect* terms as well: How does the extent and the degree of racial discrimination affect the market for goods, services, and factors of production? What kind of institutional arrangements increase or reduce the amount of discrimination? How do the experiences and reactions of various ethnic minorities compare in terms of improving or worsening their economic situation? What sorts of markets are more likely to discriminate in selling goods, or in hiring or promotion policies, and what sorts of markets are more likely to hire or promote on individual merit and to sell products to everyone on the same terms? There is no racial economics in the sense of a different kind of analysis for black people than for white people, or for Jews and Gentiles, but there is an economics of race in the sense that the basic principles of economics can be applied to deepen our understanding of the social problems that revolve around race.

The term "race" will be used here in the broad social sense in which it is applied in everyday life to designate ethnic groups of various sorts—by race, religion, or nationality.

The economic and social conditions of ethnic groups are not limited to races as biologically defined. Indeed, given the complex racial mixtures found in both majority and minority groups in the United States, there would be few pure races to discuss if race were defined biologically rather than socially. For our purposes, social groups will be analyzed as races or ethnic groups if they are generally regarded, and regard themselves, as a socially distinct group with inherited characteristics that set them apart and cause them to encounter different attitudes and behavior than those encountered by the general population. Ethnic labels will be chosen for simplicity and convenience, within the bounds of taste and clarity. There will be no philosophical implications in the use of "black" and "Negro," for example.

One reason for the relative neglect of special racial studies by economists and others has been the feeling that ethnic distinctions and discriminations were a form of "irrationality" which time would tend to erode, if not eradicate. From this viewpoint, there seemed to be little reason for exploring the elaborate context and complex crosscurrents of racial or ethnic phenomena. History, however, gives little support to the view that time automatically erodes racial aversions, fears, and animosities, or even tames the overt behavior based on such feelings. There has been no one-way movement toward improved group relations, but instead many detours, oscillations, and even severe backward movements. Religious intolerance was far less in the Roman Empire than in medieval or modern Europe. Anti-Negro laws and practices became much more prominent and much more severe in the South between 1900 and 1920 than they had been from 1880 to 1900. The Nazis' ruthless campaign of genocide in the middle of the twentieth century exceeded anything ever attempted in the eighteenth or nineteenth centuries. Other examples could be cited of increased group animosity over time, as well as counterexamples of reduced animosity and increased cooperation. The point here is that time as such is not the key factor. It is necessary to look at conditions which influence attitudes, and—particularly in an economic analysis—to study the structure of institutions and the constraints of the market, which affect the translation of subjective attitudes into overt behavior.

The most extreme form of racial-economic relationships, race-based slavery, will be analyzed first (chapter 1), followed by an account of its aftermath in the United States (chapter 2). This is also an important part of the background for understanding the most serious of current American racial problems. In part two the historical experiences of various other American ethnic groups will be analyzed for their economic implications, and for purposes of comparisons among themselves. After these essentially historical explorations, the economics of race is then considered in the third section—first in market transactions (chapter 6) and then in economic activities directed or controlled by the government (chapter 7). Finally, some general conclusions will be developed about the past (chapter 8) and the future (chapter 9) of racial factors in the economic aspect of life.

Contents

PART ONE

Slavery and its Aftermath

Chapter 1

American Slavery

Slavery has existed in various kinds of societies for thousands of years, but American Negro slavery had a peculiar combination of features, whose effects are still felt more than a century after its abolition. Slavery was not an incidental aspect of southern society, but a key feature of the southern economy and the source of the wealth and power of the dominant class in southern society. Earlier in history, dominant classes had held slaves, but the *source* of their domination was elsewhere; in most cases, the slaves were an effect rather than a cause of their wealth and power.

Slavery was, however, the keystone of the southern economy. The crops which slaves raised were the major cash crops of the region. Transportation networks followed the shipping needs of these crops. Social values and customs followed those of the slave owners. Ideas were welcomed or proscribed according to whether they supported or undermined the "peculiar institution" of slavery.[1] Although only a small fraction of the white population of the South owned any slaves,[2] this was—economically, socially, and politically—the most important fraction, and the bulk of the white population shared the vicarious feeling of being part of the dominant race. It was in fact, noticed by many that those whites who did *not* own slaves were usually stronger supporters of slavery and/or more antagonistic toward the slaves than those who did.[3]

The two other key features of American slavery were that it followed racial or color lines and that it was slavery in a democratic country. The fact that it existed in a democratic country meant that it required some extraordinary rationale to reconcile it with the prevailing values of the nation. Racism was an obvious response—a racism far stronger than that which accompanied slavery in undemocratic countries.[4]

Slavery shares certain economic characteristics with other systems of forced labor, such as serfdom, prison labor, and the military draft, but it also has its own distinctive features, and slavery as it existed in the United States prior to the Civil War was a unique institution, even as compared with other slaveholding societies at other times and places. The complexities and contradictions of American slavery derive in part from the economic constraints and imperatives inherent in a system of forced labor, and in part from the historical and institutional peculiarities of American society and of the South in particular.

The most obvious economic feature of slavery is that it is the ultimate in the transfer of wealth from one group to another. An economic system, however, must *produce* as well as *transfer* wealth, and here the peculiarities of slavery become important economic handicaps. The range of work that can be performed under slavery is limited by the need to guard against escape, and to maintain surveillance of the work. Slavery favors those kinds of work in which a large group of workers can labor under the immediate control and direction of a small group of overseers. It is not well adapted to those kinds of work that require wide dispersion of the work force, individual initiative, or considerable trust. Where slaves are a substantial enough proportion of the total population to constitute a potential danger to the system and to the safety of the slave owners, security in a more general sense requires severe limitations on the degree of knowledge—formal education and cultural exposure—which an enslaved people can be permitted. Thus the South made it a crime to teach slaves to read and write,[5] whereas slaves in ancient Greece and in the Roman Empire were often highly educated.[6] In short, a slave economy—as distinguished from isolated slave ownership—reduces the range of work that is feasible with men of a given level of ability, and also reduces the level of ability that it is feasible to develop from men of a given potentiality.

The incentive system of a slave economy further handicaps production. The normal incentives—the desire to keep the current job, the hope of advancing economically, personal pride, the need to secure references for future jobs, etc.—have little application in a slave economy. The basic incentive of fear of punishment is substituted, but the effectiveness of this substitute varies greatly according to the nature of the work. It is most effective for simple work where the quantity and quality of work performed by many can be immediately observed by a few, and where individual workers who fall short of expectations can be easily singled out for punishment. Even here, however, there is little incentive for individuals to exceed expectations. For work requiring individual initiative or judgment, or where the quality of the product will be revealed in later use, or where the identification of the individual worker responsible for good or bad results is not economically feasible, the slave incentive system is ineffective. This further restriction of the range of work in a slave economy applies not only where it is impossible to check up on performance but also where the cost of checking up would be so great as to make it unprofitable.

Forced labor in general is applicable to crude tasks and tends to be performed inefficiently in those. Prison inmates can be forced to produce auto license plates but not watches or cameras, much less works of art or science. Even casual observation of draftees at work on a military post will make clear the meaning of "soldiering" on the job. Human resentment tends to add an element of deliberate sabotage to the regular avoidance of uncompensated work. By all historical accounts—from the southern apologetics of U. B. Phillips to the black militancy of W. E. B. DuBois—all these elements were present in American Negro slavery. Contemporary accounts show innumerable ways in which slaves passively resisted, neglected, sabotaged, and frustrated the workings of the system.[7]

In an agricultural society such as the antebellum South the work restrictions imposed by slavery had devastating consequences. A diversified agriculture requires a wide-ranging knowledge of farming techniques and considerable versatility, care, and initiative in applying it. Slave-based agriculture is therefore less likely to be of this sort and more likely to be essentially a one-crop agriculture with simple routine applied on a mass scale. This was in fact the dominant pattern on southern plantations. The repeated planting of one crop, without rotation, tended to exhaust the soil nutrients, so that plantation owners became known in the South as "land killers." [8] As vast areas of land were exhausted, the slave owners would move on to other land, which would also be exhausted in a matter of years. Under these conditions, "a constant supply of fresh soils" becomes "indispensable." [9]

The tendency of slave agriculture to destroy the fertility of the soil had far-reaching implications. It meant that the South was necessarily *expansionist*. It had constantly to seek the expansion of slavery into the new states as they entered the United States. Where a state was not voluntarily inclined to be a slave state—as in the cases of Missouri and Kansas in the 1850s—organized violence and terror were used by southern invaders against the local settlers.[10] Southerners were among the main instigators and supporters of wars of annexation against Mexico.

The negative effect of slavery on economic efficiency was not limited to the reduced productivity of the slaves and the premature exhaustion of the soil. The slave system on large plantations depended heavily on the policies and practices of the overseer who was directly in charge of the slaves, even though the plantation owner was their legal proprietor. Overseers, who were typically paid according to the size of the current crop, tended to maximize the current output without regard to how this might exhaust the soil or exhaust the slave labor force.[11] Short-run gains were all that mattered. The capital loss on exhausted soil and/or a prematurely aged labor force were borne by the plantation owner. High current production meant that the overseer received not only a larger current income, but also a long-run capital gain in the form of a reputation for demonstrable "results," which would enable him to command a larger salary from future employers.[12] A common comment among contemporary observers of the antebellum South was that slaves were more often overworked and badly treated on plantations where the owner was absent and an overseer left in charge.[13] Such plantations were also in general less well maintained.[14] Southern lore sometimes depicted the overseers as a particularly depraved class, but the economic incentives made their behavior individually rational, and such behavior has tended to follow similar incentive systems in other societies—such as plant managers or farm directors under modern centrally planned economies.[15]

With all its inefficiencies, slavery was still profitable for slave owners, according to modern studies.[16] However, these studies have not attempted to answer the broader and more basic question, whether slavery was efficient from the point of view of the whole society, or even from the point of view of the white population of the South. Here the evidence is harder to specify, much less obtain. It is obvious, almost at a glance, that the area of the United States in which slavery flourished has long been the poorest section of the country, for whites as well as for blacks. Moreover, those parts of the South where slavery was concentrated—Mississippi and Alabama, for example—have long been among the poorest parts of the South. This is not a consequence of the Civil War; it was true well before the outbreak of that war. Nor is it due to climate or the initial fertility of the soil, for the South had an advantage over many northern states in both regards. In short, just as slavery permitted some whites to benefit at the expense of blacks, and overseers to benefit somewhat at the expense of slave owners, so it could permit the whole slave system to profit while imposing a loss on the larger southern society of which it was a part.

The larger southern society paid the price of slavery in many ways, one of which was in the negative attitude toward economic activity in general and work in particular which developed among its white population. The overwhelming majority of white southerners owned no slaves, so that their economic well-being depended upon their own efforts. The southern culture, bred by a slave-owning aristocracy, downgraded economic efficiency, economic motivation, and especially hard, steady work by a white man. Slave societies in general tend to make work somewhat dishonorable in the eyes of free men. Whatever the psychological mechanism or principle, it is empirically apparent from numerous contemporary accounts of the antebellum South that its white people worked less, less carefully, less steadily, and less effectively than those in the rest of the country. They were characterized by a contemporary as "too poor to keep slaves and too proud to work." [17] Frederick Law Olmsted observed, after his celebrated travels throughout the antebellum South: "To work industriously and steadily, especially under directions from another man, is in the Southern tongue, to 'work like a nigger. . . .' " He found most southern whites "disdaining" such a way of life as "beneath them." [18] Where they did work it was in a "thoughtless manner." [19] The large class of southerners known as "poor whites" worked only at intervals—when pressed for money—but not at regular jobs on a regular basis.[20] In Tocqueville's classic *Democracy in America* (1837–38), he contrasted the attitudes toward work among southern and northern whites as so great as to be visible to the casual observer sailing down the Ohio River and comparing the Ohio side with the Kentucky side.[21]

The economic and social conditions among southern whites reflected their general characteristics. Olmsted found that in the South, "the proportion of the free white men who live as well in any respect as our working classes at the North, on an average, is small. . . ." [22] This "lazy poverty" [23] and deprivation existed even where natural resources were readily at hand. The southerners' tendency to "make do" with makeshift arrangements rather than apply themselves to repair was a recurring theme in the literature of the period. [24] When Olmsted found work done efficiently, promptly, and well, in his travels through the South—when he found good libraries, well-run businesses, impressive churches, and other institutions—he almost invariably found them to be run by northerners, foreigners, or Jews. [25] It should be noted, however, that whites in the antebellum South did not come from any substantially different background—genetically or socially—than whites in the North. A different culture developed in the South, around the institution of slavery. Thomas Jefferson argued that slavery was destroying the white people of the South as well as the black. [26]

Part of the cost of the system of slavery is a system of security, not only to prevent escape but to prevent violence and insurrection by those enslaved. Only a part of the cost of this security was paid for by the slave owner himself. Another part—perhaps the largest part—was paid for by the society at large. This cost included not only a military and civil apparatus of force which had to be available, but also an intangible yet very consequential cost in inhibited intellectual development throughout the region.

Slavery not only made it necessary that the black population be kept in ignorance, but ultimately imposed a heavy censorship on what the white population could be allowed to read, [27] including state censorship of the U.S. mail, [28] a clamping down on academic freedom throughout the South as slavery became increasingly controversial in the nineteenth century, [29] and a campaign to stop sending southern young men to northern colleges. [30] These were not simply losses of freedom to a particular generation of antebellum white southerners, which might have represented a temporary psychic loss. It made the South a *permanently* less hospitable place for learning and intellectual life—which meant an enduring economic handicap for the whole region. Southern education has never fully recovered from the atmosphere generated during the slavery controversy and the pressures for orthodoxy which developed their fullest severity after the bitterness of defeat in the Civil War. That this repressive attitude toward education was due to slavery is indicated by many things, aside from the many specific statements by those who promoted it. Prior to the northern antislavery movement of the nineteenth century, which set off the violent southern repression, the southern states were the first to establish state universities.[31] Virginia spent more on colleges than did Massachusetts,[32] and academic freedom was commonplace.[33] In the early 1830s an antislavery speaker was cheered at the University of North Carolina and was shortly thereafter elevated to the state supreme court.[34] By the 1850s all this had changed drastically. Moreover, those parts of the South that escaped the legal repressions, economic retaliations, and mob violence were in areas where there was little slaveholding.[35]

Plantation slavery affected the development of civil institutions—law enforcement, medical facilities, schools, churches, libraries, etc.—throughout the South. Plantations implied vast tracts of land, with widely scattered owners and a slave population with virtually no effective demand for the services of social and economic institutions. The "lazy poverty" life style of the poor whites meant that they too had little effective demand for many of the civilized amenities. The "isolated character of Southern life with its scattered homes and indescribably bad roads did much to hinder the diffusion of education." [36] The fact that the southern white population was widely scattered meant that the cost of providing services was very high in both money and time. Sporadic visits by itinerant preachers had to replace regular church services—thereby tending to produce a dramatic "revival meeting" style of religion suited to occasional redemptions rather than a day-to-day ministry. Law enforcement over vast areas of sparsely inhabited land was also more expensive and never very effective—thereby promoting reliance on individual fighting and killing. Population density was also insufficient to supply public libraries, medical facilities, and other such social institutions. The scattered pattern of living dictated by plantation slavery imposed a very high cost on the white southerners in general, with much of that cost still being paid today.

Modifications of Slavery

One of the indications of the inherent economic deficiencies of slavery is the extent to which it had to be modified in order to get certain kinds of work done. Slaves in lumbering—which required both dispersion and initiative, unlike plantation work—had to be given more freedom and financial incentives, with no slave-driving by the white overseers even attempted.[37] Slaves working under these conditions exhibited an ability to work and a general straightforwardness of manner that was in considerable contrast to the plantation slaves or to the stereotype of the "racial" characteristics of Negroes.[38] Similar results were found among slaves used in diving operations in the Carolina swamps. Here again individual initiative— "the discretion and skill of the diver" [39]—was essential to the task, and therefore the typical slave work pattern had to be broken to get the job done. Slave-driving was replaced by a series of financial incentives, supplemented by an increase in personal freedom on and off the job. Here again the slaves were found to be "admirably skillful" and to insist on continuing to work even when visibly ill [40]—in marked contrast to the behavior of plantation slaves. An additional cost of working with slaves dispersed through large woods or swamps was the greater probability of escape. This, in turn, meant that their treatment and reward had to be such as to diminish the incentive to escape. Yet despite these extra costs to the slave owner under such conditions, the extra productivity of slaves while being "managed as free men" [41] was sufficient to make it profitable. Tobacco manufacturing processes likewise required attention, intelligence, and initiative, and Virginia tobacco factories using slaves relied on financial incentives and more personal freedom, so much "at variance with the basic mores of the plantation system" that *other* whites "hotly opposed" the manufacturers and invoked government power to try to stop them from undermining the plantation slave system.[42]

Urban slavery provided the largest exception or modification of the classic plantation slavery system in the South. While plantation slaves were typically field hands or house servants, urban slaves engaged in a wide variety of occupations, skilled as well as unskilled, in addition to those who worked as domestic servants for their owners. A very large number of slaves were hired out to work for others, the arrangement being made either by the slave owners or by the slaves themselves. The hiring of slaves for craft or industrial work created a situation often requiring "isolated" or even "occasional" work for a variety of individuals, where "the regular supervision of labor was impracticable." [43] To make slavery work economically under these circumstances required, as in other cases, a movement in the direction of personal freedom and payment for work. Slave owners in the city "early and increasingly fell into the habit of hiring many slaves to the slaves themselves, granting to each a large degree of industrial freedom in return for a stipulated weekly wage." [44] The slave owner in such cases was in practice an employment agent collecting a share of the worker's pay without being directly involved in his actual day-to-day work. The net result was that "urban slaveholders were not complete masters" and the necessity of approximating an employer-employee relationship, or an employment agency-worker relationship, "was an admission that the slave concerned could produce more in self-direction than when under routine control, a virtual admission that for him slavery had no industrial justification." This implication was clear even to the leading apologist for southern slavery, U. B. Phillips.[45]

The system of "hiring out" slaves to others, or permitting "self hire" whereby the slave found his own work and shared the proceeds with his owner, were characteristic of urban slavery, and had many social and economic implications. Like independent work in the woods or in the swamp, it presented increased opportunities for escape, increased opportunities to save enough to purchase one's own freedom, and necessitated a reduction of the harshness of plantation slavery and an increase in rewards, both in financial terms and in terms of personal freedom. Frederick Douglass, who was a slave both in the country and in the city, described the urban slave as "almost a free citizen." [46] Douglass, of course, did not mean this as an apology for the system, but merely to point out a contrast, for both urban slaves and even "free persons of color" were subjected to many restrictions and oppressions.[47] The point is that the inherent economic limitations of slavery are demonstrated by the necessity of movement toward employer-employee relationships in work situations involving dispersion, initiative, or trust. There were narrow limits on what could be accomplished by orders and whips.

Although a slave-owner's power to punish a slave was virtually unlimited by either law or custom,[48] there were economic limits on the profits to be derived in this way. Harsh punishment often increased the incidence of slave escapes,[49] and even though the escapees might be recaptured after some period of time, the costs of capture and the loss of a slave's work for weeks or months in the meantime were not negligible considerations—and there was always the possibility that he might never be recaptured. Among newly enslaved Africans, suicides were a significant factor in the sharp decrease of their numbers between their African homeland and the American plantations.[50] Various acts of sabotage—of the work, of the slave-owner's property, or even of the slave's own person

—were other common responses.[51] Arson by slaves was also a significant factor throughout the antebellum South,[52] and a major fear even where it was not a reality. While sufficiently severe and thoroughgoing repression could theoretically stop all of this, the cost of an army of guards or extraordinarily formidable fences and obstacles around a plantation would have eaten up the profits that might have been achieved by more severe slave control. In short, despite the theoretically unlimited power of a slave owner, there were increasing costs associated with the actual exercise of that power, since the slaves also had some options, including sabotage, escape, or individual or collective insurrection. These options had high costs to the slaves, but all occurred with greater or lesser frequency. In Virginia alone there were 198 documented cases of whites (including many slave owners and overseers) killed by slaves over an 84-year period.[53] There were also 91 convictions of slaves for conspiracy, 90 for arson; and rape—despite southern legend—was well down the list, occurring only a fraction as often as murder.[54]

Urban slavery was sufficiently profitable to the slave owners to continue expanding for decades, despite increasingly restrictive laws and despite the large capital loss involved when a slave ran away. Escapes were much easier in the city for a number of reasons: slaves acquired extensive knowledge of the city and extensive contacts with other slaves and with free Negroes, who could conceal them and/or direct them toward freedom. Urban slaves were also more likely to be able to read and write and to be experienced in taking care of themselves and exercising judgment on a day-to-day basis. Many cities were also river ports or ocean ports, which facilitated escape. Moreover, the very size and anonymity of the city enabled some escapees to continue living and working in the same city without being recaptured.[55] The numbers of escapes in the cities were very large. Police records for 1856–57 in New Orleans alone showed 913 arrests of escaped slaves over a fifteen-month period—and for cities in general those who were never caught have been estimated as being "several times as numerous as those who were captured." [56] By contrast, permanent escape from a slave plantation was the exception rather than the rule,[57] though temporary running away was common[58] enough to provide a living to professional slave hunters and specially trained dogs.[59] For a slave owner to move a slave from a plantation to the city, or for a city slave hirer or slave trader to bring a slave into the city, was therefore to increase greatly the risk of a large economic loss. The fact that urban slavery expanded for many years despite this is further indication of the greater productivity of labor under freer conditions with financial incentives. It also exposes the weakness of the arguments that the economic deficiencies of southern slavery were due to deficiencies of Negroes, as such, rather than of slavery as a system.

Whatever benefits urban slavery might confer on a slave owner or a slave, it seriously undermined the institution of slavery as a whole. It was therefore constantly opposed, restricted, and ultimately reduced by a succession of laws and concerted campaigns to crack down on it and its consequences. The security necessary for a slave economic system is only partly the result of overseers, fences, patrols, and slave-retrieval institutions. It depends also on psychological preventive measures, including keeping the slave overawed, dependent, and regarding his condition as somehow inevitable or even "natural." Urban slavery made all this more difficult than on a plantation. Urban slaves either exercised considerable independence themselves or daily saw others of their race who did. Instead of working under the direct supervision of a white overseer and being supplied their food, clothing, and housing by the slave owner, many urban slaves found their own jobs, working for employers they chose and leaving to work for someone else if they did not like the job, managed their own money, and exercised their own judgment in providing themselves with the necessities of life, making sure to pay their owner his share of their earnings in order to continue to enjoy some degree of freedom. Moreover, they were in constant contact with the "free persons of color" who were concentrated in the cities. This alone undermined the attempt to have them regard slavery as a natural or inevitable consequence of being black. While most free Negroes were far from prosperous, some had achieved enough financial security, education, and even some distinction to at least raise doubts about the racial stereotypes which were an indispensable part of the security system of the slave economy. Though wealthy men were very rare among the black population, they were—in absolute terms—numerous.[60] And only a few prosperous free Negroes were necessary to undermine a lifetime of mind conditioning of slaves to acceptance of inferiority.

Urban Negroes, slave and free, engaged in all sorts of commercial transactions with whites—legal and illegal—under conditions which frequently undermined all pretense of racial superiority and inferiority.[61] The laws against teaching Negroes to read and write were unenforceable in the city, and were openly flouted in urban centers throughout the South.[62] Free Negroes taught slaves, slaves taught each other, or they even organized schools. One contemporary observer noted that: "The very prohibition has stimulated exertion" toward education.[63]

One of the economic weaknesses and sources of instability in all systems of forced labor is the greater economic value of a given individual's labor as a free man than his value as a subjugated worker. Where a man can be owned as a capital asset, even the purely economic value of that asset is greater to himself than to anyone else. Anyone can own his value as a forced laborer, but only the man himself can own his value as a free man. Where any economic asset has different values to different potential owners, it tends to be traded from those who reap a smaller return to those who stand to reap a larger return. In an ideally functioning economy, selling a slave to the highest bidder would mean selling him to himself—even if he had no desire for freedom, as such, but only bid on the basis of his anticipated future returns. Despite this abstract tendency in economic theory, the actual circumstances and institutions in real life may inhibit, reduce, or totally thwart such mutually beneficial arbitrage. However, it does not always or inevitably do so. In European serfdom, the value of the serf's time to himself exceeded its value to the lord to whom he was bound, and so, over a long period of time, the serfs bought their way out of feudal duties. In the Roman Empire, where slaves were more of a business and less of a "way of life," slave owners maximized their profits by selling slaves their freedom. In the antebellum South, there were many individual instances of slaves purchasing their freedom, but it was not a major social phenomenon. Here, however, it was prevented by very severe legal restrictions on the freeing of slaves—these restrictions, like the restrictions on urban slavery, based on the principle that the dangers to slavery as an economic system superseded the individual benefits of individual slave owners or slaves.

A growing population of free Negroes raised the cost of maintaining slavery merely by their existence as examples of free black men. In addition, they were a potential source of knowledge, help, and encouragement to escaped or rebellious slaves. Where they were freed without adequate preparation for life as free men, they were a potential social problem and entailed social costs. In all these ways, "free persons of color" created large costs for a slave society, even though it was usually beneficial economically for slave owners and slaves to arrange for the purchase of freedom. In a thoroughgoing slave system, such as that of the southern plantation, it was almost inevitable that freed slaves would be unprepared for freedom, since the qualities needed for life as a free man were the opposite for those needed for life as a slave. Independence, initiative, pride, and self-direction, were not assets but were personally dangerous attributes in a slave.

In the earlier history of the United States, freeing a

slave was a relatively easy and straightforward procedure, so that slaves might buy their own freedom, or be rewarded with freedom for outstanding service, or be freed by individuals conscience-stricken at the moral implications of slavery (the Quakers) or during times of high concern with ideals (as in the wake of the American Revolution), or by individuals on their deathbed, viewing the world in a new perspective. Such manumissions created a small but growing class of free Negroes, but at no time did it reach proportions that would threaten to erode slavery itself, for the manumissions were much less than the natural increase of the slave population.[64] Nevertheless, the implication of a free black population was not lost on supporters of slavery as an economic system. As early as the seventeenth century, laws began to appear restricting the freeing of slaves,[65] except for unusual conditions, with elaborate documentation, troublesome requirements, and involved and costly legal procedures. Some southern states required a special act of the state legislature for freeing each slave.[66] The laws were so strict that some free Negroes legally owned their own family members as slaves, simply because there was such difficulty in formally freeing them. Indeed, *most* ownership of slaves by free Negroes was only this purely formal ownership of relatives for lack of legal authority to free them.[67] These laws spread and grew in severity as time passed and the free black population grew. Several southern states specifically prohibited the freeing of slaves by last will and testament.[68]

Peculiarities of the South

Why did other slave societies permit the purchase of freedom by slaves, while this became almost impossible legally in the antebellum South? Why the pervasive and deep-reaching racism which characterized American slavery much more than slavery in ancient times or even the contemporary enslavement of Africans in the rest of the Western world, including Latin America? In short, why was American slavery *unique,* and why was the South unique as a region of the United States? The peculiarity of American Negro slavery as compared to other slave systems has been commented on by many scholars. So too has the peculiar regional economic and social pattern of the South, which has been characterized as "not quite a nation within a nation, but the next thing to it." [69]

Many individual features of American slavery can be found in other forms of slavery, but the peculiar *combination* of these features would be difficult, if not impossible, to find elsewhere: (1) slavery in a democratic nation, (2) slavery as the dominant feature of the whole southern economy, (3) slavery in a country where local control was the dominant political fact of life, (4) slavery under climate and soil conditions that permitted and promoted the most extreme form of direct slave-driving, and (5) slavery based upon highly visible differences in race.

Democracy and Racism From its very beginning, whatever its institutional or social realities, the United States of America symbolically represented freedom and democracy—to itself and to the world. In seeking its own freedom, America had "fired the shot heard round the world"—and echoing for generations to come. Slavery, the most obvious antithesis of everything the country stood for, could be reconciled with American social and political philosophy only by regarding slaves as a special exception among human beings—or as subhuman beings. The American Dilemma made famous by Gunnar Myrdal was in fact present from the inception of the country, and deeply felt, by all indications. During the full fervor of American revolutionary ideals, some escaped the dilemma by simply freeing their slaves. Voluntary manumissions increased greatly in the period immediately following the Revolution.[70] In addition, a succession of northern states prohibited the importation of slaves, and then abolished slavery entirely.[71] Where slavery persisted, slave codes were liberalized to make manumission easier[72] and to offer some protection to slaves against cruelties.[73] Thomas

Jefferson became prominent in the campaign to get slavery abolished nationally, and George Washington expressed his hope that slavery would ultimately be abolished, declaring in his will that all his own slaves should be freed.[74] Antislavery spokesmen were common in the North after the Revolution,[75] and even in slaveholding Virginia, many of its most prominent leaders—including Jefferson, Washington, Madison, and Patrick Henry—publicly advocated emancipation,[76] as did innumerable less famous southerners at this time.

Slavery was, of course, not abolished. Nor was it seriously threatened in the South, where most slaves lived. The point here is simply that the American Dilemma—which Jefferson called "justice in conflict with avarice and oppression" [77]—was an important social and political reality. One way out of this dilemma was to proclaim black people inferior, incapable of taking care of themselves, dangerous, and the like. Racism has been common in all ages and in virtually all parts of the world. What was peculiar about racism in the South was the extremes to which this doctrine was carried and the powerful emotions behind it. What the experience of the postrevolutionary period suggests is that the ideals of the country made extreme racism *necessary* for slavery to be perpetuated. In despotic countries, where everyone is unfree to one degree or another, no special ideology needs to be invoked in defense of slavery. Throughout Latin America, under the iron rule of the Spanish monarchy, slavery was accepted much more casually than it could be accepted in the United States, and while racial arrogance and racial oppression occurred in these countries, then and now, it never approached the pervasive fanaticism reached in the United States. The difference was not one of humanitarianism. Slaves were treated at least as brutally in most Latin American countries as in the United States, and perhaps even more brutally.[78] The real difference was that these countries did not find it necessary to rationalize their actions with a racial ideology and racial stereotypes. "Sambo is a uniquely American product," according to

historian Stanley Elkins, who could find no such stereotype in Latin American countries with a black population
and a history of slavery.[79]

The Economy In the years following the American
Revolution, the complete abolition of slavery seemed to
many a realistic possibility. Not only were the ideals of the
country inconsistent with slavery, the economic and social
disadvantages of slavery were also increasingly apparent
to many. However, all hope of abolition was destroyed by
the invention of the cotton gin in 1793. Cotton production
now became immensely profitable and spread rapidly
through the South, promoting the growth of great plantations and rapidly increasing the value of slaves. The most
fertile land for cotton was a massive area of dark soil going
through several states of the Deep South, known as "the
black belt"—first from the color of its soil, and then from
the color of the slaves concentrated in this region.[80] The
South in general became the "cotton kingdom." Cotton
not only gave slavery a new economic lease on life,
precluding any early or easy abolition, it also molded the
slave system into the classic southern pattern of *plantation*
slavery. Plantation slavery was the most thoroughgoing
form of slavery, involving the greatest subjugation, isolation, and dependence of the slave. While plantation
slavery existed in other countries, and had the same
general character in other countries, it was not so exclusively the dominant form of slavery as it was in the
American South. The plantation was crucially important
in the development of the South, both economically and
ideologically. The plantation enjoyed its greatest economic
advantages over alternative systems of production where
there was a rich land suitable for one crop to be cultivated
on a large scale. There were important economies of scale
in the production of sugar,[81] rice,[82] wheat,[83] and cotton,[84]
though small-scale cotton production was also feasible.[85]
Crops such as tobacco, which needed "judicious care at
nearly every turn" [86] required small-scale production
under careful supervision. Within the South, those regions

whose soil and climate was most suitable for one-crop plantation slavery were regions of the heaviest concentrations of field slaves, who were the most severely worked and roughly treated slaves. Precisely in those regions, where economic conditions promoted the greatest working of slaves like animals, the ideology that Negroes were in fact subhuman was strongest—and remained strongest.

In the South, states of the "black belt" were the first to tighten up the slave codes that had been relaxed somewhat after the American Revolution.[87] Later, when laws restricting the free expression of abolitionist sentiment were passed throughout the South, those in the Deep South carried the strongest penalties on the books,[88] and were less likely to modify those penalties in practice.[89] In punishment of slaves for violations of the slave codes, in the Deep South, "flogging could legally be more severe." [90] Prohibitions on manumission were more severe in the Deep South.[91] Contemporary observers found the general treatment of slaves was more severe in the Deep South.[92] The more liberal parts of the South, down through the years, have been those parts which in antebellum days were "ill adapted to an economy of big plantations." [93] The South varied enormously in the degree to which the white population was dominated by large planter-slave owners or by small independent free white farmers. In the rich cotton counties of the Mississippi delta, small non-slave-owning white farmers were "not to be found" except in minor peripheral roles, while elsewhere in the South, "they comprised nearly the whole population." [94] Records of the pre-Civil War South show "all the more fertile portions of the coastal plain appear as districts of Negro majority in the population maps of 1860 and after, as an effect of the slave-plantation system." [95]

The erosion-prone Piedmont region[96] and the rocky Blue Ridge areas[97] were not conducive to massive slaveholdings,[98] and slaves were accordingly a much smaller proportion of the population than elsewhere in the South. While the pre-Civil War South as a whole, like the modern South until recent years, voted solidly for conservative

Democrats, in the western or Piedmont sections of North Carolina and Virginia and in eastern Tennessee, there was strong support for the Whigs, who were more liberal.[99] The whole state of Kentucky likewise had relatively few slaves, did *not* prohibit the teaching of Negroes to read, and had relatively mild laws on the discussion of abolitionist sentiments, in contrast to the severe restrictions elsewhere in the South.[100] Berea College in Kentucky was founded in 1858 as the only school in the South with both black and white students. Such antislavery sentiments as existed in the South were centered in this same Piedmont region of eastern Tennessee,[101] Kentucky,[102] western Virginia,[103] and North Carolina. In Olmsted's travels through the slave South, he found in North Carolina "less bigotry" and "more freedom of conversation" on the subject of slavery than in any other state.

Slaves there were more typically family servants and less often field hands.[104] It was not merely the smaller number of slaves, but the different roles they played which correlated with a less fierce racism among the whites. In short, there was not as urgent a *need* to believe blacks subhuman as in regions where slaves were driven like beasts.

Slavery in the North was nowhere a dominant economic system. Neither the climate nor the soil lent themselves to mass plantation agriculture. The longer and colder winters would have meant supporting an idle labor force much of the year, given that the diversified and individualized domestic tasks and seasonal occupations of small farmers were incompatible with the basic economic features of slavery. When the North abolished slavery, it lost relatively few workers. Moreover, its emancipation laws usually announced the *subsequent* illegality of slavery after some specified date, so that existing slaves were sold into the South. As Tocqueville remarked in his classic *Democracy in America* in 1835, "the Americans abolished the principle of slavery, they do not set their slaves free." [105] The North thereby escaped one of the basic dilemmas of slavery, namely, that the characteristics desirable in a slave and those desirable in a free man are so opposite that newly freed slaves from a system of total subjugation are seriously handicapped for functioning as free men. Many of the North's slaves were simply sent South. Later, during the abolitionist controversies, many southern whites bitterly complained that they had no such options as the North had when it freed its slaves. The large external cost of slavery would have to be paid by the South itself when emancipation came.

Where slavery existed as a pervasive economic system of total subjugation, as in the South, there was no longer an option open to white southerners to end it if and when its economic disadvantages to them exceeded its advantages. Increasingly, southerners who were aware of both the moral and economic problems of slavery were driven to defend it simply as a means of holding off inevitable social problems when masses of people condemned to slavery were faced with freedom and its responsibilities. Many southerners who called slavery the "curse" of the region nevertheless defended it as the lesser of possible evils.[106] Plans to resettle the slaves in Africa abounded, despite repeated failures of such schemes, suggesting perhaps a desperate desire rather than a realistic possibility. Although Tocqueville said, "God forbid that I should seek to justify the principle of Negro slavery," he nevertheless conceded that the southern whites had gotten themselves into an impossible situation, for it was "almost an impossibility" to get out of slavery without paying a heavy social cost.[107] This was long before the Civil War, which proved to be an even heavier social cost than anyone had anticipated.

Latin American Slavery

Slavery was begun, sustained, and ended much more easily in other countries than in the United States. Yet despite its uniqueness, southern plantation slavery was in a sense the most authentic slavery—the most thorough human subjugation. Slavery elsewhere abounded in modifications tending in the general direction of more freedom. Racism alone cannot account for the "peculiar institution" of the South, for the Spanish government and its colonial administration in America were at least equally explicit and determined that white supremacy should rule in the state, the church, the society, and the economy.[108] The difference between the American South and other contemporary slave societies was not in their original intent but in their economic, geographic, and political conditions.

Slavery was common throughout the ancient world.[109] Many of the slaves were captives taken in wars and their previous conditions and education covered a wide range, often being superior to that of their owners. Although there might be arrogance and cruelty toward slaves, there was no pervasive, emotion-laden belief in their innate inferiority. Roman slaves were often exploited by being held for ransom from their native lands or by selling individual slaves their own freedom. Laws covered what could be done by slaves and to slaves.[110] In short, to the ancients slavery was a reality but not an *issue,* and time produced many modifications and variations of the institution, allowing various degrees of freedom within slavery and permitting various ways out of slavery.[111]

Modern slavery in the European and transplanted European civilizations was more clearly *race-based* slavery—predominantly the enslavement of Africans by various Europeans. Racism was a natural consequence, but its impact varied enormously from country to country. Even within the United States racism varied noticeably with the economy and the soil, which determined the severity of slave-driving.

Cuba and Virginia provide striking examples of the differences between slavery in the American South and slavery elsewhere in the Western Hemisphere. Cuba and Virginia are of approximately equal size and contained a similar number of blacks and whites when they were both slaveholding colonies. Cuba was the colony of an autocratic Spanish government which tightly controlled all aspects of its local life.[112] Virginia was initially the colony of a freer British government which allowed much more local control; and before slavery reached its peak, Virginia became part of an independent nation.[113] Adam Smith noted that "even in ancient times, slavery was more severe in democratic countries." [114] The greater freedom of the individual from state control under democracy meant the greater freedom of the slave owner to do as he pleased with his slaves, regardless of society's interests or philosophy. In this case one man's freedom was literally another man's subjugation. In societies less dependent on popular support, slavery—like every other aspect of life—was subject to state policy. In Latin America it was also subject to the policies of the Roman Catholic church. The owner of a slave was his master only within limits set by these two powerful organizations. Perhaps equally, or even more important, slave owners were limited in the exercise of their power by economic conditions very different from those in the southern United States.

The inhabited portions of Cuba during its early years were largely urban. The interior countryside was unexplored wilderness rather than a locale for plantations. Cuba's great plantation crop—sugar—required large amounts of capital for processing equipment, and this was available only later in the island's development, long after the pattern of Cuban life and Cuban slavery had already been established. In the formative years of the colony, Cuban slaves were predominantly *urban* slaves, and even after the later development of the sugar industry, plantation slavery never accounted for a majority of those held in bondage,[115] much less a large majority, as it did in much of the American South.

In Cuba as in America, urban slavery was very different from plantation slavery. Cuban plantation slavery, where it existed, was at least as brutal and degrading as plantation slavery in the United States.[116] This suggests that it was not so much the influence of church and state (whose power extended to plantations) that made Cuban slavery as a whole milder than American slavery, but the different economic settings in which it took place. The dominant urban slavery of Cuba was one in which slaves worked in a wide variety of occupations,[117] often under the "hiring out" system in which the slave could be "a free artisan in all but name." [118] This was not fundamentally different from American urban slavery. What was different was that urban slavery in Cuba was the earliest and predominant form of slavery, developing in response largely to its own economic needs, which forced more freedom for the slaves as a means of achieving greater economic efficiency. American urban slavery developed in a society dominated by the needs of plantation slavery—indeed, dominated economically and politically by plantation owners—which was therefore constrained by the need to avoid undermining the total subjugation of slaves required by plantation slavery. In short, the *psychological* subjugation of plantation slaves was the overwhelming consideration that shaped southern policy and southern thinking, even toward Negroes who were not plantation slaves. Part of the cost of maintaining plantation slavery was borne by other parts of the economy, which were not allowed to develop according to their own economic needs.

Urban slavery in Cuba was not subjected to the constraints of plantation owners, and so developed even further in the direction of free employer-employee relationships than did U.S. urban slavery. Moreover, free Negroes were not a menace to the economic system, so that manumission need not be so restrictive. The result was that the "free coloreds" in Cuba were much more numerous and increased much more rapidly than in Virginia. Only 11 percent of the Negro population of Virginia was free on the eve of the Civil War, compared with 35 percent of the Negro population of Cuba which was free at that time.[119] The purchase of freedom by a slave was common in Latin America,[120] and voluntary manumission by slave owners was encouraged by the Catholic church and by social mores.[121]

Another important economic difference between Spanish colonies and English colonies was that many working-class white people immigrated to the British colonies in America by selling themselves into indentured labor for a fixed number of years (usually five), while there was no equivalent way for working-class Spaniards to finance their passage to the Western Hemisphere. This meant that in such places as Cuba there was a lack of white workers—skilled and unskilled—in most urban occupations, so that slaves and free Negroes came to dominate such occupations.[122] They were, in short, a valuable part of the economic system, rather than a peripheral and undermining element. This crucial fact contributed to the steady erosion of racial restrictions. While the Spanish and colonial governments were officially committed to white supremacy in principle, the economic realities led to tacit acceptance of blacks in many high-level occupations which they were officially forbidden to engage in.[123] Some black professionals and military officers, were simply listed officially as "white." [124] The erosion of racial occupational barriers continued over the years, despite official laments, to the point where official "exceptions" were issued and finally these exceptions were routinely available, on a large scale, upon payment of certain fees.[125]

The term "racism," here and elsewhere, conceals more than it reveals. Cuba was as "racist" in philosophy as the American South, but its *actual behavior* was very different, in response to different circumstances. As a cause-and-effect explanation, it is not enough to say what people's desires and intentions are. What must also be considered are the inherent constraints of the situation within which they act. In economic terms, what must be considered is the *cost* of translating subjective attitudes into overt behavior.

General Summary

While slavery and freedom are opposite in concept, in real life there are shades or degrees of freedom, ranging from the fullest possible exercise of freedom consistent with human society to the most complete subjugation of mind and body. The fullest subjugation has been found to be economically incompatible with the most efficient performance of many kinds of tasks—particularly tasks requiring dispersion, initiative or judgment. When individuals subject to forced labor—slaves, prison inmates, draftees, etc.—have been assigned to such tasks, it has usually been found necessary to give them a greater degree of freedom and/or economic incentives to get the job done right at low cost. Full subjugation has been found to be viable with simple, routine tasks, of such a nature that they can be performed under the eye of overseers, with individual responsibility for poor work being immediately detected and punished on the spot. These conditions were met for the staple crops grown on southern plantations—cotton, sugar, and rice. It was not met for tobacco, which required more individual care in growing and manufacturing, and which was therefore grown on smaller farms, by either free white farmers or by slaves not driven in the old plantation style.

Economic conditions, including soil and climate, determined where it was profitable to work slaves on plantations and where in smaller groups with varying degrees of freedom and incentives. Economies of scale and diseconomies of scale are common in all production—agricultural or manufacturing—but the quantities of output at which the diseconomies begin to outweigh the economies differ according to the product in question. This means that whatever the *inclination* of slave owners, their actual behavior was limited by the crop they were growing and this in turn was limited by the climate and soil where they were. The land most suitable for cotton production became the land where plantation slavery was most concentrated. In turn, the attitudes and ideologies of this region of slave-driving were those providing the strongest justification for slavery in terms of the most degraded picture of the Negro race. Those parts of the South least adaptable, by climate and soil, to plantation slave crops were those in which racism did not achieve the same degree of fervor in word and deed. This is a difference not only between the Deep South and other parts of that region, but reflected even more localized differences, as in the contrast between eastern North Carolina, where cotton plantations flourished,[126] and western North Carolina, where few plantation slave crops were grown, and which became the center of the state's liberalism.[127] Similarly, in Tennessee, where the soil of the eastern part of the state is "light" in comparison to the "rich" soil in the middle and the "very rich" soil in the western part,[128] slavery "maintained only a feeble foothold" in the east where the liberal elements had a "strong following." [129] Much of the liberalism of the antebellum South, and of the later South, was localized in the Piedmont region of western North Carolina, eastern Tennessee, Kentucky, and western Virginia.

The "economic determinism" suggested here does not imply that people consciously formulated ideologies to justify their economically motivated actions. It does suggest that (1) moral justification was especially important to Americans, in view of the dominant ideals of the country, and that (2) the more severe the treatment of black people, the more justification—i.e., racism—was needed. This is further indicated by (a) the tendency toward increasing freedom for Negroes right after the American Revolution—both under slavery and by freeing Negroes from slavery, and by (b) the milder racism, in word and deed, in countries whose ideologies required no elaborate justifications for deprivation of freedom.

The severe and degrading treatment of slaves in the United States had important social as well as ideological implications. The degree of subjugation required by plantation slavery was incompatible with the development of either work patterns or personality traits beneficial to a free man. By contrast, systems of slavery such as that in Cuba, in which most slaves were not totally subjugated, provided many gradations of conditions through which an individual could move on the road to freedom, acquiring the knowledge, experience, and personal development to prepare him for ready transition to the world of a free man. By the time slavery was abolished in Cuba in 1886, most Negroes were no longer slaves anyway.[130] The same was true in Brazil.[131] In the American South, the overwhelming bulk of Negroes were slaves, without any opportunity to prepare for freedom, when Lincoln signed the Emancipation Proclamation.

One of the most important differences between slavery in the United States and in Latin America was that in the latter countries, being Catholic, marriage was a sacrament that even the slave owners had to respect. Husbands and wives could not be sold separately, nor was sexual molestation of female slaves legal.[132] Both provisions were unknown in U.S. law or customs.[133] A much stronger tradition of family stability existed among Negroes in other parts of the Western Hemisphere. Even under slavery, over half the children born to Cuban blacks were products of marriage, whereas virtually none were legitimate in the United States at the same time.[134]

While in part the differences between Latin America and the United States reflect economic conditions, there were also philosophical and traditional differences as well. The utter subjugation characteristic of American slaves was paralleled in law and practice in the British West Indies.[135] In Britain, as in the United States, slavery was an alien concept for which their law had made no provision. By contrast, slavery in Spain and Portugal was centuries old and had developed elaborate legal precedents long before slavery developed in the American colonies.[136] The powerful influence of the Catholic church had no counterpart in British or American religious groups, who were either powerless to affect the treatment of slaves,[137] or even served as apologists for slavery itself.[138] In Brazil, as early as the eighteenth century, there were "not only Negro priests, but even black bishops." [139]

Emancipation in Latin America was not a sudden, cataclysmic, or providential event occurring to black people en masse. Freedom was achieved individually by degrees, in Cuba and Brazil at least, and most of the black population was freed in a continuous stream, with only a fraction left to be freed as a bloc when slavery was finally declared illegal. In contrast to the agony and destruction of the American Civil War, in Latin countries "the abolition of slavery was achieved in every case without violence, without bloodshed, and without civil war. . . ." [140]

Just as democracy entailed an elaborate hypocrisy and racism as accompaniments to Anglo-American slavery, so this powerful racism forced an elaborate hypocrisy with regard to racially mixed offspring—who were common in all contemporary systems of slavery. Mulattoes abounded in Latin America, but were also quite common in the American South. In Latin American countries the offspring of white slave owners and black slave women were openly acknowledged and often freed, while Anglo-American slave owners could not socially afford any such acknowledgment and the law prevented manumission in most cases anyway. [141] It was common to blame mulatto children on the overseers, or on "po' white trash" nearby, but at least one contemporary observer noted common resemblances between mulatto children and the children of the slave owners. [142] Some slave owners even sold the women and/or the children "to remove a future source of embarrassment." [143]

The postslavery experiences of black people in the United States have differed from those of black people in Latin America, just as their conditions under slavery differed. In general, the status of Negroes and mulattoes rose much earlier and faster in Latin American countries than in the United States. Many achieved high positions in Latin American countries even before slavery was ended. There is no evidence that those Negroes originally enslaved in South America were any different from those enslaved in North America, so there is no basis for assuming any biological or genetic differences that could account for the greater success of one than the other. However, neither can it be assumed that all differences in current success are due to differences in current racial discrimination. Black immigrants to the United States have succeeded economically, educationally, and in other ways much more than native black Americans,[144] under the existing level of racial discrimination, which is largely the same for both. It is not merely that black Americans are denied some current opportunities but that they were long denied the more basic opportunities to fully develop their abilities themselves.

Chapter 2

The Economic Evolution of Black Americans

Just as it is necessary to understand the general historical background and current institutional context within which black Americans live and move, so it is also necessary to understand that there is not, and never has been, a homogeneous black population in the United States. There have always been, not only great individual differences but, more importantly from a social point of view, great class differences among American Negroes. There have also been great changes in the American society and economy in different time periods, and these changes have accelerated, retarded, or even sharply reversed the progress of black Americans. Finally, it is necessary to understand that the internal social structure and system of values among black Americans has been changing considerably over the past two centuries, sometimes with extreme rapidity during particular periods of stress.

Among both European and Oriental immigrants to the United States, great differences have existed between those families in a particular ethnic group who arrived earlier and those families in the same ethnic group who arrived later on American soil, as well as great differences between those individual members of a particular family who were in the "first generation," the "second generation," etc. For American Negroes the parallel differentiation is not the time of arrival in America, but (1) the time of being freed from slavery, and (2) the time of movement from the rural South into a modern, industrial and commercial economy, usually—but not always—in the North.

Antebellum "Free Persons of Color"

Although slavery as it existed in the United States did not produce as large a class of freedmen before its abolition as in Latin America, nor allow them as much economic or social opportunity, nevertheless there were in absolute numbers many individuals and families in this category from early colonial times, and this free black population grew over time, amounting to more than 11 percent of the total Negro population of the United States before the Civil War.[1] This probably understates the free population a little, since free Negroes sometimes technically "owned" family members, who would be officially listed as slaves, though free in fact. Moreover, the population of "free persons of color" was far more important than their numbers alone would indicate, for long after slavery had ended they supplied a disproportionate share of the economic and cultural elite of the emerging black community.[2] Booker T. Washington was "up from slavery," but W. E. B. DuBois was not, nor were most of the founders of the NAACP or many other contemporary leaders in numerous local black communities. The differential advantages of this small class are an important aspect of the evolution of the black community in America, and an important clue to the larger question of the role of particular economic and social variables in the progress of any people.

The first Africans brought to colonial America in the seventeenth century were treated very much like the much larger class of white indentured servants, and were freed at the end of a fixed period of time.[3] By the end of the century, however, this practice had ceased, as the legal status of the black bondsman evolved toward that of classic total slavery for life for the individual and perpetual enslavement of his descendants. From this point on, until the Emancipation Proclamation, the freeing of a slave was the result of special circumstances rather than something occurring either automatically or in an institutionally predictable way. One of the most important special circumstances was that the slave owner was the father of the individual who was freed. Although it was the exception rather than the rule for slave owners to free their illegitimate offspring by slave women, nevertheless, of those relatively few slaves who were freed in the antebellum period, a disproportionate percentage were of mixed parentage. Mulattoes constituted 37 percent of the free Negro population in 1850, though only 8 percent of the slave population.[4] However, the term "mulatto" was rather narrowly defined to mean persons half or more white, but publicly identified as Negro. It excluded those "passing" as white and also Negroes with only a few white ancestors. Where slaves were freed because they were the owner's children, they were often given preparation—education and/or financial support—to enable them to get a start in life.[5]

Another source of free Negroes were those who purchased their freedom and those who simply escaped. Neither of these achievements was easy, and both generally required the slave to be in some unusually favorable position. To purchase freedom required that there be (1) free time available in which to work for oneself, (2) a ready market for one's work, and (3) a slave owner willing to permit such an arrangement and honorable enough to carry out his part of the bargain after the slave paid him the money, since there was no law or institution (such as the Catholic church in Latin America) to handle or control such a transaction. Running away was common on plantations throughout the South, but permanent escape was rare. There were no uncharted tropical hinterlands to which one might flee and survive in the wild, as in Latin America. Both self-purchase and successful escape required a privileged position among slaves. A house servant, a skilled artisan, or an urban slave was more likely to have the personal development and the knowledge of the world beyond the plantation necessary either to escape or to be able to carry out a long program leading to self-purchase. Mulattoes were again likely to be over-represented among those slaves placed in such a favorable position, both because of a general favoritism of whites toward mulattoes and because there were often illicit family ties involved. Almost half of the Negro population of the major antebellum southern cities were officially listed as "mulatto" [6] (despite the restricted meaning given the term), partly as a result of miscegenation in the city itself, due to an excess number of white men over white women and an excess number of black women over black men in southern cities. However, mulattoes were apparently not as much overrepresented among escapees and self-purchasers as among those voluntarily freed and given a start.

Newly freed Negroes usually had neither the capital, the personal development, nor the opportunities necessary for economic success. It was a struggle to stay alive, and not all won even that struggle. The free black population of the United States grew at a slower rate than the slave population,[7] despite the fact that the free population was increasing by manumission and escape as well as by natural reproduction. Initially the free Negroes experienced all the agonies of other poverty-stricken, unskilled, and despised groups, including later white immigrants and the mass of Negroes freed by the Civil War. The earlier freed Negroes also lived a life in large part determined by the changing exigencies of slavery. When slaves were a very minor part of the population in colonial America, whites were neither concerned about their own safety nor worried about the future of this incidental "peculiar institution." Although most blacks were still poor at that time, there were already some prosperous black plantation owners in the seventeenth century,[8] and they exercised most of the rights of white men of property.[9] Free blacks were more truly free during this period—the seventeenth and early eighteenth centuries—than at any time until well after the Civil War. Individual blacks achieved distinction in this period, including Phyllis Wheatley as a poet, Gustavus Vassa as author of a popular autobiography which went through eight editions, and Paul Cuffe as a shipbuilder and shipowner,[10] with Benjamin Bannecker the outstanding black intellectual of the time, as an astronomer, a publisher of almanacs, and one of those who designed the city of Washington, D.C.[11]

The mass importation of slaves into Virginia began in 1640, and in 1705 a massive tightening up of laws on free Negroes was included in a more severe slave code.[12] The right to vote was taken away from free Negroes, along with the right to self-defense, to free movement, and other basic human rights.[13] Similar—though not identical—trends appeared in other states at about the same time.[14] The idealism set in motion by the American Revolution led to a loosening of these restrictions on free Negroes toward the end of the eighteenth century, but by the early nineteenth century the laws began to be tightened up again as the cotton gin's economic revolution caused another mass importation of slaves, and a correspondingly greater concern for the institution of slavery and for the safety of the white population. Slave uprisings in the Caribbean spread panic through the slaveholding states, and the alarm increased with the Nat Turner rebellion in 1831. The slave uprisings at home and in the Caribbean, combined with the sudden growth of militant abolitionism in the North and the development of the "underground railroad" for helping escaped slaves out of the South, all combined to produce a passionate reaction in the South which increased in intensity up to the Civil War. The stamping out of the rights of free Negroes was one phase of this reaction,[15] and it proceeded to the point where little distinction was left between free and enslaved blacks.

The growth rate of the free black population in the United States fell drastically after 1810 and continued to fall until the Civil War.[16] Increasingly the free black population concentrated in the somewhat less repressive states of the upper South and in the North.[17] Even in the

North, however, a reaction was setting in during the same period against the increasingly militant abolitionist movement, which many saw as leading the country toward a bloody and devastating civil war. Moreover, as the Negro population in the North now grew rapidly through exodus from the South and concentrated in a few urban areas, anti-Negro sentiment and anti-Negro laws began to appear throughout the North.[18] In short, in terms of the law and the general social environment, the period from 1820 to 1860 was one of retrogression for blacks throughout the United States. This is not to say that their *economic* advancement was stopped, however. On the contrary, this was a period of important economic achievements for the free black population—not simply for a few outstanding individuals, but along a broad front.

Despite laws in the South against educating Negroes, clandestine schools and private instruction were common among free Negroes in urban centers.[19] There was considerable winking at these laws, especially when those violating them were local white clergy or planters, but they were not completely "dead letters." In April 1855 a group of blacks was discovered conducting an unauthorized school in the nation's capital, for which one was flogged, one imprisoned, and the others heavily fined.[20] As early as the 1820s day and night schools for Negroes were flourishing in Baltimore, with almost 200 adults among their students.[21] In Boston in 1850, more than half of the 2,000 black children in the city were attending school[22]—probably a higher percentage than among other low-income minorities at that time. Many of the schools that black children and adults attended during this period were private. A long struggle was necessary, even in the North, to get black children admitted to public schools.[23] In higher education, Negroes crowded into those few colleges that would accept them. By 1860 one-third of the students at Oberlin College were black.[24]

Many documented cases exist of Negroes in this period making transactions or leaving estates valued at $10,000, $20,000 or $40,000, and at least one estate valued at $100,000.[25] Perhaps more importantly, official documents show large numbers of "free persons of color" owning more modest but still substantial amounts. In North Carolina alone, more than fifty free Negroes were recorded in 1860 as each having property valued at more than $2,500 ranging up to $36,000.[26] The property of free Negroes in New York City in 1837 was worth $1.4 million, in Cincinnati half a million, in Charleston three-quarters of a million;[27] in New Orleans one-fifth of the taxable property in the city belonged to "free persons of color" [28] —amounting in value to $15 million.[29] The large number of prosperous Negroes in New Orleans was due in large part to its having been a French possession in which Negroes were treated according to the pattern prevailing in Latin America rather than the pattern prevailing in the English-speaking colonies. One of the most prosperous New Orleans Negroes of the antebellum period left an estate of $100,000, and in 1894 another black man from the same city, left an estate of nearly $500,000, even after a lifetime of philanthropy.[30] All told, it has been estimated that the total value of property owned by free Negroes in the United States in 1860 was $50 million.[31] Among the few rights not abrogated in the antebellum period was the right to property.[32]

Churches, social lodges, and mutual aid organizations developed and flourished among free black populations during this period.[33] Sometimes these organizations carried on educational and charitable programs among the black population at large, and sometimes they were social elitist organizations. An example of the latter was the Brown Fellowship Society in Charleston, South Carolina, where a prosperous class of blacks evolved early, and which in 1790 established a membership fee of $50.[34]

The free black population before the Civil War developed a number of small but sometimes locally notable businesses in a number of cities, serving in some cases the black community and in other cases a clientele drawn largely from the larger white society. The kinds of services offered typically reflected artisan skills or servant skills acquired under slavery. Blacks were particularly prominent in food-related establishments (caterers, tavern keepers, restaurateurs), tailor shops, barbershops, and livery stables, but also spread to such fields as insurance companies and manufacturing.[35]

How important was this class of free Negroes, and how long did their influence last in the development of the black population at large? One index of its influence is that most Negro college students were descendants of this class well into the twentieth century. Only in the post-World War II period did black students descended from the masses of those freed by the Civil War predominate in black colleges,[36] and their arrival forced wholesale changes in the general character of these institutions.[37] Descendants of the antebellum "free persons of color" similarly dominated Negro leadership at the local and national level until a generation ago.

The relationship between the small leadership class and the mass of the black population was decisively affected by the fact that the descendants of the antebellum "free persons of color" were literally generations ahead of other Negroes in education, family stability, social behavior, and economic position. They tended to be even more remote and unsympathetic than elite members of other races toward those further down the socioeconomic ladder, in part because there were in fact greater differences in cultural evolution. Where the early development of this elite was greatest—in New Orleans—they formed a separate caste having nothing to do with other Negroes. This pattern was not unique with American Negroes, but was common throughout Latin America. Indeed, only in New Orleans was this separation of the mulatto elite and the black mass as great as in most of Latin America. Yet everywhere in the United States this general tendency existed to some degree, involving not only reluctance to have social contacts but also an unwillingness to engage in the kinds of community service work and charitable organizations that characterized various other American ethnic groups in their periods of poverty. The willingness of the Negro elite classes to "write off" the mass of the race as hopeless was facilitated by the fact that the passage of these classes through a similar phase was now long since buried and forgotten in history, and the obvious color differences between Negro socioeconomic classes made it easy for them to accept the view that ancestry in a genetic sense was the real reason for these differences.

Although internal color differences were of major importance in the evolution of the American Negro population—with agonizing personal consequences for many individuals and families—the dominant white population of the country lumped all Negroes together and was in general almost totally unaware of these internal differences, much less their historical origins. One result of this was that the small Negro elite which cut itself off from the mass of the black population was also isolated from its white counterparts. As a tiny and occupationally heterogeneous group, it had virtually no basis for intellectual or other development. Given these circumstances, it was virtually inevitable that it became an insular, largely stagnant group emphasizing social snobbishness and material possessions.[38] The classic picture of them is in E. Franklin Frazier's *Black Bourgeoisie*.

There were serious economic consequences of the fact that the black masses and the black educated classes were out of phase by some generations in their respective development. The internal cohesion and the many institutional and informational self-help programs that advanced other ethnic minorities—notably the Jews and the Orientals—were much less common among Negroes, and their effectiveness was undermined by the mutual distrust among the different classes of the black population.

Negro colleges were geared to serving the social elite and had none of the adult-education, job-preparation, acculturation-of-the-masses, service-to-the-community orientation of other colleges serving low-income populations, such as the Catholic colleges and some urban colleges. However, unlike the white colleges serving a social elite, the black colleges served an elite too small, scattered, and occupationally heterogeneous to have any common intellectual interest, and too recently arrived to have developed any intellectual traditions. The education at such colleges was therefore neither "practical" nor "intellectual." Rather, the campus was a setting for elaborate and costly social activities for those who could afford them, and desperate efforts to participate by those who could not.[39] In short, one of the major institutions for economic advancement in the case of other minorities was devoted to entirely different purposes in the case of the American Negro. While Jewish immigrants were rising out of the slums of New York by going to cheap, drab, and socially undistinguished colleges and universities, the Negro colleges and universities were not even concerned with those in the black slums, but were devoted to providing an interesting social—not intellectual—experience for those whose ancestors had long since risen from such economic levels. These were the attitudes of a small social elite. Among the mass of the black population, there has always been a substantial group whose efforts to secure education have been both desperate and pathetic,[40] throughout the history of Negroes in America:

> Many a Negro leader today, with a fine education obtained at Oberlin, Yale, Harvard . . . were given their start by hard-working mothers or fathers who literally "bore the burden in the heat of the day." These mothers and fathers worked without any hope that they personally would ever "lay down their heavy load" of unrecompensed toil but they saw the triumph of their children from afar and they toiled unceasingly that their posterity might have a better, fuller, and freer life. They were the real "unsung heroes" of the Negro race. . . .[41]

Not only did untold thousands of black parents pay this high economic price, they paid a perhaps higher personal price in having thereafter to watch their children from "afar." Education has long been recognized as a destroyer of family relations in the black society, usually including "a complete break" with the whole community from which the educated person came, and often a concealment of his origins in later years.[42] "Unsung hero" seems almost an understatement for those black parents who insisted that their children be educated at all cost. Only someone who has seen the personal heartbreak it has meant—and which the parents usually *knew* in advance that it would mean—can really appreciate what they did. Fortunately, more recent generations of black students are less prone to abandon parents who put them through college.

A number of developments have eroded and discredited the traditional leadership pattern. First, there has always been a segment of the educated black population concerned with the advancement of the race as a whole, and this segment has tended to increase in numbers and influence, particularly in periods of racial crises and racial solidarity, such as the 1920s ("the new Negro") and the 1960s ("black power"). Second, the slow but steady rise of individuals from the masses of the black population has changed the general outlook of the Negro elite as well as visibly darkening its complexion, especially within the past generation.

Urbanization of the Negro

While black middle-class and upper-class membership has been heavily influenced by the date of acquiring freedom, it has also been very much influenced by a family's time of arrival in the city. Studies in New York and Chicago by E. Franklin Frazier show a striking pattern of similarities. The black urban community tends to expand from its point of origin in such a way that the newcomers—less skilled, less educated, with more disorganized families, high crime rate, and other indices of social pathology—tend to settle at the original site of the black community while the older residents with more solid families, higher income, more education, etc. move outward toward the edge of the black community, or lead an expansion into adjoining white communities. As the migrants settle down and acquire the economic and social skills to progress in the city, they too are inclined to abandon the original site of the black community and expand outward, leaving the central settlement to new migrants who exhibit the same social pathology as the migrants of a generation or two earlier. The pattern repeats again and again with successive waves of rural migrants to the city, the black community growing in definite zones showing the pattern of ecological succession—with crime, delinquency, broken homes, and other such indices declining with the distance from the original settlement, while all of these indices remain at their original high level at the site occupied by the newest wave of migrants.

This pattern of social ecological succession presents many pitfalls to the unwary social analyst. Any attempt to judge progress by changes occurring on a given tract of land is likely to understate—or even completely miss—the changes that have been going on. Many a tract of land may have the same life pattern as it had fifty years earlier, and yet those families who were in a given tract fifty years ago may have advanced economically, socially and culturally—but now on a different tract of land with other families who have advanced similarly. This pattern of ecological succession is not peculiar to American Negroes but has been common among other ethnic minorities. Indeed, the Italian-Americans are among the few minorities who tend to stay in one place as they advance economically and socially.[43]

When the general trend of rising income is superimposed on the pattern of ecological succession, a new phenomenon arises. Not only does the black community expand outward, the higher-income group leading the way, but each quality level of housing becomes accessible now to a lower class than before. Another way of looking at the same thing is that the average quality of tenant declines relative to the average quality of housing. The property is not as well cared for by the tenants, nor are they as insistent that the landlords care for it. To those who judge by looking at the fate of particular tracts of land rather than the fate of particular families and classes of people, it looks as if neighborhoods are "going downhill" generally, when in fact people may be going uphill generally. The same principle applies across racial lines as well, as when white middle-class suburbanites visit their old neighborhoods and find them more crowded, dirty, and dangerous than when they lived there. If they were to judge by the fate of particular blocs of people rather than particular tracts of land, they would discover that both they and the new inhabitants have higher standards of living than they ever had before.

Fashionable discussions of black communities as "the ghetto" tend to regard slums as the normal black community and higher economic and social levels are "exceptions" or "middle-class" neighborhoods. Sometimes they make the mistake of implicitly conceiving of the slum experience as the "authentic" black experience, more "real" in some undefinable sense. Yet at no time in history has the bulk of the American Negro population lived in urban slums, nor are most blacks today below the poverty level, or on welfare, or in fatherless homes. The slum experience—poverty, high crime rates, disorganized families, etc.—has endured for centuries as a transitional phase through which most classes of black American families have passed at one time or another in their evolution, even the "free persons of color" in the antebellum South. How long the transition takes is an important empirical question that has barely been asked, much less answered. What is quite clear from what is known already is that it is a harrowing experience; and that not every family survives it. Many turn back, and many others disintegrate on the spot with alcohol and drugs.

When the first waves of black migrants were in the northern cities toward the end of the nineteenth century, mortality rates were so high that contemporary observers seriously discussed the possibility that American Negroes were headed toward physical extinction.[44] Earlier, the slow natural growth of the free black population had raised similar questions. Such high mortality rates among newcomers to the city were not peculiar to any particular time or to any particular race. Decimation by disease, alcoholism, fire, and violence was the rule rather than the exception among nineteenth-century European immigrants living in urban slums. The innumerable prerequisites for urban life—both external conditions and internal knowledge and value systems—may be taken for granted by later generations born into these preconditions, but their historical development has been a slow and painful matter of life and death for those who had to make the adaptation to another way of life. The large numbers of returnees—among both black and white migrants to the city—suggest that many underestimated the difficulties or overestimated the rewards, perhaps basing their assessment of their own prosperity on the conditions among others who had already made the transition. The more rapid growth of the mulatto population than the black population during this period [45]—in contrast to the reverse pattern before the Civil War—suggests that the population problem was one of inadequate adjustment to conditions, since the mulattoes were overrepresented among those given their freedom early and had made the transition to urban living earlier.

General Economic Trends

At the time of the Emancipation Proclamation, over 90 percent of the black people in the United States lived in the South and the overwhelming bulk of those were in southern agriculture. This would remain true for the next generation. During the Civil War, many thousands of southern Negro slaves were used in industrial occupations for the first time, but the industries themselves were largely destroyed in the war, and with them any immediate possibility of a black industrial working class.[46] In the North, black urban workers lost ground to the growing number of immigrants and the developing labor unions.[47] When the South was invaded by the Union Army, great numbers of black men, women, and children followed them, experiencing freedom for the first time, performing miscellaneous jobs, some eventually becoming soldiers who fought in large numbers and with considerable distinction.

Immediately after emancipation, the new experience of being able to come and go at will led many Negroes to engage in "months of aimless wandering and idleness," [48] in sharp contrast to their previous confinement and toil. Indeed, a substantial class of aimless wanderers developed and persisted as isolated individuals who were later part of the great mass movement to the cities.

Politically, the Reconstruction period after the Civil War was the high tide of black power in the United States, with more political representation at both local and national levels than at any time before or since. In the economic sphere, however, this had little effect on the day-to-day life of most newly freed blacks. The wholly unprepared-for transition from slavery to freedom had to be made at a time when the South as a whole was devastated and disorganized, and not far from starvation. Massive federal aid kept blacks and whites alive while the southern economy was reorganized, and special efforts were made by the Freedmen's Bureau and by dedicated northern missionaries to advance the black population, but the Negro's relative lack of advancement during this period was one of the main talking points of southern whites and racists throughout the country.

The economic realities of white land ownership, near-monopoly of technical and business skills, and control of financial institutions meant that blacks had to work for whites on whatever terms were available. A form of sharecropping came into being in which the sharecropper was kept perpetually in debt to the local merchants (where he was often legally forced to buy) and so tied to the soil in de facto peonage. Severe vagrancy laws and harsh enforcement by local police and courts made it very difficult for many Negroes to get free even momentarily and to change their occupations.[49] Alternative ways of working on the land, such as cash tenancy or land ownership, were beyond the means of most of the newly freed slaves, but over the years more and more somehow escaped sharecropper peonage into those categories. There were, however, many painful and bitter failures among people whose only experience was being slaves, with of course no managerial functions or even responsibility for their own personal lives.[50] Some Negroes worked simply as agricultural employees, and a large number as domestic servants. Black artisans actually lost ground after emancipation, partly because of personal inability to function effectively outside the familiar institutional framework, partly because of obsolescence in the face of advancing industrial technology, and partly from the opposition of newly developing organized labor unions, as well as frequent refusals of white workers to work alongside them.[51] At one job or another, however, a higher percentage of the black population was employed than of the white population.[52]

From 1890 until the First World War, the majority of American Negroes worked in agriculture.[53] Despite many institutional barriers to their advancement, a rising proportion owned their own homes and farms. In 1890, 19 percent of American Negroes owned their own homes.[54] In 1913, fifty years after emancipation, 25 percent of the Negroes in the South owned their own homes.[55] By 1960, 38 percent of all black families in the United States owned their own homes.[56]

World War I brought a greatly increased demand for labor in the war industries, and thereby provided the first real chance for many Negroes to escape the South. They began one of the most massive internal migrations in the history of the United States. This was a spontaneous movement, not organized by any of the "leaders" vying with one another for popular favor. Three quarters of a million Negroes moved North within a four-year period during World War I.[57] The First World War also raised the price of cotton suddenly, allowing many sharecroppers to pay off their bills and finally escape from peonage.[58] Previous decades had seen a slowly rising black migration, from 68,000 in 1870–80 to 194,000 in 1900–10, but this was nearly tripled in the 1910–20 decade, and then almost doubled again in the 1920–30 decade.[59] Moreover, although the previous migrations had been predominantly to the northeastern cities, less than half of the new migration was to the Northeast; more than half went to north-central areas—principally Chicago—and a small fraction migrated to the West. The depression of the 1930s slowed black migration from the South (it *reversed* other groups' migrations) but this migration continued, at about half its rate during the preceding decade. When World War II again created a great demand for labor, black migration more than tripled during the 1940s, reaching an all-time high in that decade of more than 1.5 million, which was almost matched again in the 1950–60 decade.[60] In the 1940–60 period, slightly more than 40 percent of the migration was to the north-central area, slightly less than 40 percent to the Northeast, and the rest to the West—the movement to the West representing a sevenfold increase over the two previous decades.

The movement from the South was not only a change of region but in most cases a change from rural to urban living as well. It was not until 1960 that more blacks in the South were urban than rural, but most of the northern Negro population was urban before the turn of the century.[61] In 1920, 85 percent of the black people in northern states were urban.[62] In short, the black population had to undergo two major drastic transformations within two or three generations. They had first to adjust to freedom and individual responsibility for feeding, clothing, and housing themselves. This adjustment had to be made in an economy and society devastated by war, and with white economic agents and institutions bitterly hostile and often unscrupulous in dealing with inexperienced black consumers and workers. The second great adjustment was to urban living—an experience which had proved shattering to European immigrants from similar rural backgrounds before them. Most of today's black urban population has been in the city only two generations, and many of the poorest and most problem-ridden, less than that.

While the incomes of Negroes rose more or less in proportion to the general rise of incomes in the nation as a whole, the *ratio* of black-to-white income rose only sporadically and with many oscillations. Nevertheless, some relative advances can be seen over long periods of time. In 1939 the average income of black workers was approximately 41 to 45 percent of the average income of white workers, but by 1960 the percentage was 60 to 67 percent.[63] This somewhat overstates the progress, however, for many people are not in the "worker" category, and most of those above that category are white. Moreover, there is an increasing trend in upper-earnings levels to receive income as capital gains, perquisites, undistributed profits, etc., as a means of avoiding income taxes, so that undoubtedly a higher percentage of white economic gains does not appear officially as "income." Nevertheless, when all allowances are made, it is still apparent that blacks have advanced significantly, not only absolutely but relative to the general population.

General Conclusions

It would be difficult to determine with any precision the causes of rising black incomes and the changes in black income relative to white. However, it is possible to consider certain general hypotheses and to test them against the facts. How important, for example, is the political and social climate of opinion of the country at large as compared to developments within the black population itself? Have political and economic progress proceeded in step or varied more or less independently?

There is little evidence of any close relationship between political progress (or retrogression) and economic progress (or retrogression). The antebellum "free persons of color" were establishing themselves economically and developing educationally at precisely the period of the worst racial oppression in American history—the decades immediately preceding the Civil War. Laws and practices became much more restrictive for both free blacks and for slaves, in the city and on the plantations, in the North and in the South. Yet this was the period when a black small business, small property-owning class—as distinguished from isolated individuals—first emerged, when books by black authors appeared in substantial numbers, when black newspapers and magazines were first printed, and when blacks began attending college in significant numbers. Undoubtedly all these things would have developed more fully in a less repressive environment, but the only point here is simply to assess the relative weight of political actions by the white society and the internal development in the black community. Conversely, the high tide of black political power during Reconstruction was not a period of notable economic advance, and in fact included some important retrogressions. In short, there is little evidence that the great mass of the black population advanced more rapidly economically during the best period in history for blacks from a political point of view or that their economic advance could be stopped in one of the worst periods.

The rise of the NAACP, some favorable court decisions, and lobbying by Booker T. Washington and other Negro leaders gained some minor legal and political concessions, but the black man in America was in almost total political eclipse from the 1890s until well into the 1920s. There was even significant retrogression in the Negro's position in federal jobs in the South and in the segregation of jobs throughout the civil service system under Presidents Taft and Wilson.[64] Yet for the masses of the black population, these were years of great economic advance, particularly with the coming of the First World War, and even culturally the 1920s was a period of great development variously known as the "black renaissance" and the arising of the "new Negro." Great numbers of Negroes entered industrial occupations for the first time during World War I and set in motion a mass migration to the North which transformed the history of black America. The Great Depression of the 1930s brought the migration and the cultural renaissance both to a halt. With the rise of Franklin D. Roosevelt and the New Deal, the black vote went to the Democrats for the first time in history, after generations of going to the party of Lincoln. Although Roosevelt permanently captured the black vote for the Democrats, and was responsible for a number of "firsts" for Negroes, the period of the New Deal was not a period of black economic advance relative to whites. In fact, the ratio of black income to white income *fell* during this period, as blacks were hard hit by the high unemployment in the economy. Negroes advanced again, absolutely and relatively, when World War II created a massive new demand for workers, which was particularly beneficial to those at the bottom of the economic ladder, including blacks.

In the post-World War II era, the Truman civil rights platform of 1948 split the Democratic party and led to the formation of a major third party in the South for the first time in over a century. The celebrated Supreme Court desegregation decision of 1954 set off a series of controversies, institutional breakthroughs, and political realignments summarized as "the black revolution." Yet the actual incomes of black people reflected no such revolution, on through the mid-1960s. Black income was 56 percent of white income in 1953, the last year before the historic decision. It fluctuated *below* that percentage for the next decade, in some years falling absolutely while white income was rising.[65] From 1966 on the percentage rose steadily and substantially to 63 percent in 1969. How much of this reflected a permanent improvement and how much the usual rise of low incomes under accelerated war production can only be determined in the future.

While both political and economic developments have helped shape the destiny of black Americans, the evidence suggests that since Abolition the income and employment of the black population are far less affected by specific political programs than by general conditions in the economy. At least this has been the general pattern.

It may well be, however, that the concerted efforts of the past decade have broken down enough occupational and educational barriers at one time to improve the economic situation of Negroes significantly. Certainly the occupational and income advances of blacks within the past few years have been unusually rapid, at least for those with education or skills. The number of black families with incomes over $10,000 more than doubled between 1959 and 1967.[66] It is not clear how—or whether—this affects the typical ghetto dweller, the migrant from the rural South with no skills, inadequate education or experience, and with many social problems.

How is the economic progress of black people to be assessed? Whether they and/or the American society ought to be judged "successes" or "failures" depends obviously on the standards by which either or both are judged, and on the point in time from which this progress is measured. Negroes have been in the United States for centuries, but for only one of those centuries as free people, and for only about two generations in the urban setting in which most now live. While it would be impossible to find any other group with the same history, even among Negroes in other countries of the Western Hemisphere, it is clearly more appropriate to compare American Negroes with other groups from a similar background rather than a more different background. This simple requirement is, however, largely overlooked in comparisons that are commonly made. The incomes and other characteristics of black Americans are most often compared with those of white Americans in general or sometimes with a minority such as the Jews. It would be hard to find a minority with a more different background from black people than the Jews, who had centuries of urban experience behind them when they first set foot on American soil. A more reasonable comparison might be made with groups from a peasant folk-culture background, without an intellectual tradition, and a social pattern in which they were not only in the bottom income class but also in which there was a "caste" position from which no one expected them to rise. There are immigrant groups who approximate this condition, and their experiences in the American economy and society are remarkably similar to that of American Negroes, as were the social processes and the social pathology they exhibited. Few had advanced very far after two generations in the city, and in most cases either the people or the situation were regarded as hopeless at that point.

PART TWO

Immigrant
Minorities

Chapter 3

Nineteenth-Century Immigrants

All Americans are of course immigrants, with the possible exception of the Indians, but the term has come to mean *minority* social or ethnic groups from abroad, usually arriving later in the country's history. These immigrant groups have typically started at the bottom—economically, socially, educationally, and politically—and have faced both spontaneous prejudice and organized discrimination in their attempts to rise. The rate at which they rose in the face of resistance varied greatly among the various ethnic groups. The amount of resistance and discrimination by the larger society has also varied greatly with respect to different immigrant groups, and has changed greatly over time—not always in the direction of tolerance.

The history and economics of American immigrant groups is important, not only in itself, but also as a source of experience in the methods and characteristics of success and failure. Social philosophers have often despaired over the absence of scientific experiments which could settle conflicting social theories. To some extent, the history of other peoples and other times serves as a substitute for such experiments—without the staggering human cost of reliving all the agonies of history, though also without the same degree of certainty or relevance as a contemporary experiment.

This chapter considers the economic and social

pattern of various American immigrant minorities. Some of the questions to be asked about American minorities in general include, How did they fare economically and socially in the face of discrimination? How important have various kinds of differences—color, language, nationality —been in America? In what way did the more successful groups differ from the less successful, in terms of such characteristics as education, family structure, group identity, and political cohesion? Finally, in what ways do the circumstances facing today's struggling minorities resemble the circumstances facing the immigrant groups of the past, and in what ways are they different?

Despite the symbolic significance of America as a New World, a land of opportunity, and a pioneer in democracy, at no time in its history have race, class, religion, or financial conditions been small considerations. Many social distinctions were written into the law itself, as in colonial legislation against working-class people wearing clothes considered appropriate only for their betters,[1] or even in different punishments specified for the same crime when committed by people in different social categories.[2] Perhaps the greatest distinction among early American colonists was between those who were free and those who were in temporary bondage as indentured servants. As mentioned in chapter 1, the bulk of the work force in most colonies consisted of European indentured servants.[3] These were typically working-class people who paid for their passage to America by agreeing to work in bondage for a specified number of years. Their condition differed from that of slaves primarily in that their bondage was for a fixed period of time, and they would carry no visible evidence of their former condition, much less transmit it to their offspring.

Indentured servants in early colonial America worked under conditions similar in many respects to those of blacks, and in many cases alongside blacks.[4] Some of the earliest Africans brought to colonial America were in fact treated as indentured servants.[5] European indentured servants were subjected to cruelties in transit which many observers compared to the prolonged horrors of the Africans' notorious Middle Passage across the Atlantic.[6] Many indentured servants were sold to the highest bidder on arrival, with families being separated.[7] Like slaves, they were subject to punishment and abuse, including sexual exploitation of the women;[8] and like slaves, many ran away,[9] and in the West Indies they organized abortive insurrections.[10] Severe punishments were provided for runaways, including both corporal punishment and adding more years to their period of bondage.[11] Runaway whites were, of course, not as readily identified as escapees from bondage as runaway blacks.

With the evolution of chattel slavery and special laws dealing with slaves, both the similarity between white and black bondsmen and their association together began to disappear. Indentured servants retained basic legal rights, while slaves had no rights whatever under the laws of most American colonies or states. The passage of time converted indentured servants into ordinary working-class people. As plantation slavery grew in the American colonies, many of the overseers were former indentured servants.[12] Few ever joined the dominant planter class.[13] Ultimately, indentureship died out as a method of crossing the Atlantic, partly because of the buildup of a domestic American working class, partly because of the mass importation of slaves, and perhaps mainly because of British restrictions on voyage conditions, which made indentureship uneconomic. Indentureship had been so common in colonial America, however, that it is estimated that most of today's white American population has some indentured ancestor or ancestors.

The America to which the nineteenth-century immigrants came was not an equalitarian society, nor one in which mass discrimination and abuse were limited to black people. Many of the conditions and problems they faced were remarkably similar to those sometimes regarded as peculiar to our time or to black-white racial differences. The cities into which the immigrants poured were "engulfed in slums" and "overwhelmed with problems of pauperism and relief."[14] The immigrant communities were characterized by "broken homes,"[15] high crime rates,[16] overcrowded living,[17] filth and rats,[18] a high incidence of disease and death,[19] including high infant mortality,[20] abandonment of families,[21] early and even perverse sex among children,[22] the flourishing of policy rackets,[23] and organized gangs who terrorized whole communities with the knowledge and connivance of corrupt police.[24] In 1888, William Dean Howells noted that "the settlement of an Irish family in one of our suburban neighborhoods" strikes a "mortal pang" in the old residents, that property values "tremble" as "fear spreads" and the original residents "abandon" their homes.[25]

The development of racial and religious tolerance in the United States was not the realization of an ideal but a grudging acceptance of the hard fact that none of the numerous groups populating the country was powerful enough to exterminate or wholly suppress the others. Innumerable efforts to do so—from legal discrimination to mob violence—were made throughout the nineteenth century. Shakers were flogged, Mormons lynched, and Irish neighborhoods invaded; houses, churches, and schools were burned.[26] Not only hoodlums but also some of the most respected people of the time joined in anti-immigrant activities. These respectable people included Samuel Morse, the inventor of the telegraph, and James Harper, a founder of the family publishing house of that name.[27] Henry George applied the phrase "human garbage" to the immigrants of the 1880s,[28] and H. G. Wells at the turn of the century doubted that the immigrants in the American slums could ever be usefully absorbed into society.[29] According to a leading historian, the term "immigrant" was used "sweepingly" to imply "a slum-creating, soap-shy, illiterate, jargon-speaking, standoffish interloper, innocent of civilized values, indeed hardly human. . . ."[30]

The stereotypes of the immigrants, however distorted, unfair, or in the nature of self-fulfilling prophecies, were not wholly imaginary. Immigrants were overrepresented among the problem groups of society—those likely to get in trouble with the law,[31] to carry venereal disease,[32] to end up in mental institutions,[33] and to set off riots—many of which make the race riots of the twentieth century look tame by comparison.[34] It would be pointless to try to decide how much of the social pathology should be "blamed" on the immigrants and how much on a hostile or indifferent society. The point here is that social pathology very much like that among today's minorities at the bottom was very common among immigrant minorities when they were at the bottom—and that it did not prove to be an insurmountable obstacle. Different groups dealt with the problems in different ways and with very different degrees of economic and social success.

Economic conditions, in their homeland and in the United States, shaped much of the history of American immigrant groups. The source of most immigration to America in the age of wind-driven ships was determined by the routes followed by cargo vessels. The cost of a long ocean voyage on a wind-driven ship would have been prohibitive for most immigrants, except for the existence of unused cargo space on vessels returning from Europe to America. While trade between Europe and America had approximately balanced in value terms, this meant that a larger *bulk* of goods was sent from west to east than from east to west, since the United States was exporting agricultural products and importing manufactured products. This left considerable unused space on most Europe-to-America voyages, so that the additional cost of filling that space with people was relatively low—and safety alone required that the ships be weighted down more than they would have been by the relatively small cargoes of manufactured goods that were traded for large quantities of agricultural produce. This meant that the cost of getting to the United States was much less for those sailing from European ports to which American goods were shipped in great quantities than from parts of the continent which had much less trade with the Western Hemisphere.

The net result of this economic situation was that most American immigrants, prior to the American industrialization and cheaper motor-driven ships, came from northern and western Europe.[35] Moreover, the destination of each ethnic group in the United States was related to the location of the particular products being shipped from America on the cargo vessels which they used on the return voyage. For example, the ships on which the Irish came to America had carried timber to Europe, and were therefore returning to the northeastern United States and the maritime provinces of Canada to get more timber. This is where the Irish had to land, since the primary purpose of these ships was to carry cargo rather than people. The Germans caught cargo ships that had brought cotton to Le Havre and were returning to the cotton-rich Mississippi delta. From New Orleans there were many riverboats sailing up the Mississippi River, so that it was easy for the German immigrants to get to such places as St. Louis and Cincinnati, and in fact throughout the upper Mississippi valleys, where large German settlements developed.[36]

The economic influence on the distribution of immigrant groups in America sometimes took a different form. Those groups with a particular skill or trade were not as closely bound to the port at which they disembarked, and could seek those parts of the United States where what they had to offer was more in demand. The wholly unskilled not only had less reason to do this; they were less able to do it, usually having to go to work immediately upon arrival, in order to keep body and soul together, and seldom being able to save enough to move very far. Tradesmen, skilled laborers, and professional men were in much better positions to distribute themselves geographically to their best advantage. Thus the poor and unskilled Irish typically settled in large port cities, and some who went out on construction gangs settled in communities that grew up alongside the canals and railroads they built. The early German Jewish immigrants, being tradesmen and professionals,[37] had to disperse across the country, since concentrating in a particular community would have meant a self-defeating reduction of the market for each individual's services. Therefore they did not develop the kind of compact ethnic community developed by other ethnic groups, including occupationally very different eastern European Jews who settled in New York later in the nineteenth century. The Scandinavians, being from an agricultural background, tended to settle in areas where land was available more cheaply than in the settled East, but not on the outer frontier, which required very different skills from the ordinary farming to which they were accustomed.[38]

The development of steamships changed the economics—and therefore the history—of immigration to America. The usual thirty- to ninety-day voyage (varying with wind conditions) from Europe to the United States was shortened to a dependable ten days.[39] One result of this was a great increase in the total number of immigrants, rising from 5 million in the pre-Civil War period to 10 million in the next thirty years, and then 15 million in less than fifteen years.[40] Moreover, steamships now made it economically profitable for more ships to specialize in carrying people and for more people to afford to use them. This completely changed the *sources* of immigration. No longer was cheap immigration restricted to those parts of Europe engaged in large-scale commercial trade with the United States. No longer was the destination of an immigrant group determined by the particular product that a cargo ship happened to carry to their land. The transition from sailing ships to steamships was accomplished in a relatively few years, and the nationality makeup of immigrants to America changed drastically within those few years. In the mid-1850s, more than 95 percent of the immigrants arriving in New York came in sailing ships, but by 1873 an even higher percentage came in steamships.[41] By 1880, Italian immigration to the United States was higher than it had ever been before, and in the decades to come it doubled, redoubled, and redoubled again and again.[42] Emigration from other southern and central European countries also rose sharply.[43] Although northern and western Europeans made up 87 percent of the immigrants to the United States in 1882, southern and eastern Europeans comprised 81 percent of the immigrants to the United States by 1907.[44]

The changed economics of ocean voyages brought in immigrants who were (1) predominately *non*-English-speaking, (2) predominantly from societies with political institutions and social mores very different from those of the Anglo-Saxon world, and (3) predominately Catholic at a time when religious differences were major sources of conflict, especially with the rise of secular public school education. There was now also a substantial minority of immigrants who planned only a *temporary* stay in America, and a return to their homelands after accumulating some money—a very rare kind of immigrant in the days of long and painful voyages by sailing ships. During the 1870s, the traffic to Europe exceeded that to the United States.[45] Some skilled workers in seasonal industries even left Europe in the spring to work in the United States and returned home in the fall.[46] Transients had of course less reason to learn the language and institutions of the country, and even those who came with the thought of permanent settlement were not as irrevocably committed now as past immigrants had been, since a return voyage was no longer unthinkable, financially or otherwise. In the mid-twentieth century, with the arrival of cheap air travel, two-way migration between Puerto Rico and the continental United States became still more casual.

The Jews

The history of Jews as a distinct group goes back thousands of years before the discovery of America, and at least part of that history is important for understanding the economic and social development of American Jews. In one important respect, medieval Jews were very fortunate in the particular form of occupational discrimination practiced against them. They were forbidden to engage in those occupations that were central to feudalism—those

involving the land and many crafts destined for obsolescence—and were therefore forced into urban, commercial,
and financial occupations, which would of course later
turn out to be central to the modern capitalist economy.
Frederick the Great decreed that "no Jew shall presume to
engage in any manual trade." [47] While the intentions
behind such prohibitions were repressive, the long-run
consequences were that Jews were in many ways better
prepared for the modern world than many of their
oppressors.

Although many minorities have been oppressed and
abused down through the centuries, the Jews as an *alien*
minority, without a national home, were peculiarly subject
to being banished or driven from whatever country they
were in during periodic outbreaks of anti-Semitic campaigns. This in turn meant that it was economically
ill-advised for Jews to accumulate conspicuous, immobile
wealth, and very advisable to keep their wealth concealed
and in such mobile form as gold or diamonds—or in
intangible knowledge and skills which no one could take
from them.

Among the puzzling patterns of Jewish life, in Europe
and in America, their *intellectual* achievements have
excited much comment and provoked many theories.
Among the intellectual giants who left their imprint on
modern thought and action, it would be hard to find three
as prominent as Freud, Einstein, and Marx—all Jewish in
origin. At less Olympian levels, Jews are also greatly
overrepresented among intellectuals and among students
at outstanding academic institutions. This was not always
so, however, and the question of why it has become so is
one to consider after surveying their general development
in the United States.

There were *some* Jews in earliest American times, but
Jews became numerically and socially significant only in
the nineteenth century. The political restoration in Europe
after Napoleon's defeat included renewed anti-Semitic
repression, which caused many German Jews to emigrate
to the United States. Here they often began as poor

peddlers, carrying their merchandise on their backs, but from these ranks came a number who ended up as important merchants, owning such well-known stores as Gimbels, Altman's, Stern's, and Bloomingdale's.[48] From about 3,000 Jews in the United States in 1815 (mostly from Spain and Portugal), there grew a Jewish population of a quarter of a million (largely German) on the eve of the Civil War.[49] The really massive influx of Jews from eastern Europe came later, in the last quarter of the nineteenth century. By 1910 there were more than a million Jews in New York City alone, and by 1924 about 2 million. Only a tenth of these were part of the old German Jewish community, which was more prosperous and culturally very different from the new Jewish immigrants.[50]

Isolated Jewish individuals and families spread throughout the United States,[51] but the bulk of the American Jewish community remained in New York City. During the early years, the Jewish community was even more localized on Manhattan's run-down lower east side. This concentration had the effect of preserving a sense of community and provided the basis for Jewish stores, tradesmen, and professionals serving the special needs of their own community. Jewish dietary laws made kosher food stores especially important. By this time, however, Jews were already established as major merchants serving the general community.

The new, massive wave of Jewish immigrants from Russia and eastern Europe had little in common with the older German Jews of the previous generation. The German Jews were more often prosperous, polished, educated, and established. They provided the major merchant and financial figures of the times, in contrast to the pushcart peddlers, factory workers, and small businessmen characteristic of the eastern European Jews. In the clothing industry, the employers were German Jews, the employees eastern European Jews—though the latter became employers a generation later.[52] Statistics for 1901–06 show that two-thirds of Jewish immigrants admitted to the country during that period were industrial workers.[53] Despite the "poverty and lack of skill" among the newer Jewish immigrants, few Jewish men became common laborers,[54] and few Jewish women became domestic servants.[55] Instead, they entered a wide variety of occupations where they could acquire a skilled trade, business experience, or a profession.[56] Though the Jews progressed economically more rapidly than many other minorities, they suffered the effects of slums during their early immigration period. Small, overcrowded slum apartments were created by dividing up dwelling units intended for more reasonable numbers of people. Toilets usually had to be shared.[57] The lower east side of Manhattan was the most densely packed section of the city, with one-sixth of New York's population living on one eighty-second of its land—and suffering 38 percent of the city's deaths from fire.[58] In two judicial districts of the lower east side, more than 11,000 evictions were authorized in 1891–92, indicating something about the financial precariousness of the lower east side Jews at that time.[59]

The Jews, even during their early period of poverty in America, were different from other minorities in a number of significant ways. They had one of the lowest death rates in the city, partly as a result of their stress on cleanliness of food and body.[60] Alcoholism, which killed off many members of other immigrant groups, seldom claimed Jews, and slum saloons left over from other immigrant groups declined when Jews took over the neighborhood.[61] Few Jews were in trouble with the law and few committed suicide.[62] There was much crime on the lower east side, but Jews were victims more often than perpetrators. The economic rise of Jews and the development of subways in New York led to dispersion from the overcrowded lower east side, where 75 percent of the city's Jews had lived in 1892, 50 percent in 1903, and only 23 percent by 1916.[63]

The Jews did not escape the internal divisions that plagued other minorities. The German Jews, who were already economically established and at least partially socially assimilated when the great wave of poor uneducated eastern European Jews arrived, clearly resented the latter and openly criticized them as Oriental or Asiatic in their outlook and behavior.[64] They even attempted to restrain their immigration to America.[65] Yet, when it became clear that (1) the massive immigration of poor Jews was going to continue, and that (2) the wealthy, established Jews were going to be identified with them as Jews regardless of attempts at disavowal, the "uptown" Jews came to the aid of the "downtown" Jews with charity, training programs, and Americanization programs.[66] The programs administered by German Jews for the eastern European Jews tended to be paternalistic and arrogant,[67] and by the late 1880s the eastern European Jews were running their own community programs and charities.[68] Private charities, community hospitals, schools, etc. made American Jews a self-sufficient group, whose poor and sick did not have to go to non-Jews for help.[69] Jews were—and are—seldom intermarried. During this period there were few marriages even among the various nationalities of Jews on the lower east side, or between lower east side Jews and those "uptown." [70]

The Jews were among the most successful—if not *the* most successful—of American minorities, just as they have been among the most successful minorities in other countries. As far back as 1892 a survey showed sixty Jewish millionaires in New York City.[71] On a broader front, Jewish incomes tend to average higher than American incomes in general, as does Jewish education and Jewish IQs,[72] though a substantial minority of Jews remain working-class people, earning modest or even low incomes.[73] Yet it would be incorrect to think that Jews encountered no substantial discrimination, or even that discrimination has been steadily eroding. Anti-Semitism in the United States goes back as far as colonial America,[74] when there were barely enough Jews to notice. Anti-Semitism revived and grew stronger in the last quarter of the nineteenth century, coinciding with the arrival of more disadvantaged Jews from Europe, but also reflecting a general racist reaction throughout the country, during which Jim Crow laws against blacks emerged in the South and antiimmigrant feelings ran high throughout the country. Jews were banned from fraternities at the City College of New York, hotels excluded even prominent and wealthy Jews, clubs blackballed them[75]—including one club whose founder (in earlier and more tolerant times) had been a Jew.[76]

The Irish

The Irish were in many ways the opposite of the Jews, and their economic and social advancement reflected this. Although the peak of Irish immigration was reached at least a generation before the peak of Jewish immigration, the Jews rose much faster economically, passed the Irish before the turn of the century, and have continued to widen the gap. Most Irish-Americans have by now risen above their working-class beginnings, but they have in most cases risen just above it, settling "on the next rung" of lower middle-class living,[77] after economic progress that was "exceptionally slow." [78]

The very different economic and social patterns of the Irish and the Jews in America reflected differences in their respective backgrounds in Europe. While the Jews had been urban, commercial, or tradespeople for centuries, the Irish were from a rural, unskilled peasant background. A reverence for learning had been part of Jewish tradition, but education held no such central place in Ireland, which was the only country in Europe that did not establish a single university throughout the Middle Ages.[79] Even those few Irishmen able to go to college did so with noticeably less commitment than their contemporaries from other countries.[80] Only in suffering oppression were the Irish similar to the Jews, and even here their response was different. The Irish lived as a conquered people under British rule, under conditions which were likened to slavery.[81] Unlike the Jews, whose traditions as an oppressed people forbade even defensive violence, as likely to excite the wrath of the larger society against the whole Jewish community, the Irish fought back with sporadic uprisings and continual underground terrorism—developing a tradition not simply of lawless acts but of open repudiation of the official law and adherence to group mores instead.[82] Similar resistance would have meant instant suicide for the Jews, who lived as hopelessly outnumbered foreigners in other people's lands, while the Irish were an overwhelming majority in their own country.

In most cases, both the Irish and the Jewish immigrants arrived penniless in the United States, but the Irish more often went into hard, dirty, and dangerous labor with no future, while the Jews sought out jobs that offered the prospect of acquiring a trade, even if less remunerative at the outset than being coal miners, canal builders, and other such jobs which the Irish took. In the antebellum South, the Irish were often used in work considered too hazardous for Negro slaves.[83] When Olmsted asked about the peculiar division of labor between Negro slaves and Irish workers on a riverboat in Alabama, he was told: "The niggers are worth too much to be risked here; if the Paddies are knocked overboard, or get their backs broke, nobody loses anything." [84] Economics had triumphed over racial ideology.

Irish immigrants were used throughout the country on jobs involving muscle, dangers, and long hours. This was the role of the Irishman until well into the latter half of the nineteenth century.[85] Other immigrant groups were offered some of the more responsible or supervisory jobs, but the Irish were assigned to the lowest paying jobs.[86] The term "Irish nigger" was commonly applied to them in the early years,[87] and a popular joke of the time said that the wheelbarrow was one of the greatest inventions "because it taught Irishmen to walk on their hind legs." [88] The institutional arrangements of the jobs offered numerous opportunities for workers to be cheated, either by their employer, the company store, or by their own leaders who acted as labor contractors. Some workers were signed up in Ireland, to contracts which made them virtually indentured servants when they arrived in the United States.[89] Irishmen became famous as canal diggers, during the great era of canal building in the 1820s and 1830s, but they were also prominent in building roads and mining coal,[90] and Irish women often became domestic servants.[91] Canal building and railroad building were both dangerous as well as hard work. Malaria was so common among canal workers as to become known as "canal fever." [92] Cave-ins, premature explosions when dynamiting, and numerous other causes claimed many lives on both the canals and the railroads.[93] During the age of railroad building, it was said that there was "an Irishman buried under every tie." [94] For higher level jobs, help-wanted ads frequently said "No Irish need apply[95]—a stock phrase that had not completely died out even by the lifetime of John F. Kennedy. Some nineteenth-century ads for menial jobs even said "any color or country, except Irish." [96]

The Irish were prominent among immigrant groups exhibiting the usual symptoms of social pathology among people at the bottom. They had very high rates of death from tuberculosis—higher than other ethnic groups in the United States and higher than among Irishmen in Ireland —as well as high rates of insanity, a disproportionate number of widows and orphans and inmates of poor-houses, as well as very large overrepresentation among those arrested and imprisoned.[97] In the 1840s one observer noted that it was rare to see a gray-haired Irishman, the mortality rate being so high.[98] (In Ireland itself, three-quarters of the population did not live to be forty.)[99] Irish riots were recurrent, massive, and violent beyond anything seen in twentieth-century America. However, *non*-Irish riots were also common and violent in the nineteenth century,[100] and in some cases anti-Catholic rioters invaded Irish neighborhoods to burn churches and attack homes.[101] However, the largest and most famous riots of the nineteenth century were Irish riots, and "the fighting Irish" became noted for violence in many forms—from individual street fighting and gang warfare to mass riots, to organized terrorism.

One of the enduring differences between the Jews and the Irish has been in their attitudes toward other minorities. The Jews, even when poor, were not usually in direct competition with other low-income minorities. As street peddlers or merchants they came into contact—sometimes conflict—with other minorities, but there was seldom a direct bread-and-butter competition for the same jobs. Even working-class Jews tended to be employed in either home work or to be in sweatshops where Jews were predominant. Jews have long been political supporters of minority causes, among other liberal causes, and have been prominent among contributors to Negro civil rights organizations and black educational institutions. The largely Jewish garment unions were among the few unions open to Negroes in the 1920s.[102] By contrast, the Irish were often in direct competition with Negroes for the hardest and dirtiest work in the North or South,[103] and with the Chinese for similar work on the West Coast.[104] In New Orleans, unskilled Irishmen were hod carriers for skilled Negro slaves.[105] Animosity between the Irish and the Negroes has long been high, and marked by many conflicts between them, often taking the form of physical violence.[106] In the nineteenth century a section of New York in which black and Irish neighborhoods came together was known as "San Juan Hill" because it was such a famous battleground.[107] On the West Coast, the Irish and the Chinese were in similar conflict, with similar violence.[108] The Irish also had internal struggles between Protestants and Catholics, with Orange Day riots in New York becoming common in the 1830s and producing fifty-two deaths in 1871.[109]

The biggest and most famous riot in American history was the largely Irish "draft riot" of 1863. The military draft law used during the Civil War exempted those financially able to pay a certain sum of money instead of serving in the army, throwing the burden of fighting and dying on working-class people, among whom the Irish were prominent.[110] In addition, the Irish were opposed to the abolition of slavery,[111] and to the fighting of the Civil War.[112] They staged a riot outside a draft office in New

York which quickly spread and grew until the city was subjected to several days of terror, in which an estimated 1,000 persons lost their lives[113]—more than ten times the total loss of lives in 75 riots in 67 cities during the 1960s.[114] Negroes found in the street during the draft riot were lynched and mutilated by the mob,[115] and an orphanage for Negro children was burned to the ground.[116]

The association of the Irish with violence in the public mind was further strengthened by numerous Irish gangs and secret terrorist organizations. Among the latter, the "Molly Maguires" became legendary for bombings and murder in the coal mining region of Pennsylvania; until twenty of them were hanged in 1876.[117] Another group, the Fenians, organized an army and a government in exile, hoping to capture Canada and thereby force Britain to free Ireland. The Fenians had sufficient popular support to draw a crowd of one hundred thousand in New York in 1866.[118] About a thousand Fenians marched into Canada and were defeated by the Canadian Army.[119] One of the strengths of the Irish terrorist organizations was the unwillingness of other Irishmen to testify against them, either out of loyalty or out of fear of retaliation.[120] Whatever the rhetoric of these various organizations, the chief victims were the Irish themselves.

Among the nineteenth-century Irish, many leaders, critics and thinkers tried to change the Irish way of life. They were highly critical of their compatriots' alcoholism, violence, ignorance, intolerance, and general lack of adaptation to the needs of a modern economy and society.[121] Many schools, hospitals, orphanages, and poorhouses were built by the largely Irish-American Catholic church, which carried on social work among the poor and tried to protect the immigrants from unscrupulous elements, and whose opposition helped to destroy terrorist organizations.[122] The American Catholic church, which also served German, French, and later Italian immigrants, worked to reduce ethnic frictions,[123] and included the Negroes among the beneficiaries of its social services,[124] but refused to condemn slavery (so did many Protestant groups).[125] The Catholic church was instrumental in restoring order after the draft riots of 1863.[126]

Despite the popular nineteenth-century stereotype of the Irish as reckless drunkards and spendthrifts, their donations—out of very low wages—built many Catholic churches and supported many charitable institutions, secular and religious. In addition, they sent money to relatives still in Ireland—$65 million between 1848 and 1854.[127] Their economic and social conditions improved slowly but steadily, despite the strongest public prejudice and economic discrimination faced by any white ethnic group. The Irish were publicly ridiculed and denounced in the most sweeping terms, and it took years for them to live down the violence and terrorism in which only a minority of them engaged. As late as 1890, 42 percent of the Irish-Americans were working in personal and domestic service.[128]

Among the Irish, as among other disadvantaged groups, there were elements who not only tried to change their compatriots, but who sought to escape their social stigma by disappearing into the larger society, changing their names, and abandoning all traces of identification with them. Some immigrant children who found themselves taunted at school by "American" children tried to become Americanized and unlike their parents.[129] The Protestant "Ulster Irish" vanished into the larger American community, taking with them a higher level of income, education, and skill than that possessed by their Catholic countrymen,[130] but also removing a source of continual strife, in which many lives were lost on both sides.

The Scotch-Irish from the Protestant northern provinces of Ireland preceded the Irish Catholics to the United States by more than two generations, and were a very different social group in many ways. During the American colonial period, the bulk of the immigrants from Ireland were the Protestant Scotch-Irish,[131] most of whom came as indentured servants.[132] They scattered throughout the colonies, particularly in back-country and frontier areas,[133] in contrast to the concentration of the later Irish Catholic immigrants in a few eastern cities.[134] The Scotch-Irish brought with them a strong tradition of emphasis on education,[135] derived from Scotland, in sharp contrast to the attitude of the Irish Catholics. They also had much better relations with American Negroes, and in fact those mountain regions of Virginia, North Carolina, Kentucky, and Tennessee inhabited by the Scotch-Irish were among the most racially liberal in the South, both before and after the Civil War.[136]

The Scotch-Irish were seldom in direct competition with black workers—slave or free—in the job market. Most had been yeomen and craftsmen in Ireland,[137] and though many came as indentured servants, as a way of financing an ocean voyage, they did not come unskilled and culturally unprepared, as did the later Irish Catholic immigrants.[138] Some Scotch-Irish were drawn from the professional and merchant classes.[139] The two Irish groups were similar primarily in their fame for fighting and for whisky.[140] From the beginning, in the 1700s, the Scotch-Irish in America were very sensitive about being confused with the Irish Catholics,[141] but real hostilities between the two groups of Irishmen did not erupt in the United States until the large Irish Catholic immigration of the nineteenth century.

About 1830, the immigration from Ireland changed from predominantly Protestant small farmers and other lower-middle-class elements to a mass immigration of largely Catholic peasants and laborers.[142] This mass immigration continued to grow for twenty years, and then doubled and redoubled in the 1850s, in response to famine conditions in Ireland, and continued at lower, but still substantial rates on up to World War I.[143] The Scotch-Irish, except for the Appalachian mountaineers, began to be absorbed into American society early in their history,[144] even before the Irish Catholics were a major element in American society, so assimilation was not simply an escape mechanism. However, the very phrase "Scotch-Irish" was repugnant to Irish Catholics, for it implied an attempt of the Protestants to be distinguished from, and therefore a repudiation of other Irishmen.

The history of the Scotch-Irish in America is another example of how past conditioning exerts its influence. A leading historian once remarked how strange it was that the Scotch-Irish, from densely packed villages in Ireland, had become so celebrated as frontiersmen in America.[145] Although these individuals had no personal experience of the peculiarities of frontier life, they were descendants of people who had lived under frontier conditions in Ireland for generations, and before that in Scotland for centuries. It is doubtful that the Scotch-Irish brought to America specific skills relevant to frontier life, since they were at least a generation or two away from such a setting, but the cultural values, attitudes, and behavior patterns of the group had evolved under frontier conditions and provided a decisive advantage over other ethnic groups in pioneering on the American frontier.

The economic and social rise of the Irish Catholics came through channels very different from those followed by the Jews. Where the Jews became merchants, intellectuals, scientists, and educated professionals of many sorts, the Irish remained underrepresented in all these areas. The Irish became prominent in politics and in other areas where political kinds of skills—human relations—counted heavily, such as bartenders, priests, policemen, and entertainers. They also flourished in other areas where a combination of physical prowess and personal charisma were important—as in sports and organized crime. Wealthy Irish businessmen were often in banking, real estate, or construction, where working out "deals" with people was important, rather than in areas where cost accounting, technical expertise, or legal intricacies were paramount. The great big city political machines of the nineteenth century were built and dominated by the Irish, on into the twentieth century.

The key feature in the success of the big city political machine was that a political boss could cut through the bewildering complexity of the municipal bureaucracies and legal entanglement to *do something* for people who were not educationally, culturally, or financially able to get what they wanted in "legitimate" ways "through channels." It was a way of economizing on the use of knowledge, which was very scarce compared to what would have been required to make the formal, legal, and political system work. In addition to a long tradition of regarding the formal political and legal structure lightly— going back to the system imposed on them by the British in Ireland—the Irish had the further advantage in American society of being an *English-speaking* Catholic group, which could articulate the aspirations of other Catholic immigrant groups, such as the Italians, the French, the Germans, and eastern Europeans. This enabled the Irish to acquire political power even beyond their own considerable numbers in the big cities, and to dominate the hierarchy of the Catholic church in the United States, as well as to dominate the Catholic colleges and universities, allowing a "token" Italian or Slovak here and there.

As the Irish riots and Irish terrorist groups faded into history and the Irish became socially more acceptable, a more genial stereotype of the "stage Irishman" emerged. The stage Irishman featured singing and dancing, dialect, woman-chasing, drinking, and brushes with the law. Numerous popular stage productions exploited these characteristics for great commercial success over a period of at least half a century, but their substantive artistic merits may be indicated by the fact that none have survived as stage or literary products. These stereotypes became distasteful to second- and third-generation Irish-Americans as they began to rise, and the newspaper attacks and threats of boycott helped eventually to drive the stage Irishman to extinction,[146] though something similar continued in the comics in Maggie and Jiggs and in Moon Mullins.

The Irish became the most vocal of all immigrant groups about their public image and their group "identity." They formed the Irish American Historical Society in 1897, and its journal sought out all sorts of contributions, or just plain involvements, by Irishmen in historical events.[147] The Irish identity projected by Irish-Americans often had little or no connection with the culture of Irishmen in Ireland.[148] Despite the emphasis on "identity" many of the most successful and prominent Irish figures in American life have been un-Irish by the standards of the identity promoters. President Kennedy had more support among Jews than among the Irish.[149]

The Irish have not diversified into many different occupations. Unlike the Jews, Irish-American Catholics in general have tended to concentrate in a few familiar fields and to accept jobs which featured security rather than opportunity for high pay or high prestige.[150] The Irish began moving into jobs of low-level civil service after the Civil War and this has remained among their major occupations.[151] The Irish dominated sports and entertainment toward the end of the nineteenth century and the beginning of the twentieth century, but only a small part of the Irish-American population was involved. Generally, the Irish have shunned the chancy jobs for steady work. Even when the working class was heavily Irish, labor leaders were predominantly Jewish.[152]

The Italians

The background of nineteenth-century Italian immigrants to America was that of poor peasant communities with high rates of illiteracy and of sporadic uprisings which were quickly crushed.[153] In these respects their background was similar to that of the Irish. They differed from the Irish, however, in a number of ways that would later affect their development in America. The Italians who came to the United States were less often true peasants and more often farm laborers living in villages and small, densely crowded urban areas.[154] They were desperately poor, but more urbanized than the Irish. Moreover, unlike peasant communities, where women work on the family land, the Italian hired-farm-laborer economy, with a chronic oversupply of men, had few jobs for women.[155] Women were in an economically very dependent position, and their subordinate role provided no basis for the kind of matriarchal influence characteristic of family life among Irish-Americans and other low-income minorities. The Italian immigrants, like the Irish, came from the bottom of a society that was highly rigid, where people lived and died in their assigned place, though in Italy the barrier to social mobility was class rather than race or religion. The Italians were also much more emotionally and traditionally bound to particular villages, each with its own particular style of dress and of speaking, so that the great break with the past was not in leaving Italy but in leaving the village.

The bulk of the first Italian immigrants in the 1870s were from the more economically and educationally advanced northern Italy,[156] and their destinations were in Latin America for the most part. However, by the late 1880s, most immigrants were from the south of Italy and headed for the United States.[157] The great regional- and even village-consciousness of the Italians led to many internal divisions among Italian-Americans. The earlier and much smaller immigration of Italians to the United States prior to 1880 was largely from the north of Italy, and only about one-seventh of them were laborers.[158] Many were small businessmen of various sorts—most of the fruit stands in New York at that time were reportedly owned by Italian-Americans[159]—and they numbered between 12,000 and 20,000.[160] By contrast, today there are more than 7 million Italians in the United States, including more Italians in New York City than there are in Rome. There was not merely a great increase in numbers in the last two decades of the nineteenth century, but also a change in their origins (peasant backgrounds in southern Italy) and destinations (laborers in hard, dirty, low-paid occupations). As in the case of the Negroes and the Jews, those Italians who had arrived earlier and established themselves looked upon the later arrivals "with faintly-disguised contempt. . . ."[161]

The late-nineteenth-century and early-twentieth-century Italian-American immigrants continued in the United States to be strongly attached to local communities and local leaders who came over from Italy. Village leaders had often arranged passage in Italy,[162] and maintained a strong paternalistic sway over the group in America, where they often lived in neighborhoods consisting of people from the same province or even the same village in Italy.[163] Since the Italian immigrants spoke a foreign language and were from a very different culture from that of the big cities—notably New York—where they landed, they were overwhelmed and hopelessly dependent on a few of their local leaders to arrange work, housing, and other essentials of life. Opportunities for exploitation were enormous in such situations, and these opportunities were eagerly seized by ambitious *padrones.*[164] While every group of poor and ignorant people has been taken advantage of by their own leaders, as well as by members of the larger society, the extent to which the early Italian immigrants were taken advantage of has often been described, by contemporaries as well as by later historians, as worse than most.[165] A contemporary gypster in the 1890s found the new immigrants' innocence and gullibility such that he would consider it "downright sinful" *not* to take advantage of them.[166] The Italian immigrants continued on into the twentieth century to be ruthlessly exploited by their own small criminal elements.

Many of the late-nineteenth-century Italian immigrants began as ragpickers in the city dumps, or as bootblacks. In these occupations they simply took over from earlier immigrant groups who were now on their way up.[167] Even the small early Negro settlements of New York moved out as the Italians moved in.[168] The Italians moved into the poorest overcrowded tenements abandoned by other ethnic minorities. In the first Italian settlement in New York, populated largely by ragpickers, the neighborhood was considered so hopeless that neither cleaning nor rehabilitation was attempted, and eventually—after all the municipal delays, hearings, and false starts so familiar in twentieth-century slum housing cases—the city finally simply tore it all down and turned it into a park.[169] A variety of Italian communities then developed in other parts of the city.

The Italians arrived at the beginning of the construction of New York's vast system of subways, as well as the continuation of railroad building in general, and supplied a major part of the brawn required for these tasks, repeating the earlier role of the Irish in the digging of canals and the building of railroads.[170] Approximately one-half the Italian-Americans were still laborers at the end of World War I, but fifteen years later the proportion was down to just one-third.[171] Their rise on the economic ladder was accompanied by a much wider diversification as to industry and occupation.[172] By the 1920s the Italians had replaced the Jews as workers in the needle trades, as the latter moved on from this skilled and semiskilled field to higher occupations.[173] Since then, Italian-Americans have branched out into many professions, the creative and applied arts, industry, and business.[174] Italian-American organizations for mutual aid and other group purposes reflected their highly local attachments and heavy reliance on local leaders. Although these local organizations ran literally into the thousands, there was no substantial national organization of Italian-Americans, such as characterized the Irish, the Jews, or the Negroes.[175]

The relationship of the Italian-Americans to the Catholic church was somewhat different from that of the Irish. Italy had achieved national unity in a process generating much hostility between the Pope and the secular nationalist leaders.[176] The Irish, who already dominated the Catholic church in America when the Italians began arriving in the late nineteenth century, were hostile to Italian nationalists and revolutionaries, which included many who had arrived in America as refugees after the abortive revolutions of the 1830s and 1840s. The earlier nationalists had established a fiercely anticlerical tradition, both in Italy and in America, so that hostility between Irish-Americans and Italian-Americans existed even before the bulk of Italian immigrants arrived.[177] The bulk of the Italians however was neither anticlerical intellecutals nor revolutionaries. Nevertheless, the Catholic church, which in Ireland was a church of the masses persecuted by the ruling Protestants, was in Italy the dominant church historically allied with the ruling aristocracy and therefore suspected by the peasants.[178] Moreover, the particular way in which Italians regarded and acted toward the church as a religious as well as a temporal institution was very different from (and offensive to) the attitude of the Irish.[179] The friction created by these differences was such that Italian-American immigrants were even referred to from the pulpit as "Dagoes" and made to sit in the back of the church, with the Negroes.[180] One measure of the alienation of the Italian-Americans from the Catholic church in America during this period was that they contributed only 5 to 10 percent as much per capita as other Catholics in the United States.[181] In short, the Irish and Italian immigrants were not united by their common religion, but divided by it. Had they been of different religions, there might have been fewer occasions for group conflict.

Italian immigration, which had never reached 10,000 annually prior to 1880, rose rapidly to 100,000 per year by 1900 and reached a peak of more than 280,000 per year in 1914.[182] Eighty percent of these immigrants came from the less prosperous and less developed south of Italy.[183] They arrived late—after earlier immigrant groups had established themselves in various neighborhoods and occupations, after the rise of strong labor unions presented a barrier in many fields, and when national sentiment against immigration was growing in the United States. They had few skills of any value in an industrial economy, and illiteracy was high among them.[184] The early Italians played a negligible role in the development of the labor union movement, either in terms of general participation or the supplying of leadership. This may be due in part to the particular mixture of Italians in the United States, because 40 percent of those from northern Italy were union members in 1910, while only 10 percent of those from southern Italy belonged to unions at the same time.[185] In countries such as Argentina and Brazil, where northern Italians composed a large proportion of the emigrants from Italy, Italians were prominent both among the members and the leaders of labor unions.[186] Indeed, Italians played a much larger economic and social role in the general development of Argentina and Brazil than in already industrialized America, where many other groups had already staked out claims.

The Italians in many cases replaced the Irish in hard, dirty, low-paid work. For many this was clearly a temporary expedient, for the men usually came alone and a high percentage returned to their native land with their earnings. For decades the total number of Italians in the country was less than the number emigrating during that decade alone.[187] By 1920—just before the restrictive immigration laws—the Italian-American communities became permanent. The village way of life, the great respect and loyalty to leaders found in southern Italy, remained typical in the American city. In marked contrast to the pattern of ecological succession in housing found among Negroes, Jews, and other minorities, the Italian-American neighborhoods tended to remain Italian-American neighborhoods, even as the group rose economically.

Like other people from a peasant folk culture, Italian-Americans are underrepresented in institutions of higher learning and in intellectual life generally, though advancing steadily in both respects.[188] Unlike the Irish and the Negroes, the Italians maintained strong family traditions —part of their general emphasis on strong immediate attachments and corresponding disinterest in wider ties with the ethnic group as a whole, much less with the larger society. By contrast, both the Irish and the Negroes, with much less strong family ties than the Italians, have long had larger scale and more effective group-wide organizations. Part of the reason for this may lie in the history of the respective groups. The Irish and the Negroes were both oppressed and degraded by another race. The Italians suffered this treatment from their fellow countrymen and could expect help or consolation only from their family or neighbors. Like the Irish and the Negroes, however, the Italians experienced the law as something made by others and imposed on them—often in blatantly discriminatory ways—and so it had very little legitimacy in their eyes. By contrast, the Jews for centuries owed their survival as an outnumbered and hated minority to respect for the laws, and within their own ghettos they made their own laws.

In the public mind Italian-Americans have long been associated with organized crime. However, in this as in other ways, the Italians are internally segmented. Italian leaders of organized crime have been chiefly Sicilian (which is *not* to say that most Sicilians are in organized crime). Moreover, the Italians did not originate organized crime in America, but rather took it over from the Irish and the Jews in the 1930s.[189] For the Italian population as a whole, the crime rate even during their immigrant period was not as high as the crime rate for immigrants as a whole.[190] A study of Italian-American crime in 1929, during the age of Prohibition-spawned gangs, showed them to be *under*represented in the financial crimes (robbery, burglary, fraud, etc.) as compared even with native-born Americans.[191]

Italian-Americans have gone into business much more often than the Irish, but the businesses tend to be smaller than the businesses of the Jews, and do not as readily lead to further socioeconomic advancement.[192] In general, Italian-Americans tend to rise slowly, with fewer occupational differences between generations than with some other European immigrant groups.[193] This may reflect the barrier to higher education presented by the traditional peasant culture, in which movement into the educated professional elite means a separation from family and friends.[194] Those who do go on to higher education tend more toward the "practical" than toward the purely "intellectual" subjects.[195]

By 1968, the average income of Italian-American families ($8,808) had overtaken that of Irish-American families ($8,127),[196] although the latter had preceded them to America by two generations. This was not achieved by breakthroughs of Italians into higher-paid professional or managerial positions—where the Irish still retain a slight lead[197]—but by earning more in the working class brackets. The proportions of Irish and Italian families earning over $15,000 per year in the United States are virtually identical (10.4 and 10.5, respectively), and the percentage earning over $25,000 favors the Irish, 2.1 percent to 1.6 percent.[198] The Italians simply advanced economically along a broad front. Even in education, where they still lag slightly behind most other major immigrant groups (and behind Negroes) in school years completed, in percentage completing high school and percentage attending college, the Italians are also advancing at a faster rate between generations—only about 6 percent of those 35 years of age and older have completed college, but 12 percent of those from 25–34 have done so.[199]

The higher incomes of the Italians compared to the Irish is a difficult phenomenon to explain. Certainly it cannot be explained by the usual factors such as education (the Irish had more education, on the average, than the Italians), occupation (the Irish had a higher percentage of their population in professional and managerial employment), by time of arrival in the United States (the Irish had arrived before the Italians), or by linguistic or other cultural advantages (the Italians spoke a foreign language and had customs which were less like those of the United States than the customs in Ireland). Where did the Italians have an advantage—an advantage powerful enough to overcome the many other advantages of the Irish?

One clue may be in the respective attitudes of the two groups toward work and toward dependency and escapism. Irish-American immigrants had a high incidence of dependency on public charity, particularly in their early years when they were making the painful adjustment to a new way of life. Italian-Americans at a similar stage of their immigration experience were at least equally poor, performed many of the same low-level jobs formerly performed by the Irish, and often lived in slums formerly inhabited by the Irish. But the Italian immigrants would take virtually any job at virtually any wage to avoid accepting charity.[200] Those Italian immigrants who were ultimately driven to accept charity were often found to be half-starved and physically wasted. Even as late as 1906, "the Irish had more paupers, beggars, and inmates of almshouses than the Italians." [201]

These and other differences between the Italians and the Irish in America go back to the economic and social conditions in their respective homelands. The southern Italian working class youngster became a man early in life—during what would be adolescence in the American culture.[202] The Irish peasant, by contrast, remained a "boy" well into what would be middle age by American standards.[203] These differences in turn were a result of the economic constraints within which each group operated. The family farm in Ireland, among the class of people who immigrated to America, was just sufficient to support one family, and it typically needed all the hands available to do that. A young man could not expect to marry and add another child-producing family to his parents' farm and household, nor was he able to afford to buy his own farm in most cases. He therefore continued living on his parents' farm, being called and being treated as a "boy" on into late adulthood, until his father retired or died and the farm became his. During these long years the son was assigned tasks and chores by his father, his food and clothing were supplied by the family, the money he got was doled out by his father, and if he occasionally earned any money himself on outside jobs, it was expected to go into the family coffers.[204]

The Italians who emigrated from southern Italy and Sicily were usually either agricultural laborers or peasants. Even where they were peasants, the family farm was often too small and unproductive to absorb all the labor of the family, and the young boys were sent out to work in the labor market during their adolescent years. The young

Italian was likely to be self-supporting at an early age and could marry young and become head of his own household. This class of Italians was not any more prosperous than their Irish counterpart, but the human relations growing out of their particular economic circumstances required early self-reliance and no lifelong subservience or dependency, in hopes of inheriting the family property. The family property was either nonexistent or insufficient to live on in any case, among those southern Italians who immigrated to the United States. Because the self-sustaining or prosperous Italian farms were typically huge estates in Italy, there was a demand for farm laborers. Because more Irish farms were self-sufficient family plots, there was less possibility for an Irish peasant boy to become an independent farm laborer.

The Irish young man in a peasant family was not able to assume the ultimate role of husband and father until after a prolonged adolescence, and in the meantime his masculinity could be expressed only episodically in violence, drinking, and passing romances—all of which became prominent features of Irish life. Donnybrook is an Irish town, and Lynch is an Irish name. Alcoholism has long been a chronic problem in Ireland, and the rate of alcoholism among Irish-Americans remains several times as high as among Italian-Americans.[205] The need for alcoholic escape seems less a result of absolute poverty than of an unsatisfactory role in life in terms of human relationships. A similarly unsatisfactory set of human relationships—though for different reasons—is associated with a high incidence of alcoholism and narcotics addiction among American Negroes, though it has been estimated that the toll of alcoholism among nineteenth-century Irish immigrants was higher than alcohol and drugs put together among twentieth-century American Negroes.[206]

Neither the Irish nor the Italians lived in America as they had in their homelands. Both concentrated in large metropolitan areas working at urban occupations, in contrast to their rural backgrounds. However, each brought to the United States a cultural pattern reflecting early conditions, and these different patterns had substantially different economic results.

Chapter 4

Twentieth-Century Immigrants

Twentieth-century immigration to the United States differs from nineteenth-century immigration not only in numbers—a drastic reduction caused by tighter laws in the 1920s—but also in its ethnic composition. The German, Irish, and other northern and western European groups who dominated nineteenth-century immigration streams to the United States were already beginning to be displaced by the southern and eastern European groups toward the end of the century.

Irish immigration reached a peak of about 221,000 per year in 1851 but did not exceed 100,000 per year again after 1854 nor 55,000 again after 1891. Scandinavia sent just over 100,000 immigrants to the United States in 1882 but never sent even half that amount again in any year after World War I. Great Britain sent just over 100,000 immigrants in 1870, 1882, and 1888, but never again in the twentieth century, and never more than 60,000 for any year after World War I. German immigration reached a peak of about 250,000 per year in 1882 but did not go over 100,000 again after 1892 until the post-World War II era. The shift to southern and eastern European immigration can be seen in the figures for Italy and Russia. Italian immigration reached 100,000 per year in 1900 and remained above that level until it reached a peak of more than 280,000 per year in 1914. Emigration from Russia and the Baltic states passed the 100,000 per year mark for the first time in 1902 and remained above that level until 1914, reaching a peak of more than 290,000 per year in 1913.[1] However, the largest streams of people into the country after the restrictive immigration laws of the 1920s were the Mexicans, whose peak recorded annual immigration was less than 90,000.[2]

The rise of fascism in Europe in the 1930s brought a new wave of immigrants, similar in race but very different in socioeconomic background from most of those who came to the United States in the nineteenth century. These political refugees were often highly educated professionals, intellectuals, and scientists, and their adjustment to America was usually faster and more successful than that of either their predecessors or successors. Sometimes they are pointed out as examples of how people can readily succeed in America, even when they arrive penniless on these shores. While many of these refugees were forced to flee without their material possessions, they brought with them vast capital assets in the form of education and high-level experience in modern societies very much like the United States. The material possessions they were forced to leave behind were an effect rather than a cause of their prosperity. Their experience does demonstrate, however, the enormous importance of "human capital"— the investment of knowledge, skills, habits, experience, etc.—and of the return on this capital which often substantially augments what may look like payment for current exertions.

Since none of the twentieth-century minorities is comparable in size to the massive waves of Germans, Irish, Italians, or Jews in the earlier period, those discussed here will be chosen as illustrations of the role of various factors in the economic advancement of ethnic minorities in the face of language, color, and other economic and social barriers.

Japanese-Americans

Japanese-Americans have been the most successful nonwhite immigrant group in America, whether success is measured in income, education, and similar achievements or in low rates of crime, mental illness, and other forms of social pathology.[3] This was not always the case, however. When the Japanese first began emigrating to America in significant numbers at the end of the nineteenth century and the beginning of the twentieth century,[4] they went into many hard or menial jobs which native Americans did not want, and they received much lower wages for doing the same work. They were resented for lowering American wage standards and encountered a wide variety of discriminatory practices and even legislation barring them from certain occupations or from owning land.[5] Immigration laws were tightened against them and unofficial "gentlemen's agreements" with Japan greatly restricted the further emigration of Japanese laborers in the early twentieth century.

The Japanese were—and remain—a very small minority, even in the areas where they are most concentrated.[6] They have never had a substantial political base in the United States, as the Jews, the Irish, the Negroes, and others have had. Japanese-Americans also differ from most other immigrant groups (except the Italians) in having had a very large *return* migration to their homeland in the early decades of their life in America, this return migration exceeding the inmigration in many years.[7] Undoubtedly, the level of hostility they faced in the United States—and their political and physical vulnerability to it—had much to do with this.

Because many Japanese-Americans were denied citizenship by laws passed during the "yellow peril" hysteria in the early twentieth century, they were also thereby denied access to a number of professional and white-collar occupations which require a license and were also denied access to agricultural land—an important economic factor in the Pacific Coast states in which they settled. This left them manual occupations and small business. They early managed to achieve prosperity in these limited areas by the same hard work and thrift that had made them so feared as competitors in other fields. By the 1940s, many had achieved a modest success in the limited occupations open to them, and their children—as native-born Americans—had access to wider occupational opportunities. At this point came the cataclysm of this group's life in America—the attack on Pearl Harbor by Japan and their mass internment during the hysteria and race-hate that followed.

More than 100,000 Japanese-Americans, most of them native-born citizens of the United States, were rounded up and put into internment camps after Pearl Harbor, many losing property that they had worked for years to acquire, including some who lost literally everything they owned.[8] The rationale for this drastic measure was that Japanese-Americans were dangerous enemy aliens, but neither then nor at any time since was a single Japanese-American charged with a single act of espionage, sabotage, or disloyalty of any sort during World War II. It would be difficult to find any other group of Americans with such a record. Moreover, "enemy alien" status did not cause German-Americans or Italian-Americans to be rounded up and interned during World War II. Clearly, color prejudice and the fact that Japan had inflicted a devastating loss on the United States at Pearl Harbor were major factors. The fact that the Japanese had acquired enough property for others to profit by getting hold of it under duress was also a factor. The internment took place under a presidential executive order, and the general who carried it out declared: "A Jap's a Jap. It makes no difference whether he is an American citizen or not. . . ."[9] It would be necessary to re-create the atmosphere of the times to understand how such public statements could be made or accepted. Japanese-Americans in Hawaii were *not* interned, even though all the "reasons" given for interning Japanese-Americans on the mainland applied even more so in Hawaii, which was closer to Japan, more vulnerable to attack or invasion, and in which the disastrous attack on Pearl Harbor had taken place. The gross inconsistency is explained by Hawaii's long history as a multiracial society where substantial numbers of Orientals lived.

In the internment camps, Japanese-Americans were pressed to renounce their American citizenship by Japanese-American militants who resorted to threats and violence, with the apparent knowledge and connivance of the American officials in charge. Years later, these coerced renunciations were ruled void by a U.S. District Court,[10] and still later the whole operation was ruled illegal by the U.S. Supreme Court, now presided over by a man who originally supported and participated in their internment —Earl Warren. While the Japanese-Americans in the internment camps were considered enemy aliens, they were also—inconsistently—subject to the military draft as American citizens.[11] Even more amazing than the policies toward the Japanese-Americans during World War II were their own reactions to these policies. Those drafted and assigned to a segregated combat unit in Europe distinguished themselves as one of the most decorated units in any branch of service.[12] Others taught at U.S. Army language schools or worked for U.S. intelligence.

The internment period was a turning point in the history of Japanese-Americans. While the Japanese-Americans were first isolated in camps, many who were checked and cleared—about 35,000 persons—were released and allowed to go elsewhere than to the forbidden West Coast. These were primarily the younger, American-born Nisei.[13] Also, day-to-day life in the camp required Japanese-Americans to fill a wide variety of occupations, which would not normally have been open to them on the outside. The net effect was a greater residential and occupational dispersion than before, removal from a region of the country where anti-Oriental prejudice was much greater than in other parts of the nation, and a releasing of the younger generation from the narrower world of family and "little Tokyos" into the wider social and economic life of the United States. With the return of peace, anti-Japanese feeling not only receded from its wartime level, but probably to lower levels than before the war. The obvious injustice of their mass internment and the brilliant fighting record of Japanese-American combat units won public sympathy, even in areas long notorious for anti-Oriental feelings and actions. One sign of the times was the overwhelming defeat of a California referendum in 1946 which would have incorporated the anti-Nisei laws of the past into the state constitution.[14]

In short, the internment of the Japanese-Americans, like some of the medieval restrictions on the Jews, eventually worked to their advantage. It gave the group greater occupational and residential mobility, released the young and ambitious native-born Japanese-Americans from the strict control of their elders, and decisively broke the back of the anti-Japanese prejudice and discrimination which had held them back for decades. Despite irreparable personal and financial damage to individuals, Japanese-Americans as a group prospered more after they returned from the internment camps than before. In 1940 more than 25 percent of all Japanese-Americans were laborers, but by 1960 only 5 percent were in this category, while Japanese-Americans have as high a proportion of professional men as the white population (15 percent)—which represents nearly a quadrupling in twenty years.[15] Legally, Japanese-Americans never received full restitution for their wartime losses, even after the courts declared their internment illegal and the government authorized settlement of their financial claims. The actual settlement payments amounted to no more than ten cents on the dollar.[16] The Japanese-Americans, however, did not put their main emphasis on trying to get justice, but rather on trying to get ahead. This they did. Here they succeeded better than any nonwhite minority, earning incomes comparable to the white groups.[17]

West Indians

West Indian Negroes living in the United States are a minority much overlooked by scholars and researchers, even in an era of massive study of blacks. Yet they are a group of great importance, not only in terms of their past achievements and their current roles, but perhaps even more as a means of gauging the socioeconomic effect of being black, as such, as compared to the effect of the many cultural and institutional factors historically associated with the evolution of the American Negro. West Indians in the United States have long had a distinctive life style, set of values, and educational, economic, and cultural achievements very different from those of American Negroes. Though only a small fraction—perhaps 1 percent—of the black population in America, they have long been overrepresented among prominent blacks. Sidney Poitier, Harry Belafonte, Godfrey Cambridge, Shirley Chisholm, and Stokely Carmichael are all from West Indian backgrounds, as were Marcus Garvey, Claude McKay, and James Weldon Johnson during the black renaissance of the 1920s, and Malcolm X more recently. West Indians have long been prominent among "the first Negro who" pioneered in various political and legal positions in New York.[18] West Indians are disproportionately represented among black professionals.[19] Their education, income, home ownership, etc. have been obviously greater than among native American blacks,[20] and their indices of social pathology, such as crime, much less.[21] Like other very different subgroups of the same ethnic community, American-born Negroes and West Indian Negroes have had much mutual antagonism and conflict. There was open conflict in the 1920s among black leaders of American and Caribbean birth,[22] and in New York City among the native-born and foreign-born Harlem populace as well.[23] But even in later and quieter periods, the differences between American and West Indian blacks have continued.[24] One study has indicated that there is virtually no social intimacy between them, even when they are next-door neighbors.[25] How have two black groups come to be so different?

The history of West Indian Negroes, like the history of American Negroes, has been largely a history of slavery—a slavery very similar in some respects and very different in others. This history may provide some clues as to which particular features of slavery produce the most severe and long-lasting handicaps, and which features can be more readily overcome. Slavery in the British West Indies was plantation slavery to an even greater extent than in the United States, with an even higher incidence of absentee ownership (from England),[26] and—almost inevitably—involved even more severe treatment of slaves.[27] Sexual exploitation of slave women was more blatant and more organized than in the United States.[28] As in the United States, the planters deliberately tried to keep the slaves from learning to read,[29] and were probably more successful, since urban slavery was less common in the West Indies. The percentage of the Negro population that was free was small and not significantly different from that in the United States. In short, the West Indian Negro suffered brutality, the destruction of family life, and enforced ignorance to an even greater extent than his American counterpart. Yet a hundred years later the West Indian in the United States is not only more prosperous and better educated, but also has a much more stable and patriarchal family life. At the very least, the causal weight of these much discussed variables needs to be reexamined, and other factors sought as well.

West Indian plantations concentrated on one cash crop—usually sugar, but also coffee—to an even greater extent than in the United States, but because there was no readily available commercial supply of food in the islands, the slaves were forced to grow most of their own food on land set aside for this purpose and during periods of time set aside for this purpose.[30] Thus, even under slavery, West Indian Negroes had direct personal responsibility for an important part of their own well-being, and also acquired experience in economic activity on their own, since they cultivated their individual plots without supervision and were usually allowed to sell any surplus in the market.[31] American plantations, by contrast, were not forced to rely on such methods nearly as much, because their food needs could be supplied or supplemented through the market, given that there was a very large white, nonplantation population in the South and in the United States, which could supply many things needed on the plantation. In the West Indies there was no large white population, and most of the small white enclave were directly connected with the plantation.

The great population imbalance in the West Indies—90 percent black, 10 percent white—had a number of important ramifications. Not only did it force the slave-holders to allow the slaves some area of economic autonomy in order to achieve plantation self-sufficiency in food, it also made slave escapes and slave rebellions much more feasible than in the United States. The climate and geography of the West Indies also facilitated escapes and rebellions. The tropical climate made exposure less of a hazard to the escapee, and tropical vegetation made food more readily available in the wild, as well as providing cover in the largely unexplored interior of the island. The chance that an escaped slave would encounter even isolated white men—much less organized groups or settlements—back in the jungles or mountains was very small, as compared to the chance that an escaped plantation slave in the United States would run into white patrols, white workmen, or white rural settlements in the South. Moreover, the geography of the United States was well known to white men, though not to Negroes, whereas in the West Indies it was equally unknown to both and the whites were more reluctant to venture into the jungle. The importance of knowledge of the terrain and of survival prospects in the wild is shown by the great difficulty of enslaving Indians in the United States, whereas American mainland Indians transported to the Caribbean were more readily enslaved.

The greater self-reliance of blacks in the West Indies, deriving from the economic necessities of the plantation, combined with the greater prospects of permanent escape and survival off the plantation, made resistance and rebellion more feasible, since there was not the near certainty of being crushed that there was in the United States. Individuals and even groups of slaves escaped into the interior jungles and mountains, where they set up communities and even waged guerrilla warfare against the whites.[32] In short, out of West Indian slavery emerged a more self-reliant, independent, and defiant population than emerged out of U.S. slavery. Much of what is attributed to race as such, or to slavery as such, is a function of special historical circumstances beyond anyone's control. A further indication that it was circumstantial differences rather than racial differences that were involved is that white indentured servants were also more rebellious in the West Indies.[33] West Indian blacks and American blacks are not only both African in origin, but the West Indies was the "seasoning" station for enslaved Africans from various tribes and regions, and American Negroes were usually imported from the West Indies rather than directly from Africa. West Indian and American slaves were drawn from the same pool on the same island and differ, therefore, primarily in their experiences under slavery in the two settings. The West Indian setting permitted and fostered more self-reliance, more economic experience, and more defiance of whites. As a preparation for life as free men, these characteristics apparently outweighed the greater suffering, sexual exploitation, and enforced ignorance of the West Indian slaves.

The differences in emancipation between the West Indies and the United States were not unusually great. In the West Indies, as in the United States, mulattoes were either freed earlier or given special treatment on the plantation, and they remain a relatively privileged class long after emancipation.[34] However, it is worth noting that it is *not* the mulatto class that has emigrated to the United States, but rather those from the black population. While emancipation in the British West Indies was not as wholly unprepared for or as literally overnight as in the United States, neither was it as extended an evolutionary process as it was for most of the enslaved populations in Latin America. The British government announced eventual emancipation in 1823, through intermediary stages to be completed a decade later.[35] However, in this case, as in the American South, emancipation was the action of a distant central government over the strong objections of local whites, and while the local whites were in no position to launch a civil war, they did become increasingly repressive toward the slaves, toward free Negroes, and toward white missionaries sympathetic to the blacks.[36] Thus, far from the smooth transition envisioned by the British government, West Indian emancipation was marked by increased internal animosities and by increased rates of slave escapes, resistance, and open rebellion.[37] Freedom came to West Indian slaves nearly thirty years before it came to American slaves, and it did not begin in a war-shattered economy, as in the South, but nevertheless it coincided with declining economic conditions in the islands, with a disastrous setback in exports of sugar.[38] Moreover, by a variety of legal subterfuges the planters imposed conditions approaching peonage on many of the nominally free Negroes,[39] and the latter did not enjoy anything like the political ascendancy of American Negroes during Reconstruction.

Although the white aristocracy continued dominant in the top political and economic circles in the West Indies, there were far too few of them to man all the responsible positions in the economy and society. It was therefore impossible to limit black West Indians to purely menial jobs as was the case with blacks in the United States. Although great numbers of West Indian Negroes continued to experience dire poverty combined with discrimination by both whites and mulattoes, there was less often the completely closed door which so many black Americans faced in so many occupations.

The overwhelming proportions of blacks in the population made Jim Crow laws unfeasible, and therefore there were no such laws for West Indian blacks to accustom themselves to, with all the degradation and psychological problems this would have entailed. There could be a very few jobs reserved for whites only, but *only* a very few (since there were very few whites), leaving a whole spectrum of work, skills, and status for blacks. None of this implies that the British were any less racist than the Americans. Certainly the British in the West Indies were noticeably *more* racist than Latin rulers were in other Caribbean islands,[40] and fully equal to their American descendants in racism. Indeed, many of the harsh slave codes in the American South were copied directly from the slave codes of the British West Indies.[41] What differed were the economic conditions under which this racism existed and the limitations which this placed on the forms it could take.

The example of the West Indians suggests that it is not slavery alone, or even brutal treatment during slavery, that serves as a crippling handicap for generations after emancipation, but rather the occupationally and psychologically constricting world in which the American Negro developed in the United States. Their example also suggests that the current disabilities of black Americans are due not only to current discrimination but also to past deprivation and disorganization that continue to take their toll.

Puerto Ricans

Perhaps even more than other ethnic minorities, Puerto Ricans are a socially distinct group in the United States, rather than a distinct race in any biological sense. Most Puerto Ricans are white by the standards of Puerto Rico itself, which—like most Latin American racial standards—are less stringent than U.S. standards in drawing the line on the continuum from white to mulatto to black.[42] Since large numbers of Negroes and Indians on the island have virtually disappeared into thin air, as far as Puerto Rican population statistics are concerned, it is generally assumed that they have been absorbed into the white population of Spanish ancestry. Nevertheless, the majority of those Puerto Ricans who come to the United States are apparently white even by U.S. standards, so that the

Puerto Ricans as a group provide a basis for considering the importance of color as compared to other variables relative to economic advancement in the United States. Puerto Ricans represent in many ways a repetition of the experience of nineteenth-century European immigrants, though of course they are not officially immigrants at all, since they are U.S. citizens from an American commonwealth. Nevertheless, they speak a foreign language, come from a different culture, and in the continental United States they begin at the bottom of the economic ladder. Puerto Ricans have lower average incomes than American Negroes,[43] more children per family than native blacks or whites,[44] and a higher percentage are on welfare. They experience the classic problems of the nineteenth-century immigrants: high rates of delinquency, broken homes, tuberculosis, and mental illness,[45] as well as a problem more characteristic of twentieth-century disadvantaged groups: high rates of unemployment.[46] As in the case of the other ethnic groups with problems, however, it is necessary to keep in mind that most Puerto Ricans do not have most of these problems and that many do not have any of these problems. For example, six-sevenths of Puerto Ricans are *not* on welfare.[47]

Puerto Ricans are among the most recent arrivals in the continental United States. There was a net migration of less than 10,000 per year prior to 1930, and the massive immigration of Puerto Ricans has been a post-World War II phenomenon.[48] The Puerto Rican migration has been characterized by a very large *return* migration, so that the net migration figures greatly understate the number of persons traveling back and forth between the island and the mainland. Unlike the Italians and the Japanese who returned home in substantial numbers in the early decades of the twentieth century, the Puerto Ricans tend to return not to spend American money in a cheaper economy—the cost of living in Puerto Rico is similar to that on the mainland—nor in frustration or defeat. They return simply because it is relatively easy to move back and forth between the mainland and the island, just as other

Americans move from one state to another. It takes only a few hours to fly between New York and Puerto Rico, and the trip is not very expensive. The trip in either direction may therefore be for either a short-term, or a long-term stay.

Puerto Ricans are not only highly mobile between the island and the mainland—particularly New York City—but also highly responsive to changing economic conditions in both places. The net migration of Puerto Ricans has closely followed the ups and downs of the U.S. business cycle.[49] Before World War II, recessions or depressions in the United States caused a net loss of Puerto Ricans. Persistently high rates of unemployment in Puerto Rico during the postwar high-employment period in the United States has coincided with a mass influx. In 1950 there were a quarter of a million Puerto Ricans in New York, and by the early 1960s an estimated *three*-quarters of a million.[50]

Puerto Ricans who immigrated to the United States generally came from an urban background on the island, though not from such an overwhelmingly large city as New York nor from one with a similar culture. Although the Puerto Ricans followed the classic pattern of other ethnic minorities in crowding into the cheapest and poorest quality housing available, they did not have the option available to most earlier minority migrants of expanding from the initial settlement into surrounding neighborhoods. The initial Puerto Rican settlement was wedged into East Harlem and was therefore blocked from expansion to the west by the poorer members of another large minority who found it difficult to move. A small Italian community—traditionally immobile even when economically able to move—also blocked their expansion, as did a high-rent district and the Harlem River. The net result was that the rapidly expanding Puerto Rican "community" became in fact a large number of patches of settlements here and there across the length and breadth of New York City. Moreover, Urban Renewal programs have destroyed many Puerto Rican neighborhoods, scattering families and destroying what group life had developed.

One of the contrasts between the Puerto Ricans and the nineteenth-century European immigrants is that the Puerto Ricans lack many of the strong community-based organizations—churches, mutual aid societies, group rights organizations, etc.—which earlier immigrants possessed at a similar stage of their evolution. Partly this may reflect the scattered residential pattern of Puerto Ricans, but this is hardly a full explanation, since there are some very sizable Puerto Rican neighborhoods, comparable to those of earlier immigrants who produced more numerous and stronger local ethnic organizations. Additional reasons for the relative lack of Puerto Rican community organizations include the high residential mobility of the group within New York and between New York and Puerto Rico, and the fact that numerous city, state, federal, and commonwealth agencies now handle problems previously handled by ethnic community organizations. However, even in matters outside the scope of government and unrelated to residential mobility, such as the establishment of newspapers serving the ethnic community, newspapers serving the Puerto Rican community were founded and are owned by non-Puerto Ricans.[51] The Catholic churches in the Puerto Rican community are also largely run by non-Puerto Rican priests,[52] in sharp contrast to the Catholic churches serving the Irish community in the nineteenth century, though not too different from the Catholic churches serving the Italian community in its early years.

One consequence of the relative lack of ethnic organization among the Puerto Ricans is that, despite their substantial numbers, they have received relatively little political patronage—even in a city traditionally given to ethnic patronage and "balanced" tickets of candidates— and are less well represented in government jobs than the Negroes of New York.[53] They have also filed relatively few complaints of discrimination with the agencies handling such matters.[54] One reason for this might be the generally less aggressive attitude of Puerto Ricans noted by a number of observers.[55] This more easygoing nature has also had its positive effects, in enabling the scattered Puerto Ricans to get along with numerous other ethnic groups in New York with a minimum of friction,[56] in marked contrast with such groups as the nineteenth-century Irish or the Negroes. Puerto Rico itself is a multicolored society with substantially less racial friction than the mainland United States.

To an even greater extent than other ethnic minorities in poverty, Puerto Ricans have a very high birth rate, double that of the general population.[57] The usual explanations of absence of birth-control knowledge or the opposition of the Catholic church seem not to apply here. A massive birth-control information program began in Puerto Rico in the 1940s, over the largely ineffective opposition of the Catholic church, but the problem was that birth-control devices were not used, for reasons both cultural and associated with overcrowded sleeping conditions.[58] Sterilization operations—which avoid both these problems—are unusually widespread among Puerto Ricans, both on the island and on the mainland.[59] This is a striking indication of the naïveté and arrogance of those who conceive of these problems—and other such problems—in terms of a need to bring their superior "knowledge" to the "unenlightened" group. On the contrary, it is the situation of those suffering the problem that needs to be studied by presumptuous outsiders.

The higher socioeconomic classes use conventional birth-control methods but much of the migration to the U.S. mainland is from the working class. The history of Puerto Rico's population problem is very much like that of other less economically advanced countries. The lifesaving methods of modern medical science are imported without importing also the lower birth-rate patterns that developed in step with these mortality-reducing techniques in the Western world. A sharp reduction in mortality, unaccompanied at first by any change in child-bearing patterns, leads to rapid population growth, followed later by declining birth rates. The birth rate began to decline in 1950 in Puerto Rico.[60] Among Puerto Ricans on the U.S. mainland, declines in birth rate tend to follow rises in socioeconomic position. As among Negroes, the birth rate among middle-class or well-established working-class families tends to be drastically below that of the group as a whole.[61]

Although Puerto Ricans living on the mainland had until recently lower average incomes than Negroes, they have established many more businesses.[62] These have been almost exclusively small businesses serving the local community. The larger number of Puerto Rican businesses may reflect the greater specialization required because of having a different language and having special food preferences which are understood and served by the *bodega*. But it may also reflect a greater cultural tendency toward business as a means of advancement than among upwardly mobile Negroes, who are more likely to enter professions, where they are better represented than the Puerto Ricans.[63] Puerto Rican immigrants are dominant in small businesses in the Virgin Islands,[64] where they are regarded as unusually hard-driving businessmen—by Virgin Islands standards—and have a stereotype very much like that of Jewish merchants in Western societies, Chinese merchants in Asia, or East Indian merchants in Africa. In short, the "unaggressive" attitude of Puerto Ricans is relative to U.S. and specifically New York standards. Puerto Rican businesses have not, however, taken the decisive step taken by some nineteenth-century ethnic minorities—notably the Jews—of going beyond serving the local ethnic community, which provided an initial base, to serving the society at large. Many earlier ethnic minorities have still not taken that step, and in a world of large, well-established chain stores and giant corporations, that step may be harder to take today than in the nineteenth century.

Although Puerto Ricans have until recently been lower on the income and occupational scales than American Negroes,[65] they are rising faster and passed the latter by 1970. As in the case of the Negroes, those Puerto Ricans who come to public attention tend to be "problems" while the majority who are not problems are overlooked. In the case of Puerto Ricans this is even easier to do, since more of them are not readily distinguishable in color from the rest of the population and some are deliberately "passing." As in the case of some earlier immigrants, the occupational distribution of the second generation is noticeably different from that of the first, and in an upward direction.[66]

Like other ethnic minorities, the earlier Puerto Rican migrants, once established economically and adjusted socially, tended to resent the later arrivals, both for their behavior in itself and for the effect of that behavior on the public image and public acceptance of the group as a whole.[67] Puerto Ricans have developed most of the social pathology of earlier minorities, including juvenile gangs, but unlike some earlier minorities these juvenile gangs do not generally have adult criminal counterparts.[68]

Mexican-Americans

Although there are more than 5 million Mexican-Americans in the United States[69]—making them one of the largest minorities in the country—they tend to receive much less attention than other ethnic minorities, and are in fact sometimes referred to as the "invisible" minority.[70] Sometimes even governmental reports or scholarly studies simply lump them together with Puerto Ricans, Cubans, and other "Spanish surname" immigrant groups.

The classification of people as "Spanish surname" does not correspond to any actual social grouping in the United States. Major Spanish-origin groups, such as Mexican-Americans, Puerto Ricans, or Cuban-Americans, usually marry within their own respective groups, with little intermarriage among these groups. Indeed, where members of these groups intermarry, it is usually with someone of non-Spanish origin.[71] This is in part due to the great physical distances between these groups, Mexican-

Americans being overwhelmingly concentrated in the Southwest, while Puerto Ricans are overwhelmingly concentrated in the Northeast. In short, while Americans of Spanish origin may share certain characteristics, they do not behave or interact as one ethnic group.

Mexican-Americans are an important group, not only in and of themselves, but also as a group whose cultural characteristics permit some comparisons and estimates of the effect of language, color, and foreign origin as factors in economic progress. While Mexican-Americans are similar to Puerto Ricans in language, religion, and other cultural characteristics, they are different in legal status (Mexicans are foreign immigrants while Puerto Ricans are American citizens) and in skin color (a smaller percentage of Mexican-Americans being "white" by U.S. standards).

The percentage of Mexican-Americans in each age bracket is very similar to the percentage of the Puerto Rican population in each bracket, and very different from the distribution of Americans in general. Mexican-Americans or "Chicanos" are much younger than the population as a whole, reflecting a much larger family size, with many small children. One indication of the magnitude and implications of the differences in family size is that the per capita income of Mexican-Americans as a whole is lower than that of Negroes, even though the average income of Mexican-American families is slightly higher than that of Negroes.[72] Mexican-American families are simply larger than Negro families, and much larger than the average American family. As with the Puerto Ricans, the Catholic church is apparently much less of a factor in this, or in Mexican-American life generally, than it was (or is) in the life of the Irish-Americans. Again, this goes back to the history of the church in the country of origin. In Mexico, as in Latin America generally, or in Italy, the Catholic church was identified with the economically and politically dominant classes, whereas in Ireland the Catholic church suffered persecution along with the masses of the poor for centuries.

Although most Mexican-Americans (85 percent) were

born in the United States,[73] their native tongue is Spanish in 72 percent of the cases.[74] Most other Spanish-origin minorities in the United States also grew up speaking Spanish at home—83 percent of Puerto Ricans, for example.[75] Although this is a common pattern among second- or third-generation Latin groups (including Italian-Americans), it is in sharp contrast to the pattern among nineteenth-century Jews and Germans, who began to speak English very early in their group history. The differences can hardly be due to the languages involved, since Spanish is linguistically closer to English than the languages spoken by Germans or Jews. However, the Mexican-Americans, like the Puerto Ricans and the early Italian and Japanese immigrants, have a very large *return migration* to their homeland. For many Germans and other ethnic minorities who migrated to the United States in the nineteenth century, the move was considered permanent from the outset, and for millions of Jews fleeing persecution there was neither a desire nor an interest in returning. The temporary or tentative nature of the Mexican migration to the United States is indicated not only by the preservation of a foreign language but also by the low percentage of Mexican immigrants who become naturalized citizens, as compared with immigrants from other countries.[76]

The extent to which a group makes such a major investment as the learning of a new language and culture is very much related to the expected period of payoff on the investment, which is to say how long the average individual or family in the group expects to be in the new environment. With Mexican-Americans being concentrated in the American Southwest, along the border of Mexico, numerous temporary or permanent returns to the Mexican culture are feasible. Given a skin color difference between most Americans and Mexican-Americans, and a long tradition of racial segregation, a mere change of language would not mean as much toward opening economic opportunities as it would to the white nineteenth-century immigrants. However, the explanatory weight of this latter consideration should not be overemphasized, since Puerto Ricans usually retain Spanish as their mother tongue also—particularly those Puerto Ricans of dark complexion.[77] All these various group patterns represent very rational investment decisions for those involved. It is also very logical that the different degrees of assimilation tend to be reflected in different degrees of economic progress among the various groups.

Like most American ethnic minorities from very low income agrarian background in their homeland, Mexican-Americans have averaged lower incomes than the American majority, and lower than such minorities as the Jews and the Japanese-Americans. However, as compared to other similarly disadvantaged minorities—the nineteenth-century Irish and Italians, or the Negro or Puerto Rican population—the economic experience of Mexican-Americans has not been unusual. The median family income of Mexican-Americans in 1970 was $6,002 compared with $5,879 for Puerto Ricans and $7,891 for Americans as a whole.[78] The incidence of "broken homes"—16 percent of all Mexican-American families—is higher than the national average, but lower than among contemporary black families,[79] and still lower than among the Irish in New York at the time of World War I.[80] Youth crimes, including gangs, are common in Mexican-American urban communities,[81] but this has been the rule rather than the exception among low-income minorities in both the nineteenth and the twentieth centuries. The age distribution of the Mexican-American population has a disproportionate number of individuals in those age brackets where there is a high crime rate, so that the Mexican-American crime rate would be higher than the national average even if it were identical to the national average within each bracket. In general, the Mexican crime rate has been above average, but not outstandingly so.[82]

Although Mexican-Americans have vast internal differences in the time of family arrival in the United States (some Mexicans were in the Southwest when the area was first taken over by Americans), rural location and life style, average level of income (varying widely by localities), as well as the usual differences between generations, these have not generated as much open strife as among other minorities, such as the Irish and the Jews in the nineteenth century or among Negroes in the twentieth century.

Like other groups without an intellectual tradition in their homeland, Mexican-Americans have put little emphasis on education in the United States. American Negroes average more years of schooling than Mexican-Americans, nationally and in every state,[83] and are functionally illiterate only half as often.[84] Mexican-Americans attend college less often than either black or white Americans, and tend to enroll in the less prestigious colleges when they attend college at all.[85] Mexican-Americans organize very few institutions of their own—businesses, mutual aid organizations, or civil rights movements.[86] In housing, Mexican-Americans are more crowded than either blacks or whites,[87] and in general they suffer a high incidence of premature death from the traditional poverty diseases.[88]

Like other poor minorities, in both the nineteenth and twentieth centuries, Mexican-Americans have had much negative experience with the institutions of society, from police to schools.[89] Chicanos have had perhaps more trouble than any other ethnic minority with immigration officials, for the ease of crossing into the United States from Mexico has led to large-scale illegal entry and therefore to large-scale campaigns to deport Mexicans, in which native-born Mexican-Americans are often stopped, questioned, or raided, in the search for illegal aliens. During one such campaign in the 1950s, nearly 4 million Mexicans were deported in a period of five years.[90] Obviously far more people than this had to be investigated in order to find those residing illegally in the country.

As with some other minorities, the progress of Mexican-Americans has not been constant, but has been interrupted by important periods of retrogression. In parts of the Southwest where Mexican-Americans were landowners or otherwise locally important persons in the nineteenth century, both political and social equality were common, but by the turn of the twentieth century, with the massive influx of outside whites and the economic decline of the old Spanish families, this tolerance gave way to increasing discrimination.[91] The later waves of poor, unskilled, and uneducated Mexican immigrants faced strong anti-Mexican stereotypes, practices, and ideology. The degree of discrimination has varied greatly from place to place (Texas cities vs. Los Angeles, for example) as well as over time.

The labor shortages of World War II provided Mexican-Americans with opportunities to enter higher occupations than before, and also broke down some of the legal and social segregation.[92] As with other minorities, major opportunities came to the Chicanos not as a result of any special programs directed toward them, either by their own leaders or by the leaders of the larger society, but by major economic events unrelated to race as such. Most Mexican-Americans seized the opportunity to advance themselves economically and socially, but one segment used this prosperity to dress in flamboyant "zoot-suits" and launch gang attacks on U.S. military servicemen.[93] This dealt a damaging blow to the public image of Mexican-Americans, and brought on internal condemnation from the Chicano community—one of the few instances of major internal conflict.

While Mexican-Americans have been characterized by a Mexican-American sociologist as a "nonachieving minority," [94] their average income and other social indicators compare well with those of minorities from a similar socioeconomic background in their respective homelands. Given the extreme unreliability of official immigration figures,[95] due to the large illegal immigration to America, it is difficult to say how many generations most Mexican-American families have been in the United States. This is especially so in view of the large number of Mexican-Americans repatriated over the years, voluntarily and involuntarily. However, the first great wave of official immigration, ranging from about 40,000 to almost 90,000, was in the 1920s, with another very large wave beginning in the mid-1950s and still continuing today. Since many of the earlier immigrants went into rural or agricultural pursuits, most urban Mexican-Americans today are probably no more than second-generation city dwellers. Compared to others at a similar stage, the Mexican-Americans' record is at least creditable.

Chapter 5

Comparisons
of Ethnic Groups

Comparative studies of ethnic minorities can provide some empirical basis for assessing the relative importance of various factors (language, color, tradition, socioeconomic background, etc.) in the economic advancement of a people. A further analysis of the particular periods of history in which various groups arrived in the United States, or in the urban economy and society, provides further clues. In this way, history provides a useful though imperfect substitute for a controlled experiment, which rigorously scientific analysis would require, but which cannot be achieved with human beings.

It is difficult enough to try to draw valid conclusions of a cause-and-effect nature without attempting also to assign praise or blame to whole groups of people for the way they did or did not advance economically. All of them lived in a world they never made, both in terms of the American society they entered and in terms of the traditions and skills they inherited from ancestors long dead. It is even pointless to grade cultures in any absolute sense, for some cultural features that produce success and prosperity within an industrial and commercial economy and society might well prove futile and embittering in a peasant economy or in a fishing and hunting community. For example, a number of efforts by Jews to settle in colonies on the land in nineteenth-century America ended in total failure in very short order. This most successful of American ethnic minorities—in an urban setting—failed in agricultural colonies from New York state to Oregon to Louisiana, making such basic mistakes as purchasing the wrong kind of land. These colonies failed even though organized and supported by many Jewish leaders and subsidized by leading Jewish organizations.[1]

What can be done is to ask (1) *whether* cultural differences greatly affect the progress of American ethnic groups, or whether this is largely determined by the degree of "racism" in the larger society toward the particular group, and (2) *what* particular cultural characteristics are related to economic development. Since times differ as well as people, it will also be necessary to consider how the circumstances faced by contemporary ethnic minorities differ from those faced by the minorities who arrived in America in the past.

Intergroup Comparisons

The economic and social history of American minorities provides at least suggestive and tentative answers to many of the questions that arise concerning current ethnic problems. These include (1) the role of group identity, (2) the significance of political power, (3) the causes of family disorganization, (4) the significance of color, and (5) the conditions for economic advancement.

Group Identity None of the major ethnic groups in America has escaped serious internal divisions. Neither has the dominant majority of Protestant Anglo-Saxons, for that matter. The only difference among the various minorities in this regard is how they dealt with their internal differences.

During the rise of the Jews in nineteenth-century America, their internal *social* differences—aside from politics or ideology—were serious enough to make intermarriage among various subgroups of Jews uncommon, even though most of them lived in New York City. The differences between German and eastern European Jews were particularly deep and long lasting, but other subgroups of Jews—the Hasidic Jews, for example—maintain a separate identity within the Jewish community to this day. Jews were split not only by nationality but also religiously—from the most rigidly tradition bound through various gradations of religious liberalism to complete agnosticism—and ideologically they ranged from the most conservative pillars of society to the most radical revolutionaries. Neither cultural, religious, political, social, nor ideological unity was ever imposed or achieved among the Jews. Yet the Jews developed some of the strongest social service, philanthropic, and cultural institutions of any ethnic group, making it unnecessary for Jews to receive charity from Gentiles, and promoting many interests of the Jewish community as a whole. In short, uniformity was not made a prerequisite for community cohesion.

Among Irish-Americans, a very different pattern emerged. They split along lines of Protestant versus Catholic, as in Ireland itself, as well as along socioeconomic lines between the so-called shanty Irish and the lace-curtain Irish. The Protestant-Catholic split was a source of violence and bloodshed for many years on Orange Day, and their clash on that day in 1871 led to more than fifty deaths. The theological differences between the two denominations of Christianity may be no greater than those among various denominations of Jews, or between religious Jews and nonreligious Jews, but the accompanying social distinctions and social animosities were obviously much more divisive and self-destructive among the Irish. The outnumbered Irish Protestants (the "Scotch-Irish") tended to assimilate into the larger society, draining off a better-educated and more economically successful part of the Irish-American community. In short, where uniformity was made a prerequisite for community, it was the community which suffered.

The later history of American Negroes followed much of the pattern of the Irish. The factions led by Booker T. Washington and by W. E. B. DuBois, respectively, in the early 1900s were not nearly as far apart in substance as popular stereotypes sometimes suggest,[2] and were probably not as far apart as various Jewish groups who worked together, but the bitter rivalry between Washington and DuBois consumed much energy in internal struggles that could have been more effectively used promoting the interests of black Americans as a whole. The rise of Marcus Garvey's movement in the 1920s was another source of bitter internal strife among Negroes, as was the later split between "militants" and "moderates" in the 1960s.

Group "identity" is a shifting concept. It sometimes refers to a simple awareness of similarity, sometimes to a positive pride in group membership, and sometimes to a cultural or ideological uniformity associated with group membership. The mere recognition of group membership is common both to economically successful and economically unsuccessful ethnic groups. Pride in group membership is apparently greater among the more successful than among the less successful groups, but this obviously might be either a cause or an effect. It is by no means clear that promoting group identity promotes economic success. Some of the most successful minorities have been very Americanized. The Jews became rapidly acculturated to American society in the course of their rise, probably more so than the Irish, and certainly more so than the Italians. Japanese-Americans are so acculturated that they are not socially accepted as Japanese in Japan. West Indians in the United States have long preserved a special identity— not a black American identity or an African identity, but more often a *British* identity.[3]

A distinction must also be made between having a special identity and making a public *issue* out of identity. Among nineteenth-century immigrants, the Irish made perhaps the greatest public issue about their identity. They organized protests and boycotts against those who depicted the Irish in unworthy roles in literature or on the stage.[4] They organized a society to study Irish history and to publicize it.[5] The Gaelic language and special Irish food were also objects of great concern. In politics, their bloc vote helped them control many big-city political machines. None of this implied that the Irish had any more "identity" than anyone else, or that such identity as they manifested was either deep-seated or authentic, in terms of its faithfulness to Irish culture as it existed in Ireland. In many ways what Irish-Americans projected as their "Irishness" was wholly foreign to Irishmen in Ireland.[6] By contrast, Jewish identity was preserved through a variety of religious, social, and cultural organizations and patterns of behavior, but was not nearly as much of an *issue*. There were probably far more nineteenth-century Jews who spoke Yiddish than there were Irish-Americans who spoke Gaelic, but Yiddish was not a public issue. Again, the twentieth-century pattern of Negro Americans repeats much of the nineteenth-century pattern of the Irish. The emotional surge of black identity in the 1960s has fastened upon many cultural items—the so-called Afro hair style, for example—that were foreign to most Africans. Black history became as much of an issue as Irish history had been—and neither history was seriously studied by most of those who made a great issue of it. Swahili, like Gaelic, became an issue, but again without much serious study of it.

Group cohesion has sometimes had an important economic effect by providing a sheltered market in which members of the given ethnic group evolve as businessmen and professionals serving the ethnic community. This was important at one stage or another in the development of most American ethnic minorities. However, the real progress of the group was often marked by a diversification *beyond* this pattern to a pattern of working in a wider variety of occupations in the mainstream of the American economy. The small Jewish peddler tended to concentrate on selling to the Jewish community, but the great Jewish stores—Macy's, Gimbels, Stern's, Wanamaker's, Bloomingdale's, etc.—served the whole American society. The turning point in the rise of the Japanese-Americans came when they were forcibly torn away from their home communities and many of their younger members were scattered through the interior of the United States. Before that happened, however, they had already developed economic skills in their enclaves as the Jews had done in the nineteenth century. In short, the ethnic community has been a useful incubator for economic skills, but once those skills were developed, it has been a confinement that has had to be transcended for any substantial economic achievement to take place.

One of the more promising periods in the evolution of American Negroes was the late nineteenth century, when blacks dominated particular small businesses serving the larger society, such as catering, barber shops, and some high-prestige restaurants. This was *before* the rise of the black urban ghettos. However, the racial tensions which developed with the rise of massive black urban communities, made up largely of unskilled and uneducated migrants from the rural South, doomed the existing black businesses serving a white clientele, without developing a major business class in the ghettos themselves. Black business, having begun at a stage which other American ethnic groups reached only later in their development, was unable to readily go back and begin again in the ghetto and retrace its progress out to the larger society. Possibly confidence was as important as skills and experience, and redeveloping confidence after losses and retrogression may be harder than developing it the first time from scratch. There were at all times *some* black businesses, but one of the remarkable characteristics of American Negroes has been the relative smallness of their business class compared to that of other ethnic groups—even poorer ethnic groups, such as the Puerto Ricans—and the fact that black West Indians, in New York at least, pioneered and were greatly overrepresented in such black businesses as existed.

Many minorities have faced a painful dilemma when the earlier arrivals, having developed economically and socially to the point of achieving some degree of prosperity and respect, are threatened by a later (and sometimes larger) wave of migrants of the same group, whose general unpreparedness for American life revives racial stereotypes, prejudices, and discrimination against the group as a whole. The Jews went through this more than once after the earlier German Jews had established themselves in the first half of the nineteenth century, only to have their successful and conservative community suddenly augmented by radical refugees from the unsuccessful revolutions of 1848 in Europe, and then inundated by the great immigration of Eastern European Jews after the 1880s. The later wave of Jewish refugees in the 1930s aroused further apprehensions among American Jewish groups, some of whom were ambivalent or even opposed to further large-scale immigration of Jews to the United States. Similarly, the antebellum "free persons of color," particularly where they were most prosperous—as in Charleston and New Orleans—viewed the emancipation of slaves ambivalently and often resisted any social contact or public identification with those freed by the Civil War.

Later, when the great waves of Negro migrants reached northern cities, the smaller, established black communities already there opposed the migrants in their press[7] and fled toward surrounding white communities when they arrived.[8] European immigrant groups in general opposed further immigration, once they were established, even at a working-class level. Organized labor in the nineteenth and twentieth centuries—composed primarily of immigrants or the sons of immigrants—was the most zealous advocate of restricting immigration, and ultimately achieved laws that brought large-scale immigration to an abrupt halt in the 1920s.

However justified or unjustified the actions and attitudes of the earlier arrivals toward their later compatriots might be from a moral perspective, their fears were not without foundation. The arrival of large numbers of unassimilated Jews coincided with a renewed wave of anti-Semitism which closed many doors previously open to American Jews—economic as well as social doors. In the South, the virulent racism which created the Jim Crow laws and widespread lynchings occurred in the wake of emancipation and Reconstruction. During this period, many families descended from the "free persons of color" who had after long struggles achieved a secure, if peripheral, place in the world, suddenly found themselves regarded and treated as "niggers" like everyone else of their race. In the North, the migration of uneducated and unacculturated blacks from the South directly disrupted the existing black communities and the heightened prejudices which followed their arrival destroyed many black businesses serving a white clientele. Unacculturated European immigrants were a very direct threat to organized labor, not only because of their willingness to work for lower wages, but also because their linguistic and cultural differences among themselves made it hard for them to cooperate—a fact exploited by employers, who deliberately sought a *mixture* of foreign workers, just as early slave owners had deliberately sought a mixture of people from different African tribes.

Established minority-group members have generally followed a variety of policies and practices with regard to later, poorer, and less acculturated members, ranging from social separation and public repudiation through attempts at getting them acculturated, through fiercely proclaiming group solidarity and promoting the group culture in defiance of the larger culture. All these policies have been followed by American minorities to varying degrees, but the variation in the mixture is notable and related to other variables. Group solidarity can be maintained at lower cost where (1) the economic and cultural differences between the earlier and later groups are not too great, (2) the earlier group is sufficiently large relative to the later arrivals that the latter are not a heavy burden to finances or patience, (3) the later arrivals are neither financially nor culturally so far behind Americans in general that a very long period would be required to bring them up, and where (4) the larger society either has not had strong prejudices toward the particular group, or would be unable to readily identify members of the group. Where these variables tend to make the cost of group solidarity very high, there tends to be less group solidarity. In extreme cases, successful group members may simply disappear into the larger society en masse, as in the case of the nineteenth-century Irish Protestants. Isolated members of other ethnic minorities have changed their names or life styles and entered the larger society, but the number who have done so is in most cases only a fraction of those who could have done so if they chose. The cost of severing relationships with family, friends, and the previous culture is higher than most people are willing to pay. A more viable alternative for many is class separation, with or without public repudiation of the newer arrivals.

One of the important and practical ways in which group identity and pride have been maintained has been through *mutual aid* organizations. These organizations not only spare the poor, sick, or homeless individuals the humiliation of accepting charity from outsiders, they spare the group as a whole the loss of self-respect which charity entails. The Jews developed extensive mutual aid societies and specialized institutions—hospitals, orphanages, schools, etc.—soon after arriving in America in great numbers in the 1880s. Despite great poverty, disease, and death among them initially, seldom was a Jew in a position of accepting charity from Gentiles. This was not only a current benefit to individuals but an important *investment* in group pride and independence as well, which would pay off in later generations. Similarly, Japanese-Americans, even during their years of economic struggle, provided many mutual aid organizations to spare the members of their race from having to accept help from whites—and to spare the group as a whole the demoralizing consequences. The *early* history of American Negroes shows a similar pattern among the "free persons of color"—but like so much of their progress, it was wiped out in the social upheavals following emancipation, Reconstruction, Jim Crow, and the mass migration to the North. Mutual aid societies among "free persons of color" were found as early as 1775 in Boston,[9] and in 1859 in the same city it was noted that Negroes were seldom seen in the poor-houses, because of the "many" benevolent societies in the local black community.[10] Black mutual aid organizations of various sorts were organized in Philadelphia in 1787, and in Charleston in 1790.[11] There were eleven such organizations among Negroes in Baltimore in 1813, and one hundred by 1838.[12] The principle of self-help was well established and well functioning in black communities throughout the country[13] when these communities were suddenly inundated with masses of wholly unprepared blacks, first in the wake of emancipation and later in the mass migrations to the northern cities. The task of incorporating these masses into a mutual aid system, a culture that had evolved over several generations, or of caring for them out of the modest incomes of a tiny fraction of established blacks was so obviously over-whelming that it was seldom seriously attempted. Poor blacks were largely abandoned to dependency on public charity. Mutual aid organizations continued to exist and even to grow in the black communities, but they were now hopelessly inadequate for the needs of the whole commu-nity. Moreover, the early attempts to develop thrift among newly freed slaves through the Freedmen's Bank and numerous local banks met a disastrous end when they collapsed in business failures which destroyed the pain-fully accumulated savings of thousands of newly freed slaves. The immediate economic disaster—bad as it was—was probably less disastrous than the long-run conse-quences of discrediting thrift and investment. W. E. B. Du-Bois claimed that ten more years of slavery would not have done as much harm to the development of the Negro race in America as the failure of the Freedmen's Bank.[14] Fortunately, the Freedmen's Bank, run largely by whites, was succeeded in later years by smaller banks run by Negroes themselves, and though many of these were later wiped out in the general wave of bank failures in the 1920s, banking is now one of the leading black businesses, and the source of wealth of at least a few black million-aires. It is interesting that here, too, the Negroes and the

Irish are so similar in the kind of businesses at which they achieve their greatest success. It is further ironic that banks dependent upon many small savers should take root among two ethnic groups popularly thought of as reckless spenders.

Group identity has external as well as internal meaning: the "public image" of a minority as perceived by the outside majority. The two groups that have been most vocal about their public image are the Irish and the Negroes. The stereotypes of the two groups were in fact remarkably similar; the nineteenth-century image of the Irishman has been likened to "Sambo" in behavior, even though not in appearance.[15] That image has of course changed drastically since, so that in the mid-twentieth century to call attention to a man's Irish background is now regarded as a genial gesture.[16] The change of image, however, did not occur in response to deliberate image-remaking efforts but resulted from the economic rise of the Irish and particularly the decline of Irish violence, under the combined influence of the Catholic church and the group adaptation of the Irish to a minority status in America, in which the tactics developed as a majority in their homeland had to be discarded.

The special identity of ethnic groups erodes not only as their members deliberately or unconsciously become acculturated to the larger society, but also as the larger society borrows from their culture. Many Jewish, Irish, Negro, and Latin expressions, foods, and other cultural features are now *American* cultural features.

While the naive "melting pot" concept of American ethnic groups can no longer be accepted, it would be equally naive to conceive of these groups as isolated enclaves preserving the purity of their "cultural heritage." Even where ethnic minorities have a distinctive cultural style, that style often evolved on American soil and bears little resemblance to the culture of their ancestors' homeland. It is well known that chow mein and chop suey are not indigenous Chinese foods, but dishes developed by Chinese-Americans primarily to serve to white Americans.[17] The "Afro" hair style of American Negroes is likewise not the hair style of native Africans, except for those Africans who now imitate American fashions against the opposition of traditionalists. In a similar way the Irish-American St. Patrick's Day Parade evolved in the United States, and has only in recent years been exported to Ireland. Even with more serious cultural features, such as the mutual aid organizations which virtually all American ethnic groups developed, these are usually organizations quite foreign to the same groups within their native land. The same is true of ethnic political organizations and in some cases newspapers. An Irish-American, Italian-American, etc. cultural feature is often just that—a feature peculiar to their current setting but unlike the culture of Ireland, Italy, etc., or that of the United States. Many individuals steeped in their ethnic culture, and proud of the ethnic distinctiveness it gives them in the United States, have visited their ancestral homelands only to discover that this same culture brands them instantly as Americans to the natives.

The "melting pot" concept covered not only cultural assimilation, but biological amalgamation as well, perhaps best symbolized in such works of fiction as *Abie's Irish Rose*. For Negroes, Jews, Puerto Ricans, and Mexican-Americans, such biological "melting pot" concepts are very much fiction. However, among men of Irish, German, Polish, and British ancestry in the United States, it is the rule rather than the exception to have a wife of a different ethnic group.[18] In each case, however, more men in these groups are married to women of the same group than to women of any other specific group; the in-group marriages constituting between one-third and one-half of all marriages. Moreover, marriages outside the group are not random; the second most frequent source of wives is typically some related ethnic group—marriages between Russians and Poles, for example. Even the close Italian in-group society is not immune. Only 52.5 percent of Italian-American men marry Italian-American women.[19]

The extent to which these ethnic intermarriages

constitute a dilution of ethnic cultural identity depends on the extent to which the individuals adapt one or the other's culture, or become cosmopolitan instead. On this, statistics tell us very little. It seems probable, however, that much of the intermarriage occurs among individuals already outside the cultural orbit of the ethnic enclave, so that such marriages are symptoms rather than causes of assimilation, and may have little effect on the culture within the enclave.

Political Power Most American ethnic groups have striven to acquire greater political power, using various tactics with varying degrees of success. More fundamental than the question, What tactics have worked best? is the question, Has political power promoted economic and social advance, as hoped? Clearly political power is not a necessary condition for economic advance. Japanese-Americans have always been so overwhelmingly outnumbered, even where their largest communities were located, that political power was out of the question. Yet they are among the most successful of American minorities, despite much discriminatory legislation, particularly in West Coast states in the first half of the century. By contrast, the Irish were the most politically successful of American minorities. They dominated political life in a number of American cities by the middle of the nineteenth century. Yet, despite an impressive list of Irish political "leaders" (plus militant extremist "martyrs"), the bulk of Irish-Americans was still predominantly in unskilled and menial occupations in the last decade of the century. The Jews were no match politically for the Irish. Even in the Jewish stronghold of New York City, it was the middle of the twentieth century before Jews were able to wrest political control from the Irish, even though they had passed them economically in the preceding century. Negroes, in some respects, have had more political representation than Jews. In short, those American ethnic groups that have succeeded best politically have not usually been the same as those who succeeded best economically.

Bloc voting has not always been a powerful weapon, particularly when everyone knew in advance which party was going to receive that bloc vote. The political party that "owned" the vote had little reason to make concessions to earn it, and the opposition party had little hope of winning a committed bloc vote by offering concessions. This was largely the history of the American Negro vote, which was automatically Republican for two generations after Lincoln freed the slaves, and which became automatically Democratic after Roosevelt's New Deal. The development of more independent voting by blacks has led to more concessions by politicians in general than a bloc vote was able to get in the past. The size of the vote has obviously been a factor here too. However, even a large minority which shows little interest in politics, such as the Mexican-Americans, may be ignored by the politicians.

Political success is not only relatively unrelated to economic advance, those minorities that have pinned their greatest hopes on political action—the Irish and the Negroes, for example—have made some of the slower economic advances. This is in sharp contrast to the Japanese-Americans, whose political powerlessness may have been a blessing in disguise, by preventing the expenditure of much energy in that direction. Perhaps the minority that has depended most on trying to secure justice through political or legal processes has been the American Indian, whose claims for justice are among the most obvious and most readily documented. Yet the economic level of most American Indians is lower than that of most other disadvantaged minorities. In the American context, at least, emphasis on promoting economic advancement has produced far more progress than attempts to redress past wrongs, even where these historic wrongs have been obvious, massive, and indisputable.

Family Life   Among the many ways in which American ethnic minorities have differed from one another is in the pattern of their family life. The question here is whether, or how, this relates to their economic progress.

Do the more successful minorities have a different family pattern from the less successful minorities, and if so, is this a cause or an effect of their economic success? Is it the love and authority relationship among the family members themselves which matter most, or the particular values with which the family endows the children? To what extent is family life shaped or influenced by the physical surroundings—"urban blight," etc.?

While some of the less successful minorities—notably the nineteenth-century Irish and the Negroes—have had a high incidence of broken homes, such family breakups have always been extremely rare among Italian-Americans,[20] who also rose slowly in income, education, and social position. The Italian-American family has been not only highly stable but also highly patriarchal. However, strong stable families have been characteristic of such successful minorities as the Jews, the Japanese-Americans, and West Indian Negroes. Puerto Ricans and Mexican immigrants to the United States have had a highly male-dominated family pattern, where the male is present, but both have also had a large incidence of broken homes in the United States.

In their family patterns as in other aspects of their social and economic patterns, American ethnic minorities reflect their past history and culture. The value of family life, and the particular kind of family life, was usually established long before the immigrant groups arrived in America. The maintenance of their family pattern under American conditions has been a continuing problem for most minorities, the Puerto Ricans being particularly unable to maintain the male-dominated extended family with highly protected children in the American setting.[21] Italian-Americans have succeeded, however, in maintaining a very similar kind of pattern through a culture that is highly centered on the family and the immediate community—with less emphasis on the larger Italian community as a whole than with other ethnic groups[22]— and by allowing the safety valve of *male* freedom to hang out on the streets with neighborhood boys.[23]

The example of Italian-American families raises the basic question of what is meant by "group identity." Theirs have been the most powerful ties to family and immediate friends—often composed of people from the same part of Italy or even the same village in Italy or Sicily[24]—but with no strong *group-wide* organizations, such as Negroes and Jews have.[25] In Fiorello La Guardia's 1941 campaign for mayor of New York City, for example, he carried the city but lost the Italian-American vote to his Irish opponent.[26] Group identity has always been extremely strong among Italian-Americans, but the group in question was the family and associated friends. Strong loyalty to such small groups was a major factor in the exploitation of Italian-American workers in the nineteenth century by their own labor contractors who dealt with the American employers. It has also helped Italian-Americans to drive out other ethnic groups who controlled organized crime before them,[27] and to survive the challenges of later ethnic groups to their control. The point here is that group identity is not simply strong or weak, but that it may be strong and weak at different levels for different groups.

Clearly it is not simply the *stability* of the family which correlates with economic success. While there are no highly successful ethnic groups who have *unstable* family life, stability alone has not been sufficient to create economic advancement. Stable families imply emotional strength and stable values transmitted to the children, but the particular nature of these values influence the uses to which the emotional strength is put, and therefore the chance of economic progress. The Jews, the Japanese-Americans and West Indian Negroes emphasized such traits as work, thrift, and education—more generally achievements involving planning and working for the future, implying the emotional control for self-denial in the present and emphasizing the logical and mundane over the emotional, the imaginative, and the heroic. The opposite characteristics can be seen among the Irish and the Negroes, where advancement has been achieved in emotional and imaginative areas, such as oratory, lyric literature, and music, and which have produced many dramatic "leaders" and heroes. A more revealing contrast, however, may be with the Italians who have had strong and stable families without the rest of the pattern of Jews, Japanese-Americans, and West Indian Negroes. The Italian-Americans, like the Irish, came from a rural background in which the small village community was essentially the whole world as far as the individuals within it were concerned. To a certain extent, this was also true of Negro and Puerto Rican migrants to northern cities. Such settings have never produced large-scale visions of philosophy, economic opportunity, or great concern for education in the broad sense of knowledge of the world rather than training in particular skills. In short, groups developing in such settings have tended to organize their daily lives around the immediate "practicalities" of a *given* setting, and either to avoid the abstract and speculative or to reserve it as a place for emotional release in religion, song, or small-time heroics in defense or some half-thought-out concept of personal "honor" or status, rather than approaching the abstract with a systematic, disciplined, long-term effort which produces science, large-scale economic ventures, scholarship, or major socioeconomic changes. American minorities from peasant backgrounds may admire great intellectual, economic, or social advances, dream of duplicating them, or even occasionally make efforts to that end, but they are not likely to be dedicated or sustained efforts, such as they put into vehicles of emotional expression, such as music, fighting, or the colorful use of words.

Where groups from peasant backgrounds have excelled in areas outside the daily routine, it has typically been in feats of immediate performance with emotional appeal—athletics, music and other forms of entertainment, oratory—rather than in the culmination of a lengthy preparation in formalized abstractions, such as scholarship, science, law, medicine, or economics. Efforts have been made to depict those who have created less in areas of formalized abstractions as intellectually inferior. However, there is not so much a difference in intellectual level as in the kinds of intellectual activity involved. The kind of intelligence required in athletics, music, or oratory is an immediate, almost impulsive intelligence—perhaps exemplified in a great broken-field runner or an improvising jazz musician—rather than the kind of intellectual capacity developed and trained over a long period of time. This is not to claim that there is no need for training and experience in popular music or oratory, or that there is no place for inspiration in science or scholarship, but only to point out that the relative proportions of these qualities are very different in these different fields. The nature of these different intellectual orientations is so obviously related to the kind of culture from which the groups came that there is no need to attribute them to innate biological differences among people.

Unlike other groups from a peasant culture, the Italian-Americans have successfully run businesses—but usually *small* businesses under the immediate direction of the owner and often in close touch with the local community, rather than businesses requiring a broader vision and a wide range of abstract skills.[28] A disproportionate percentage of the Italians who have succeeded in a big way in broader fields have come from the *north* of Italy or from *non*peasant classes in southern Italy.[29] With the economic and social rise of Italian-Americans, increasing numbers go to college but specialize more in "practical" pursuits rather than in "the more intellectual and speculative" subjects.[30] The effect of patterns developed centuries ago and thousands of miles away remains strong.

One of the more remarkable contrasts between ethnic groups is that between the family patterns of American Negroes and those of West Indian Negroes living in the United States. The high incidence of broken homes, and the greater influence of the black woman (as compared to American women generally) in the family have been major features of studies of American Negroes, from the pioneering research of W. E. B. DuBois at the turn of the century to the controversial Moynihan Report of the mid-1960s.[31] By contrast, the family life of Negroes who emigrated from the West Indies is both highly stable and highly patriarchal. What does this imply for some of the "explanations" given for family disorganization among black Americans? Clearly, any explanation based on genetic racial characteristics or on the African cultural background must be discarded. African families are strong, extended families, and patriarchal. The more popular explanation that slavery is responsible[32] must also be seriously reexamined.

Slavery made it impossible for black men to have any real authority over either their women or their children, or to protect the women from being sexually exploited by white men, and the large number of mulattoes born during slavery indicates that such exploitation was common. However, slavery in the West Indies was at least as bad as slavery in the United States, in this respect as well as in others. In the West Indies during the era of slavery, it "was no uncommon thing for a planter to line up his slave girls before his guest who was invited to take his choice for the night." [33]

The matriarchal family and many broken homes tend to be prevalent in situations where there is always steady work available for the women, while the men face recurrent unemployment. The nineteenth-century Irish and the Negroes through much of the present century have been in precisely this situation—the women in constant demand as domestic servants while the men are hired and fired from a series of unskilled and unsteady jobs. Modern statistics show the unemployment rates among black males to be highly correlated with black divorce rates a few months later.[34] The segregated southern school system created another set of steady jobs for black women, which persisted and grew as domestic service declined. The rise of steady clerical work for women at a time when automation was destroying many of the manual-labor jobs for men continued this pattern. It is not that the men earned less than the women, but that their income was less dependable, and less comparable to the income of males in the larger society than is the income of black females relative to females in general. In short, the black husband is often in no position to play the economic role which the general mores project, while the black woman is both able and forced to play a larger role than that generally projected for wives. The *relative* position of the sexes is crucial: black families have been breaking up at a rapidly increasing rate during a period of rising black incomes—but one in which black women's incomes are rising at a much faster rate than that of black men.[35]

While the family situation of contemporary American Negroes is a major social problem, it is not historically unusual, much less unique. The incidence of broken homes among blacks is about 30 percent, among Puerto Ricans slightly higher, among Mexican-Americans slightly lower. But among the Irish in New York at the time of the First World War family breakups were *much* higher—50 percent of their families had broken homes.[36]

Another demoralizing and alienating influence between the sexes within a group is widespread female prostitution involving males of other ethnic groups. This history is also common to both the Irish and the Negroes. Most prostitutes in many American cities in the nineteenth century were Irish, as were most prostitutes in London in the eighteenth century. Prostitution has also flourished in many black communities in the United States, attracting a large white clientele. The attitudes, emotions, and behavior generated by this situation reached well beyond those directly engaged in it.

The great similarity in the experience of the Irish-Americans and of American Negroes, and the great differences between the family patterns of American Negroes and black West Indians, completely undermines the argument that current black family problems are a product of slavery. So does the existence of similar problems among white Puerto Ricans, among Mexican-Americans, and to some extent among unemployed aerospace engineers. Women-centered families are in fact common among low-income whites in America,[37] whether the family is "broken" or intact. Similar patterns are found in working class families in England and in the Caribbean.[38]

Cultural factors cannot be entirely ruled out as influences, along with the economic factors. In the late nineteenth century, Italian immigrants were poorer than the Irish or the northern urban Negroes at that time, and yet they did not suffer family disintegration to a comparable extent. One reason may be that the patriarchal tradition that the man alone worked had been very strong in southern Italy, where it was easily sustained by a shortage of jobs. Further, this lack of work experience among Italian women made them less employable in America. The fact that the Italian immigrants often settled together in a neighborhood with relatives and close friends from the same village in Italy meant that there was, in effect, a pooling of risks, so that the temporary financial help needed during periods of unemployment could come from the group without forcing the wife to work (the settlement of Italians in groups was not simply quaint peasant folkways). Child labor was also common among Italian immigrants, in defiance of school and labor laws, and whatever its other drawbacks, it did not tend to break up the family. Finally, many of the Italians who first came to America during the period of the worst hardships were single males, many of whom returned to Italy as planned after making some money in America. In short, the Italians who bore the brunt of the first entry into American society were less often families than in the later period.

The number of children per family is also highly correlated with income level among blacks. In the lower income brackets, black families have more children than white families at the same income level, while in the upper income brackets, black families are *smaller* than white families.[39] Black families headed by professional or technically trained men do not have enough children to reproduce themselves. The great maldistribution of children by income class is further aggravated by the fact that income distribution is slightly more *unequal* among blacks than among whites.[40] That is, the top 10 percent of blacks earn a higher proportion of the total income of the black population than the top 10 percent of whites earn of the total income of the white population. There are a number of important social consequences of this situation:

1. The painful struggle from poverty to middle-class income, which a certain proportion of American Negroes makes in each generation, has to be largely done all over again in the next generation, because middle-class blacks have so few children to inherit their advantages.

2. The bulk of black children come from those classes with the least income to support them, and the least education or successful experience to impart.

3. The enormous economic disparities within the black population—between the only child of a doctor or engineer and the huge family of a laborer or welfare mother—creates great emotional strains—envy, suspicion, guilt, etc.—within the black community, inhibiting cooperative efforts to advance the race as a whole.

The reasons for the extremely small size of black middle-class families—ranging from 0.7 to 1.6 children in various studies—[41]are undoubtedly many, but it would be difficult to assess their relative importance. One factor is that blacks of the same middle-class *income* level as whites have less *wealth*,[42] and so are less able to afford children. They would tend to have less wealth because they are more likely to be *newly* middle class, from families too poor to have left them even a modest estate and with relatives who would be less able to help them in an emergency and more likely to require help from them in an emergency. The newly achieved middle-class-income position is probably of more value to the blacks, both because it is new and hard won, and because it removes them from the worst forms of racism. Finally, middle-class blacks are more likely to come from lower-class homes with excessive numbers of children and to react strongly against their own childhood experiences. Perhaps as generations pass and middle-class blacks become familiar with and more confident in their new status, some of the reasons for severely restricting their family size will erode, and a more normal distribution of children will evolve in the black population.

It has been a common phenomenon in most races and nationalities, at most periods of history, that the poor have more children than the rich. Among low-income blacks, families have been even larger than among most low-income Americans. This is clearly not a racial characteristic, as shown by the opposite pattern among middle-class blacks and by the unusually small families of most urban blacks before the twentieth century. Whatever the reasons, its consequences are very serious, and reach beyond the individual family to affect the economic and social progress of American Negroes as a whole. For example, much publicity has been given to the fact that a high percentage of black males fail the U.S. Army mental test, and this has even been used to support the theory of racial inferiority. However, *three-quarters* of all black males who failed the mental test came from families with four or more children. Half of them came from families of six or more children.[43] Among either blacks or whites, mental development tends to be greatest among small families. Many studies of high-IQ children, of prominent men and women, and other "success" groups, have typically found a great overrepresentation of the "only child" or the firstborn, who was necessarily an only child for at least a time. Conversely, twins—who share divided attention from the moment they enter the world—average lower IQs than children born one at a time. In short, family size has implications well beyond the family itself. The direct financial cost of supporting a large family, serious as that is, may be less important than the racial and social consequences of sending forth large numbers of people with less preparation than is needed to cope with the complexities and frustrations of modern life.

Since family size varies by income and education, a

considerable part of the ethnic variation in number of children is in reality a variation in income and education among ethnic groups. The fact that Negroes of high income and advanced education have fewer children than whites in similar categories, even though blacks in general have more children than whites in general, is only one example of this. Puerto Ricans have more children born per woman than Americans of Irish, Italian, German, Polish, or Negro origins. Yet Puerto Ricans who have finished high school have fewer children per woman than any of these ethnic groups—and fewer than the national average for high school graduates. Even Mexican-Americans, who have the largest number of children per woman in child-bearing years of any major ethnic group, do not have as many children per woman as *any* of these other minorities (other than Puerto Ricans), when comparing high school graduates only—and they too have fewer children than the national average for high school graduates.[44]

Color There is little doubt that color differences have aroused even more racial antagonism than the other ethnic differences which generate group animosities. The peak levels of hostility against Orientals have been comparable to those against blacks, though black-white hostility has a longer history in the United States. Color differences are important not only because of the degree of racial antagonism associated with them, but because color is an enduring difference from generation to generation which time does little to erode, as it does with language, religious, and other ethnic differences. For the foreseeable future, color is a difference that will either have to be accepted or remain a source of social friction and hostility. The question is, *Can* color differences be accepted in American society? How important has color been as a variable affecting the economic development of ethnic minorities?

For most of American history, color differences have not been accepted, where acceptance means simply the ability of a person to go unmolested, uninsulted, and to work or live wherever his capabilities would enable him to do so. Very often it is assumed that an approach to such acceptance must be the product of "education," with "leadership" being taken by governmental and civic leaders in organizations, and that "time" is bringing us closer toward such acceptance, though there are varying estimates of the rate at which this is happening. Like so much that is said about race, these propositions are generally judged by their moral quality or their intellectual symmetry, and almost never examined empirically. In those situations where there has been more acceptance of color differences, has this been the result of campaigns for racial tolerance by leaders and organizations? Has time been a major variable, in the sense that progress has been the rule, with only the rate of progress being problematical, and with no important worsening of race relations taking place over time?

Consider those times and places where there have been closer approaches to acceptance of color differences. One of the earliest such periods was the early seventeenth century. As mentioned earlier, Africans brought to the American colonies in bondage were, during the early decades, treated according to the same rules as white indentured servants; mixed freely with white indentured servants, married, or otherwise produced children with them, were freed at the end of the customary indenture period, and enjoyed most of the usual rights of people in whatever position they managed to achieve. It was not a Utopia, but it was a lot better than what was to follow. This situation was not the result of any moral exhortations, governmental programs, or organized campaigns. On the contrary, the progressive enslavement of blacks was the product of organized political campaigns backed by ideology and economic special interests.

Early American colonists were not only vocally opposed to slavery, but even southern colonies such as Virginia and Georgia passed laws prohibiting it while South Carolina put increasingly heavy duties on the importation of slaves.[45] All of these colonial laws were *nullified* by the British government, under the influence of special interests who profited from the slave trade. It was precisely stateways which changed folkways. In short, in early colonial America up to the seventeenth century, the natural behavior of people in everyday life was not nearly as bad as their political response to an issue that was whipped up emotionally.

Despite the supposedly beneficial effects of time, the status of the black man in America deteriorated over most of the next two hundred years, as his bondage was progressively made more complete, more irresistible, and more difficult to escape. An exception was the period after the Revolution until the early years of the nineteenth century. During this time, organized campaigns led by men of the stature of Thomas Jefferson and Benjamin Franklin did produce some good, though they failed in their attempts to get slavery abolished. In view of the number and importance of the men involved, the net result must be considered rather meager—a reflection on this particular approach rather than on the individuals. Men of lesser stature, both in history and in their own time, were able not only to thwart them but to clamp down harder than ever in the period from 1810 to 1860.

Another oasis of sorts was the urban slavery which allowed some Negroes some measure of freedom and exposure to wider horizons. Here again the loosening of the bonds of slavery was not the result of any deliberate organized effort to that end, but was a natural by-product of a situation in which the full brutalities of the plantation were not needed or even useful. Again, the natural behavior of people in everyday life was much better than the repressive laws or the organized demands to keep the Negro in his place.

One of the great moral crusades revolving around the American Negro was the abolitionist campaign beginning in the early part of the century and continuing on up to the Civil War. This coincided with the greatest sustained and progressive repression of the Negro—slave and free,

North and South. Rights enjoyed for years were taken away, one by one. Jobs once held securely were now reserved for whites only. Free black individuals and communities once living peacefully by themselves were set upon by white mobs. How much of this was a reaction to the abolitionists' making an issue is still a matter of judgment among historians. It is clear, however, that the immediate conditions of blacks was not improved by the moral crusade. Whether the abolitionists brought on the Civil War is an even more controversial question. Government policy, of course, ultimately freed the slaves, but it was government policy—primarily at the state level—which had kept them enslaved, not only in the general sense that governmental sanction was necessary for slavery to exist, but in the sense that legal barriers to manumission kept American Negroes from being freed individually as readily as blacks in Latin America were.

Another period of moral crusade, but this time with political power behind it, was that of Reconstruction in the South. Here organized campaigns were responsible for major political gains for blacks and for emergency economic aid under desperate postwar conditions. The moral climate also brought forth many northern missionary teachers whose work has been deservedly praised by both contemporaries and later commentators across the spectrum of social and political opinion. There is no denying the great immediate benefits of this particular moral crusade. Nevertheless, this was also a period in which economic retrogressions existed side by side with political advance. The great number of black skilled workers—four-fifths of all the skilled mechanics in the South in 1865 were black[46]—declined drastically during Reconstruction and the decline continued well on into the twentieth century. The reaction after Reconstruction brought on the notorious Jim Crow laws and the greatest wave of lynching in American history. It would be hard to balance the immediate benefits and the ultimate losses from the moral crusade and Civil War. For present purposes, it is sufficient that they were unable to create as acceptable a social climate as had existed spontaneously in some past and future periods.

In the late nineteenth and early twentieth centuries, northern urban Negroes began to achieve a level of acceptance not to be reached again until generations later—and not yet reached again in some respects. Profitable and prestigious black businesses serving white customers, housing integration even in Chicago—these seem like optimistic visions today. Yet they were achieved without campaigns, programs, or "moral leadership." They were destroyed precisely when race became a public and political issue, with the arrival of large numbers of southern Negro migrants.

The record is not unequivocal, but it lends little empirical support to belief in the effectiveness of organized campaigns to promote color tolerance, and provides at least some basis for believing that color acceptance is not impossible in the United States.

General Conclusions

There are some strong resemblances between the experiences of most ethnic minorities in America and some other equally strong differences in the patterns of their development. Few ethnic characteristics could reasonably be regarded as racial in any biological or genetic sense, because in many cases various cultural subgroups have completely different behavioral characteristics from those of their own race representing different cultural traditions. Very different family-size patterns among American Negroes of different economic levels is one obvious example, as well as numerous differences between American-born and West Indian-born Negroes. The differences in income, education, and general outlook between Protestant Irishmen and Catholic Irishmen—both in the United States and in Ireland—are other obvious examples. Among Italians there are great differences in the behavior and achievements in America between those whose ancestors lived in peasant villages in the south of Italy and those whose ancestors lived in a different social or cultural background. Nor is this simply a matter of internal differences in genetic ability. Those of a given group who "succeed" in American economic and social terms typically do so in particular kinds of work which reflect the values developed long ago in different settings. A successful Italian-American whose ancestors lived in a peasant village is unlikely to be in the same field as an equally successful Jew whose ancestors lived in medieval urban ghettos, or a successful black whose ancestors were enslaved in the South. What is more important than simply noting ethnic differences is seeing whether there are certain patterns which hold true from one ethnic group to another—whether certain traits tend to produce certain results, at least in the American setting, regardless of who has those traits.

Some traits commonly thought of as causes of economic failure and social pathology are low-income origins, overcrowded and substandard housing, prejudice and discrimination, inadequate educational opportunities, and a general failure of public services—such as the police, schools, and garbage collection—to do their jobs properly in minority neighborhoods. All those things impeded the progress of all American minorities; but it is by no means clear that the more successful minorities had any less of such handicaps than the less successful minorities.

Most American immigrants arrived broke and had to live from hand to mouth, as did American Negroes after being freed from slavery. The overcrowding in the tenements on the Jewish lower east side in the nineteenth century exceeded anything seen before or since.[47] A recent survey of a lower east side slum now inhabited by poor blacks shows that there are only *one-third* as many people in a given area as there were when it was a Jewish slum in the nineteenth century.[48] Indoor toilets were then the exception rather than the rule, and the smell in some neighborhoods was often described as unbearable by outsiders not used to it.[49] So too was the smell in the overcrowded ships bringing immigrants to America. From the middle of the nineteenth century on, indoor toilets developed—for the joint use of several families.[50] A study in New York City in 1894 showed only 51 private toilets in nearly 4,000 tenements, and only 306 persons out of more than a quarter of a million had bathtubs in their homes.[51] Epidemics of various diseases were common in immigrant neighborhoods.[52] Hundreds died just from summer heat in New York in 1896, even though the temperature averaged only 91 degrees and never reached 100 degrees.[53] What would be a moderate hot spell today was literally killing heat in overcrowded tenements with virtually no ventilation. As for the police, their graft collections were a regular part of doing business on the lower east side.[54] And it was not uncommon when a Jew was attacked for the police to arrest the victim and let the attacker go free. This was also common practice on the West Coast when Japanese-Americans were attacked. To say that such things are morally revolting is not to say that they are historically rare. What is rare and relatively recent in history are serious attempts to force the police and the courts to administer justice to minorities—and to the poor generally—in an impartial manner. It was commonplace for immigrant children to be taunted by their "American" classmates or to be treated with contempt by their teachers, and for the parents to be too intimidated to do anything about it.[55] At some time or other, they were all thought to be "hopeless" by outsiders—and had little or no hope themselves.

It would be very difficult to discover any relationship between the different rates of economic advance by different minorities and the various "causes" of poverty. However, it is not so difficult to relate the rate of advance of certain cultural traits. Among the characteristics associated with success is a *future* orientation—a belief in a pattern of behavior that sacrifices present comforts and enjoyments while preparing for future success. This may manifest itself in building up a business, acquiring a skilled trade, or in long years of educational preparation for a professional or intellectual career. Those groups who did this—the Jews, the Japanese-Americans, and the West Indian Negroes, for example—all came from social backgrounds in which this kind of behavior was common before they set foot on American soil. The Jews' urban, commercial, and intellectual orientation was centuries old when they arrived in the United States. The Japanese-Americans, though poor upon arrival, had come from a *middle-class* rural background in Japan—not a peasant background, as in the case of the Irish, the Italian-Americans, or American Negro migrants from the South. Negroes in the West Indies worked at responsible jobs for generations, and had personal economic responsibility even under slavery. There is no place for praise or blame for individuals here; rather it is a question of cause and effect for large groups. The Jewish boy who is conditioned to book learning from his earliest years is as much a creature of circumstances beyond his control as the children of other minorities whose interests are channeled into completely different areas, and who may grow up regarding books as something odd. Nor is it even a matter of superior foresight by one's ancestors. It would have been wholly irrational for peasants in past centuries to promote book learning and school attendance in view of the desperate need for anything the children could contribute to the family's immediate subsistence, and the long odds against their being able to rise economically or socially in highly rigid societies. Uninhibited conviviality and a seizing of passing pleasures is by no means unreasonable for people whose "place" in life has been rigidly fixed beyond much hope of change, as it was in Irish and Italian villages in past centuries, and among past generations of blacks in the American South. Nineteenth-century immigrants from a peasant background seldom used the free libraries available, and resisted compulsory education laws.[56] By contrast, Jewish immigrants crowded into every free educational institution available.[57] Attitudes, once formed, acquire a momentum of their own, however, which persists even under very different circumstances. It is important to understand which cultural patterns prove successful, nevertheless, because attitudes can also change, even if not suddenly.

A high value on immediate "fun," "excitement," and emotionalism has characterized the less successful minorities. For both the Irish and the Negroes Saturday night acquired a great importance as time to release emotions in music, lively social activities, and fighting.[58] Holidays in general have been very important for such groups as emotional releases—in sharp contrast to the major Jewish holidays devoted to such somber things as atonement or recalling their ancestors' passing over from slavery to freedom. The Jews never had a secure "place" even at the bottom of society, had to be prepared to move, if need be, and to take something with them—in their heads if not in worldly belongings. Carefree abandon is unlikely to be generated in such situations. Although Jews were confined to fixed occupations, the nature of those urban and commercial occupations was such that their earning opportunities varied considerably according to how knowledgeably and diligently they worked. By contrast, the prosperity of peasants depended greatly on the weather and the market for their products—neither of which was within their control. It is not surprising that peasant cultures tend to emphasize fate and luck rather than individual preparation for and control of one's future. Centuries of experience gave each of these very different sets of attitudes great historical momentum, which carry them well into the modern world in a wholly different national and social setting. In the American economic setting, these different attitudes will of course lead to very different results for the various ethnic minorities.

The family has been found to be tied up with many other aspects of life. Groups characterized by a high incidence of broken homes have also been characterized by high incidences of exaggerated "masculinity" in the form of violence, liquor, obstreperousness, and sexual exploitation. The Irish were commonly associated with violence in the nineteenth century; they continue to have a very high rate of alcoholism (fifty times that of the Jews),[59] and long ago acquired the title, "playboy of the Western world." These same characteristics have also been observed by many in the American Negro, with drugs to some extent replacing alcohol in recent years. Yet the stability of the family has an effect economically only insofar as its values promote economic success. The highly stable Italian family and community tends to *inhibit* some forms of economic advancement insofar as its antiintellectual bias makes it necessary for the individual Italian-American to make a painful break with his past as the price of pursuing an intellectual career. A Jewish individual wishing the same kind of career and having the same talent for it has no such price to pay, and is in fact more likely to be encouraged by those around him. Where family and cultural ties are weaker, the price of going against group values is lower. How much of an asset strong ties are depends in part on what the specific values of the group are in relation to the aspirations of the individual or the opportunities in the larger society. The family may be an asset up to some point and a liability beyond that point. One of the turning points in the evolution of Japanese-Americans was the partial undermining of family authority during their internment in World War II, and the subsequent release of many of the younger Japanese-Americans from the camps to seek their individual fortunes throughout the country without parental guidance or authority. From their success, apparently the family had given them what they needed to succeed, except for greater individual freedom, which they now acquired as a by-product of unusual circumstances.

Leadership patterns among minorities tend to fit the rest of their social patterns. Groups given to excitement, violence, and emotionalism in general tend to produce flamboyant leaders, great orators, and individuals with personal charisma. Both the Irish and the American Negroes have produced numerous men of this sort, over the years, though it would be hard to think of an American

Jew or a Japanese-American leader who could be characterized as charismatic. The charismatic leadership tends heavily toward politics and other grand designs as means of advancing the race. Black leadership has also tended to be messianic, heavily political, and given to all sorts of grand designs, from Marcus Garvey's back-to-Africa movement, to Father Divine's religious cult, to modern schemes to create an independent black nation out of several states of the United States. By contrast, the Jews and the Japanese-Americans have proceeded with very mundane organizations for limited social ends within their own communities. Leadership for them has meant the ability to organize, administer, and plan, rather than messianic zeal or ideological purity. The West Indian Negroes are a somewhat different case, for they have gained political power largely as representatives of the black community as a whole, but aside from Garvey, they have tended to promote down-to-earth schemes of various sorts.

There are, apparently, traits that do and traits that do not produce economic advance, and there are historical conditions that do and do not produce these traits in various groups. However, all ethnic groups have adapted to American conditions to some extent, and virtually all have risen significantly as a result.

Intemporal Comparisons

In comparing and drawing inferences from the experience of various ethnic minorities, it must be kept in mind that these minorities passed through their economic evolution at different periods of history. The world around them was changing while they were changing. In some ways the situation faced by blacks, Chicanos, Puerto Ricans, and other contemporary disadvantaged minorities is very different from that faced by the Irish, the Jews, or the Italians in the nineteenth century. In other ways, it is quite similar. Without attempting to measure with any precision, it may nevertheless be possible to consider some of the larger kinds of similarities and differences.

One of the questions often asked is why the contemporary American Negro (or Puerto Rican or Mexican-American) is unable to "make it" in terms of economic success, the way earlier immigrant minorities did. Answers have often run in terms of reduced job opportunities for low-skilled labor, the greater strength of color prejudice, vanishing entrepreneurial opportunities, family disorganization, and a greater subjective "alienation" and hopelessness among blacks and other minorities today. Before considering these "explanations," it may be worthwhile to consider whether there is in fact really something substantial to explain. Are today's minorities in fact any further behind than nineteenth-century immigrant groups at similar stages of their development?

While blacks have been in the United States for centuries, they have been free for just one century—and they have been in black urban communities for only two generations or less, in most cases. From the experience of other ethnic minorities, it is apparent that how long a group's culture has been an urban, industrial, and commercial one is a key factor in its success in urban, industrial, and commercial America. Black urban communities are relatively new, in historical terms. Harlem, the first major black urban community in the United States, was still predominantly white in the early years of the twentieth century. It became black around the time of the First World War, and it became a slum with the massive migration of southern Negroes to the North in the 1920s. Black urban communities in most major cities date from about the same time or a little later. Blacks born in the city as children of the original migrants in the 1920s would now be fifty-year-old second-generation urban dwellers, and their children would be urban third-generation young adults. It has been estimated that it took the Irish three generations to climb out of poverty, and that no major immigrant group got out in less than two generations. Puerto Ricans and Mexican-Americans are even later arrivals in urban America than the blacks.

Statistics on differences in income among ethnic groups must be analyzed very carefully. A substantial fraction of the current income differences between ethnic groups is related to the average age of the respective groups. Americans of Irish and Italian origin have a median age of about 36 years, while Americans of Mexican and Puerto Rican origin have a median age of about 18 years. In a society where employment and earnings are highly correlated with experience, the first two groups would have significantly higher earnings even if there were no differences whatsoever in worker capability or in employer bias as among these groups. In some cases, the differences between groups are rather striking, as in the median age of the population, which is ten years older (28) for Cuban-Americans than for Puerto Ricans and Mexican-Americans.[60] This has important economic implications in an economy where twenty-eight-year-olds usually earn substantially more than eighteen-year-olds. It means that if each Cuban-American of a given age earned exactly the same as a Mexican-American or Puerto Rican of the same age, Cubans as a group would still earn more than Mexican-Americans or Puerto Ricans as a group. In reality, Cubans as a group earn more in the United States than Mexicans, even though they earn *less* in the prime earnings bracket (25–44 years old) than the Mexican-Americans,[61] and may well earn less in every age bracket. There are also very substantial differences in age distribution among Negroes (median age 23), Japanese-Americans (29), Russian-Americans (47!) and other groups.[62] Average annual income for individuals of the same age would vary much less from one ethnic group to another in the variations in raw averages. The median family income of various American ethnic groups in 1968 is shown on page 151.

Differences in unemployment rates are likewise highly correlated with age. For example, Negroes have higher unemployment rates than whites, but in both races men in the prime working ages (25–44) have unemployment rates

	MEXICAN	PUERTO RICAN	NEGRO	IRISH	ITALIAN
Median Family Income:	$5,488	$4,969	$5,074	$8,127	$8,808
Median Age:	17.8	18.3	22.8	35.9	35.5

Source: U.S. Department of the Census.[63]

that are only about one-third of the unemployment rates among males in the inexperienced brackets (16–20). Indeed, Negro males in the 25–44 bracket have had lower unemployment rates than white males in the 16–20 bracket for each of the past twenty years.[64] Given this large disparity in unemployment rates by age, the fact that the black population has a higher proportion of younger workers automatically makes their unemployment rate higher than it would have been otherwise, which is not to deny that significant differences in unemployment rates by race remain.

When the family income of ethnic groups is compared on the basis of people in the same age bracket (25–44), the results are:

MEXICAN	PUERTO RICAN	NEGRO
$6,261	$5,097	$6,684

Source: U.S. Department of the Census.[65]

Data are not available for the Irish and the Italians by age brackets, but their average age would fall near the middle of the 25–44 bracket, so their overall median family incomes are probably not very different from their median family incomes in this particular bracket. In short, the incomes already cited for the Irish and the Italians can be compared to those given immediately above for Mexicans, Puerto Ricans, and Negroes. The narrowing of the income differences among these five ethnic groups when adjusting for age in this general way suggests an even further narrowing of differences could be shown for individuals of the same age—say, males age 30. However, the gap was not completely closed in 1968. One of the peculiarities to be taken into account is that the average income of Negroes varies greatly as between the North and the South. The national average cited above includes millions of Negro families in the rural South. Negro families outside the South had a median income of $7,769 in the 25–44-year-old age bracket in 1969,[66] less than $400 behind that of the Irish who preceded them in northern urban communities by about two generations.

Mexican-American incomes have also been rising rapidly in recent years. For the United States as a whole, Mexican-American family income was greater than that of Negroes in 1970, though not the incomes of Negroes outside the South:

AGES	NEGRO (national average)	NEGRO (outside the South)	MEXICAN- AMERICAN	U.S. AVERAGE
14–24	$5,013	$5,159	$5,534	$ 7,037
25–34	6,605	7,658	7,567	9,853
35–44	7,569	8,970	8,058	11,410
45–54	7,357	9,663	7,491	12,121
55–64	6,438	8,360	7,997	10,381
65 and older	3,282	4,199	a	5,053

Source: U.S. Bureau of the Census.[67]
a *Not available.*

Puerto Rican family income rose to $5,975 in 1970, slightly less than for Negroes, and for persons 25 years old and older Puerto Rican individual income averaged slightly higher than that for Negroes.[68]

Despite the rise in income among disadvantaged

minorities between 1969 and 1970, there was no corresponding reduction of individuals or families below the poverty level among Negroes, Mexican-Americans, Puerto Ricans, or in the general population.[69] Apparently increasing prosperity in a group, or in the country as a whole, has little immediate effect on those at the bottom of the income distribution. In short, the growth of affluence among today's disadvantaged minorities does not indicate that those members of these minorities in poverty are getting out of poverty. Among all three major disadvantaged minorities, the problem of getting people out of poverty remains unsolved, even though the bulk of all three groups are advancing at rates quite comparable to those of earlier disadvantaged minorities, and have now reached income levels quite comparable to them in absolute terms.

Among the obstacles faced by twentieth-century disadvantaged minorities are institutions created by nineteenth-century minorities to protect their hard-won advances. Labor unions are an obvious example. American labor unions have a long history of exclusionary practices. Such practices have sometimes been aimed specifically at keeping out Negroes, Orientals, or other minorities, but even where they simply favor relatives and friends of existing members, their *net effect* is still to put various areas of the economy off limits to aspiring minorities. One indication of the power of union exclusionary activity is that Negro railroad workers and skilled craftsmen were far more common in the middle of the nineteenth century than in the middle of the twentieth century. That this is due to union influence is suggested by the fact that job opportunities for skilled Negro craftsmen were reduced less in the South than in the North,[70] not because the South was more liberal but because unions were less successful in organizing in the South.

Earlier minorities discriminated against in hiring and promotion have long favored "objective"—i.e., nonjudgmental—employment criteria, such as civil service exams, seniority, diplomas and degrees, etc. Such standards protect the already developed minority from discrimination by the Anglo-Saxon majority, but they are additional major obstacles to minorities currently in the process of development. Contemporary established minorities would have had a very hard time escaping from poverty if such obstacles had existed in the nineteenth century. In many cases, the relationship between the criteria and the jobs range from tenuous to absurd—vocabulary and general intellectual achievement tests for civil service jobs as unskilled laborers being an obvious example of the latter. The fervent support of many objective job criteria is often based on their historic role as protection against individual or group discrimination, rather than on any demonstrated relationship to actual job performance. Where such criteria have become in effect protective barriers against contemporary minorities, they are of course themselves discriminatory.

A general standardization of jobs, wages, and promotions patterns has also made it harder for contemporary disadvantaged minorities to advance than for their nineteenth-century counterparts. Under either "objective" or judgmental hiring and promotions standards, most minorities new to the urban, industrial, and commercial society would be at a disadvantage relative to minority or majority members from families with generations of experience in such settings. However, this by itself is only one of many kinds of inequalities among applicants for jobs and promotions. In a world where markets and firms were less structured, as in the nineteenth century, the less skilled, less able, or less desired workers could readily find employment, though with different earnings or promotions prospects than those workers considered more desirable. Piece-rate methods of payment in particular made workers of widely different efficiency—even children—equally employable. Those who were more productive earned more, those who were less productive earned less; those judged promotable could be promoted and those judged unpromotable could be left where they were—but still working.

As jobs came more and more to be formally defined

and standardized, with standardized rates of pay—by *time,* not varying with individual productivity—the range of individual abilities which it paid the employer to accept has contracted. As the rates of pay rose in response to public sentiment or union power rather than productivity alone, the less skilled, less experienced, less reliable, or otherwise less desired workers became "unemployable" to a greater extent. "Rising pay" and "higher job qualifications" both have a good ring, but they also mean more "unemployability." No one is employable or unemployable absolutely, but only relative to given rates of pay.

As formal promotions patterns developed in government and in private industry, the low-level jobs on which the least employable workers depend for a living began to become steps in the promotions ladders, and employers increasingly hesitate to hire workers with less prospects of rising on the ladder—even when they are perfectly capable of performing the low-level job itself. The net effect of all this is that, where a poor nineteenth-century worker without skills or experience could find a job to support himself, and could later rise personally or at least see his better-prepared children rise, his twentieth-century counterpart with similar background must *immediately* be worth high wages and show promotions prospects or face a serious risk of having no steady job at all. One consequence of this is that where nineteenth-century disadvantaged minorities were often overworked, twentieth-century disadvantaged minorities are often unemployed or on relief. The question here is not which of these conditions is better for the individual immediately involved, but which offers better prospects for the group as a whole to advance. Dependency and lack of job experience affect not only the first generation, but the generations that follow. A job is not merely a source of current income but an investment in job skills—meaning not simply the ability to perform certain acts, such as operating a lathe or printing photographs, but developing *work habits,* discipline and attitudes needed on any job. High unemployment rates mean not only reduced current income but delayed acquisition of these prerequisites, and increased risk of falling into the vicious cycle of family dependency.

In some ways, twentieth-century society does more to promote better opportunities for disadvantaged groups—through specific safeguards against racial discrimination in employment and public services (never 100 percent effective, but not 100 percent ineffective either), and through more impersonal economic and social mechanisms generally. These modern policies create more opportunities for those minority-group members who are currently capable or on the point of becoming so. They do little for current minority-group members in a position similar to that of the nineteenth-century immigrant who arrived in the urban industrial world without money, skills, education, orientation, or connections. There is increasing evidence that such individuals today have *less* opportunity to rise than before. Even though the number of American children living in poverty declined sharply during the 1960s, this was *not* true for children living in families headed by a woman—whether that woman was black or white.[71] In short, the disorganized poor are not being lifted out of poverty, even though society as a whole—and especially minorities—may be advancing economically. Well-organized families, with both parents present, not only advanced economically but, outside the South, the younger (under 35) Negro families in this category actually overtook white families in the same category in income in 1970.[72] In general, the Negro population is simultaneously advancing in the upper-income and occupational levels and retrogressing at the lower socioeconomic levels in terms of hard-core unemployment and increasing proportions of broken homes.[73] While these facts emerge from the great amount of research recently done on the black population, they may well be symptoms of a more general trend in the society as a whole toward institutional practices whose net effect is to foreclose opportunities to those on the bottom.

PART THREE

Race and Economics

Chapter 6

Race
and the Market

Race is a factor in many kinds of markets. The most obvious is the employment market, where in the past such phrases as "white only" or "no Irish need apply" were commonplace. The passing of such explicit phrases did not of course mean that the policies and attitudes behind such phrases had completely passed as well. Race is also an important factor in housing markets—not only as regards whether individuals from different ethnic groups have the same opportunity to buy or rent desirable housing, but also as to whether the *terms* on which they may buy or rent are equal. Finally, in the purchase of everyday consumer goods, the price and quality of such goods often vary by neighborhood, with the highest prices and/or lowest quality often being in black ghettos, Puerto Rican barrios, and other neighborhoods inhabited by poor or minority groups.

Whatever the merits of moral or philosophical arguments, cause-and-effect analysis is needed to analyze the scope, magnitude, and variation of discrimination over time, the degree to which various market and nonmarket forces intensify or reduce discrimination, the extent to which various behavior patterns within a minority group advance or retard its economic progress, and to judge the consequences of various possible approaches to dealing with the problem. Causal analysis requires much more precise terms than moral judgments. Terms such as "discrimination," "equality," or "exploitation" may be sufficiently meaningful to express moral feelings, but specific analysis of causation requires much more precise definition.

Discrimination is a good example. Its many meanings range from the most innocent one of simply making distinctions or selections to that of arbitrarily barring people from rights and benefits because of irrelevant criteria, such as race. Rather than attempt a "correct" definition of this vague term, we may simply distinguish various situations:

1. Members of a particular group are accorded fewer and poorer opportunities than members of the general population with the same current capabilities.

2. Members of a particular group are accorded the same opportunities as the general population, but possess fewer of the current capabilities necessary to achieve the same end results.

3. Individuals judged by others as possessing equal current capabilities are given equal opportunities, but the judgments themselves are biased by racial prejudices which underestimate the degree of current capability of certain minorities.

4. Current capabilities are correctly estimated as different among different groups, but these differences are due to previous differences in opportunities rather than differences in innate potential.

5. Current capabilities are correctly estimated as different among groups, but many individuals within each group differ greatly from the average of the respective groups, so that judging individual capability by group capability leads to much loss of potential contributions to the economy and the society.

6. Dislike of associating with members of certain groups leads to their exclusion from certain situations, regardless of their true or estimated current capability or native potential.

No attempt will be made here to decide which of the above is "really" discrimination. Whatever the moral implications of these situations, for cause-and-effect purposes it is sufficient that they are different situations and that the results of each situation can be analyzed logically and empirically. Such situations will be investigated here in the job market, the housing market, and the market for consumer goods.

The Job Market

Negroes, Jews, Irishmen, Italians, West Indians, Japanese, Puerto Ricans, and Mexicans have all—at some point or other in their American experience—earned less than the general American population, often at jobs more exhausting and generally unpleasant than the jobs of other Americans. Were they all (1) victims of dislike, (2) misjudged on their current capabilities, (3) lacking in current capabilities, or (4) lacking in innate potential? Was there some combination of these factors, and did that combination vary from group to group and from time to time?

Each of these American ethnic minorities was (or still is) unwelcome as neighbors, co-workers, employees, or as participants in the general economic and social life of the country. Clearly this factor alone has been insufficient to prevent their absolute economic advancement or even their relative advancement where that has been achieved. Moreover, those periods of advance have *not* typically coincided with a lessening of dislike, and in a significant proportion of the cases, periods of advancement have coincided with *increasing* group animosity. There has probably never been a period of more blatant anti-Semitism in America, from the highest social strata to the lowest, than the last two decades of the nineteenth century, which was precisely the period in which the Jews were rising at a rate unparalleled among large immigrant groups. Similarly, no other group has aroused as much intense racial animosity in a very short period of years as the Japanese-Americans at the beginning of the twentieth century—precisely when they were going from poverty to prosperity with a rapidity that made others fear that they were "taking over." Not even the Negroes brought to America in the early seventeenth century had as many rights abrogated within as few years as the Japanese, even though the Negroes eventually ended up losing all rights as chattel slaves. In short, the lessening of group animosity has not been a precondition for economic advancement, and rapid economic advancement has often been accompanied by increased group animosities.

A certain benign contempt may exist toward a group that is clearly on the bottom and showing no signs of rising. But once they reach the stage of becoming threats to others' jobs or status, a much more active and intense hatred may develop. This is sometimes referred to as "good race relations" turning to "hostility." Rising ethnic groups are the greatest threat to others at or near the bottom—including other ethnic minorities. It is not surprising that the longest and most intense animosity between American ethnic groups has been that between the Irish and the Negroes,[1] who competed for the same jobs long before the Civil War, and who fought many battles on the job[2] and in the slum neighborhoods which they often shared. The Italians and the Irish were often together in church as well as in the job market, and their relations were hardly better than those between the Irish and the Negroes.[3] On the other hand, Negroes were seldom a threat to the Jews, who worked at different jobs and lived in different neighborhoods, even when they were in poverty. However, anti-Semitism has a long history among middle-class Negroes in New York,[4] and has grown as more Negroes have entered middle class occupations competing with Jews. There is, in short, little support in history for the belief that group proximity breeds good will or that improved good will is essential for advancement. Obviously, no minority can advance in the face of total, active hostility by the majority, who can in extreme cases either intern them, enslave them, or practice genocide. However, short of such extremes, animosity has been an accompaniment of progress in many cases and eventual respect was accorded only after substantial gains had been consolidated. When social acceptance has come to ethnic minorities, it has typically come *after* their rise and has not been a cause of that rise. Obvious as this may seem, its implications are frequently overlooked by those wishing to make the fight against "white racism" their number-one priority.

Turning from group dislike to group misjudgment, we encounter a somewhat harder question. History does not always present a clear enough picture of racial minorities to enable later generations to compare the popular image of the times with the reality of the times, in order to estimate the degree of misjudgment. It would certainly be hazardous to believe that all groups possessed the same capabilities at all points of time, so that all stereotypes could be classified as misjudgments. This is particularly so when capability means capability in specific ways within a specific culture—which is what is estimated by prospective employers, investors, realtors, and others who might have economic dealings with ethnic minorities. There is, moreover, substantial evidence of real differences in capability, reliability, work attitudes, and other economically relevant variables between groups—and within groups—at a given time as well as substantial changes over time.

Education is an obvious example. Even free educational opportunities, such as public schools and libraries, were neglected by many nineteenth-century immigrant groups while Jewish immigrants crowded into them at every opportunity.[5] The antebellum "free persons of color" went to schools that they had to pay for, since they were usually barred from public schools, and in the South attended illegal and clandestine schools. Yet a few generations later, their more prosperous offspring—now the elite of the black community, but in a blind alley as far as further advancement was concerned—treated even college education frivolously. In the twentieth century, as in the nineteenth, Latin immigrant groups from peasant backgrounds put a low value on education, as indicated by higher dropout rates than among other low-income minorities and by tending toward easier colleges and easier courses when they attended at all.[6] In many cases, the education—as such—is not crucial for doing the job, but the general set of *attitudes* and *habits* exhibited in behavior toward education may be very important factors in one's capability and reliability as a worker.

A study of the earnings of thirty-five immigrant groups in 1909 showed a high degree of correlation between their earnings and (1) length of time in the United States, (2) percentage of each group able to speak English, and (3) the percentage who were literate—in any language. Literacy in a foreign language is very significant here because it is of virtually no direct value to an American employer, and yet the general attitudes and behavior patterns which lead a large percentage of a group to become literate are quite valuable on the job. The fact that only about half the Turkish and Portuguese immigrants were literate even in their own languages was not unrelated to the fact that they had the lowest average weekly earnings in 1909, while the fact that 99 percent of the Finnish immigrants were literate at least in their native language was not unrelated to their having more than 30 percent higher earnings. Even in cases where different segments of the *same* ethnic group were compared—eliminating employer racial prejudice as a factor—similar substantial differences existed between those segments which were more literate in their native language and those who were illiterate in it—between northern and southern Italians, for example.[7] Even when the same formula was applied to American Negroes—clearly a different case from foreign immigrants—the empirical results were not very different.[8]

There is little evidence of behavioral uniformity among people from vastly different cultures, nor is there much evidence that earnings differentials among ethnic groups reflect substantial misjudgments of current productivity on the job. Moreover, the substantial differences in earnings, occupations, and employment rates among different generations of the same ethnic group at the same point in time suggest that racial prejudice alone is insufficient as an explanation. If there were substantial misjudgments of current group productivity, this would mean an opportunity for some employers to reap unusually high profits by concentrating on hiring members of such low-wage groups. Even if employers of all other groups were too blinded by prejudice to seize this opportunity, it would leave a great opportunity for extra high profits by employers belonging to the same ethnic group. Yet the experience of employers hiring members of an ethnic group that has lower earning and/or higher unemployment rates does not show remarkable success, and in many cases elaborate and costly programs have produced very meager results, even when subsidized by large government grants.

Group antipathy is a somewhat different case, but not totally different. If a group is paid less, or employed or promoted less often, because it is disliked by employers, co-workers, or customers, then it may continue to suffer low wages and higher unemployment rates even if its current capabilities are equal to those of others. The functioning of the market will not tend to eliminate such differentials. However, this too provides an opportunity for other employers—including members of the same ethnic group—to reap unusually high profit by concentrating on hiring those people who are rejected by others. There is little evidence that this happens in most cases, though perhaps the hiring of many Jewish workers by Jewish employers in the nineteenth century, especially in the garment industry, and the hiring of many Japanese workers by Japanese employers in the twentieth century, would be past examples.

This analysis tacitly assumes that (1) employers are attracted by prospects of unusually high profits and that (2) there is no effective general collusion against a particular group. If employers were indifferent to opportunities for high profit or if the rate of profit they could earn was externally controlled, then any opportunities to hire members of ethnic groups whose pay was lower than their productivity could be passed up. There is little indication that most employers are unconcerned as between making more money and making less money. What does happen in a number of situations is that they are prevented from earning more by government agencies—regulatory commissions such as the ICC or FCC—or may be legally nonprofit, as with schools, foundations, hospitals, etc. When this is so, then there is no real opportunity to earn more profit by hiring misjudged minorities or in any other way. In such circumstances, the employer can hire according to his own prejudices without paying any price in terms of foregone profits.

Economic theory would lead to an expectation of more discrimination in markets with externally controlled and externally limited profit rates than in unstructured and uncontrolled competitive markets.[9] In general, this is what is found. The railroad industry, which is tightly regulated by the Interstate Commerce Commission, has long been one of the most discriminatory industries in the United States—hiring *no* Negroes at all, for decades, in many skilled jobs, and hiring substantial numbers only as Pullman porters.[10] In the middle of the nineteenth century, before regulation, Negroes dominated railroad occupations in the South, except for conductors.[11] The communications industry, whose profit is regulated by the Federal Communications Commission and by state regulatory agencies, likewise has a long history of discriminatory hiring far more severe than that in the economy as a whole.[12] Other highly controlled areas of the economy, such as banking, likewise exhibit a pattern of extreme discrimination, not only against Negroes, Jews and other minorities, but even against nonconformist personality types. It would be hard to explain this pattern by personal prejudice alone, for there is no special reason why employers in regulated industries should happen to have *more* prejudice than employers in other industries. What is different in the regulated industries is that the *cost* of discrimination is reduced or eliminated.

Regulated industries are of course regulated by politically appointed commissioners, so that while their hiring policies have fewer *economic* constraints (such as those which force more competitive industries to hire minorities), they are even more subject to *political* constraints. This means that while there is likely to be more racial discrimination in a regulated industry than in an unregulated industry during periods when there is no great public outcry against discrimination, the regulated industries would be forced to make a more sudden about-face on discrimination than the unregulated industries when political forces attack discrimination. An example of this is the telephone industry, a highly regulated industry which has long had an extremely low percentage of Negro employees, even in jobs such as operators and linemen, which require no special education or experience. Yet when employment discrimination became a major political issue in the 1960s, there were great increases in the hiring of Negroes in the telephone industry—even in occupations where the total number of jobs was declining. In the South, where political pressures were not comparable, there was virtually no increase in the proportion of Negroes hired,[13] even though the industry's employment was growing fastest in the South.[14] In the North, *one-third* of the *new* employees hired between 1966 and 1968 were Negroes.[15] Among electric and gas utilities also, Negro employment gains were concentrated in the North.[16] All these public utilities are primarily *state*-regulated; more so than federally regulated.

In short, empirical evidence confirms what economic analysis would predict: that regulated industries have *more* discrimination than unregulated industries when this depends only on economic considerations, but reverse themselves more rapidly than unregulated industries when discrimination becomes a political issue. This pattern will be worth remembering when we consider discrimination by the government itself in the next chapter.

A legally nonprofit organization is in a very similar position to the firm whose profits are limited by a regulation. It too pays no economic cost for discrimination, and could therefore be expected to be more discriminatory than unregulated, profit-seeking organizations—as long as public opinion is not aroused. But since it is typically dependent upon public contributions, grants from the government, or at least needs its tax-exempt status, it too is likely to change more drastically when the climate of opinion changes on racial discrimination. The academic world is a classic example here. In 1936, only three Negro Ph.D. holders were employed by all white colleges and universities in the United States.[17] By contrast, more than three hundred Negro chemists alone were employed in private industry in 1940.[18] Just one generation later, after public opinion became aroused against racial discrimination—all this was reversed. White colleges and universities began hiring black faculty members en masse —and lectured private industry on the need to end discrimination! It is also significant that black breakthroughs in the academic world first occurred in the money-making part of the college—varsity athletics. Hospitals are another large area of nonprofit organizations, and one which, until relatively recent times also practiced extreme exclusion and discrimination against doctors who were Jewish[19] or black.[20] This often extended to patients as well.

In general, job discrimination has a cost, not only to those discriminated against and to society, but also to the person who is discriminating. He must forgo hiring some employees he needs, or must interview more applicants in order to get the number of qualified workers required, or perhaps offer higher wages in order to attract a larger pool of applicants than necessary if hiring on merit alone. These costs do not necessarily eliminate discrimination, but discrimination—like everything else—tends to be more in demand at a low price than at a high price. The cost, of course, is of no concern to a businessman who is personally unconcerned about profit, but such businessmen are rare to begin with, and tend to get eliminated through competition, for their financial backers and creditors care about profitability even if they do not. Nonprofit organizations, however, can ignore the economic cost of discrimination—though not the cost of antagonizing the public, if the public is actively opposed to discrimination.

Under special conditions, discrimination can be made profitable. An extreme example would be if the whole white race organized into one giant monopoly to set the terms and conditions of black employment, housing, and other economic activities—and if it were prepared to retaliate against any individual white employer, realtor, merchant, etc. who violated the terms established. How feasible is this in practice? In many economic situations, it is not feasible at all. As long as each individual is seeking to maximize his individual gains—not the collective gains of the group to which he belongs—each individual white has incentives to violate the agreement, and can be prevented from doing so only by various means of policing the agreement, of widely varying effectiveness and cost. In some special circumstances, however, the cost of policing and enforcing discriminatory rules may be very small. If relatively few blacks have a certain job skill, and if the mass of white workers with that skill objects to working with blacks, then the individual employer loses little by refusing to hire blacks and risks much (in deliberate retaliation and/or lower worker morale) if he does hire a black. Similarly, if very few blacks can buy a home in an expensive neighborhood, the realtor or banker who facilitates their doing so may risk a large retaliation for a relatively small gain. Skin color makes policing costs very inexpensive—indeed, word may spread like wildfire when a Negro takes a job or buys a home in a place that has been all-white for many years.

The *cost* of collusion is crucial. An agreement or "understanding" that certain jobs, neighborhoods, or organizations are to be kept 100 percent free of the particular ethnic group can be policed rather cheaply, especially if the excluded groups have distinctive color

(Negro, Oriental) or—less effective—distinctive names or accents. It is easy for those most determined to exclude them to tell whether the tacit exclusion is being followed by others. Once the total-exclusion policy is broken, however, it becomes much more difficult and expensive to police an understanding that *only so many* of the excluded group are to be allowed in. One more Negro, Jew, Italian, Oriental, etc. is never as noticeable as the first one, and if there are many independent businessmen involved, each can say that it is not he who is "flooding" in the formerly excluded group.

It is possible for an otherwise competitive industry to behave as a monopolist in racial matters, due to the low cost of exclusion and retaliation sometimes found in racial matters, whereas the cost of collusion and retaliation on the output or prices of the product might be too high to make it worthwhile. However, even racial exclusion requires special conditions to be feasible—that a large proportion of the dominant population feels strongly about excluding a particular group from a particular place or activity; that the cost of identifying the group and policing the "understanding" be low, and that those who feel strongest about this are willing and able to retaliate against individual members of their own group who find it profitable to violate the exclusion. Once the exclusion has been violated and significant numbers of the excluded group enter despite the exclusion, the cost of keeping out the remainder rises sharply, since the cost of identifying new entrants rises, as does the number of individual members of the dominant group who now have a vested economic interest in keeping the breach open. For these reasons, it is not uncommon for a 100 percent exclusion to last for generations—and then collapse like a house of cards. A certain street may be an iron-clad boundary around a racial ghetto, and yet within a few years after the first minority families cross that boundary, the whole neighborhood may be incorporated into the ghetto. In many professional sports, Negroes were totally excluded until after World War II, but once one team began to hire

Negro athletes, competitive teams would be risking suicide on the playing field (and therefore at the box office) if they refused to do so.

The feasibility of collusive ethnic exclusion depends not only on conditions within the dominant group, but also on conditions within the excluded minority. The larger the number of minority group members who are *immediately* prepared to enter if the exclusion is broken, the higher the cost to each majority group member who helps maintain the agreement, in terms of his foregone profit-making opportunities. Since the strength of a chain is no greater than that of its weakest link, it is not necessary that the "average" member of the dominant group be prepared to relent in order to increase his personal earnings, but only that one or a few members be prepared to do so. The cost of retaliation—economic or social—is important only *relative* to the profit to be gained by breaching the agreement. Where substantial numbers of the excluded group are both willing and able to enter—a mass of blacks ready to pay higher prices for better housing, or ready to become star athletes—then individual profit-seeking is likely to cause the exclusion to give way. A new line of resistance may form elsewhere, at a neighborhood boundary farther away or at the occupational level of athletic managers and executives, but how long the new line will hold depends on how long it takes for the same backlog of qualified, excluded individuals to build up.

In situations where long or costly preparations are necessary to be able to enter an excluded area—years of savings to get a down payment on a house, a costly education for a particular profession, years of specialized training to become a skilled craftsman or classical musician—the very fact that the exclusion exists tends to prevent any backlog of qualified people from building up, and therefore reduces the cost of those who maintain the exclusion. A moderately determined resistance may therefore be effective in maintaining exclusions in such circumstances, whereas an all-out resistance may fail in other areas. Even a long and costly preparation is not an effective barrier, however, where such preparation for a particular excluded field is attained as a by-product of activities in some other fields. Even in times and places where white-collar employment has been closed to blacks, many jobs as schoolteachers in the segregated educational system were open, so that great numbers of black women acquired an education, which also qualified them for jobs in white-collar fields in general. This backlog then became a factor in forcing breaches in the wall of exclusion around white-collar jobs. Similarly, large numbers of qualified black athletes were generated by recreational activities, college athletics, and the black professional leagues, even when there was no reason whatsoever for a black man to prepare for a career in major league baseball, football, or basketball.

The Jews are an even more striking example of this. Because they tend to have a high level of education in general, they have the prerequisites for admission to many fields at once, including those in which they may happen to be excluded at a particular time and place. One such excluded field was college and university teaching, until World War II. But once a breach appeared, economic pressures ripped it wide open, for there were many Jewish scientists, economists, writers, etc. who could also teach their subject in college, at a time when college teachers were in great demand. Because high-quality college and university education prepares an individual for many different fields, a group with such education has a backlog of qualified individuals ready to move into any of a number of fields, and is in a position to break through many exclusions that would otherwise hold. This may also explain why Negroes have had far less success in breaking into skilled blue-collar fields than into other fields requiring similar time and expense in preparation. Blue-collar skills are often highly specific, so that only someone who has trained himself for the particular job is likely to be qualified, and no backlog of such persons is likely to develop as long as the exclusion itself is present.

Consumer Goods Markets

Numerous studies have indicated that prices of goods tend to be higher and the average quality lower in low-income ethnic neighborhoods.[21] In addition, numerous schemes to defraud the less-knowledgeable people in such neighborhoods have flourished for many years,[22] probably as long as such neighborhoods have existed. In the nineteenth century, Irish immigrants were cheated and swindled before they even got off the boat, and the process continued on the docks, in the roominghouses in which they usually spent their first days in America, and among travel agents who sold them fraudulent tickets to their destinations.[23] The nineteenth-century Italian immigrants were similarly exploited in innumerable ways by travel agents, landlords, bankers, labor contractors, etc.[24] In the twentieth century, the victims are more often Negro, Puerto Rican, or Mexican-American.

In Los Angeles, for example, a clock-radio selling for $19 elsewhere in the city was sold for $42 in the Mexican-American community. Gas ranges selling for $110 elsewhere sold for $200 in the Mexican-American community—and a portable television set selling for $230 in the Mexican-American community sold for $270 in Watts.[25] Comparison shoppers in New York found that the same item in the same store sold for different prices to whites, Puerto Ricans, and blacks.[26] According to another study, "In East Harlem, there are hardly any 'one price' stores." [27] East Harlem has a variety of ethnic groups, with many individuals being very new to the city. A common feature of fraudulent stores in ethnic neighborhoods is the absence of price tags, for this very reason. In still another study, the Federal Trade Commission found an item selling for $165 in the regular shopping areas of Washington that was selling for $250 in a store specializing in low-income customers.[28]

The question is not whether fraud is practiced on ethnic minorities, but how much of the price and quality differences in ethnic communities is solely a result of fraud rather than many other economic factors. What is physically the same product may have very different costs of delivery to the customer, depending upon the conditions of delivery. Supermarkets, for example, are able to operate profitably selling a standard product for less than the price charged at a small grocery store, which may be making little or no profit. This is largely because the *turnover* is faster in the supermarket; the item sits on the shelf a much shorter time before it is sold, so that a given investment in a shelf full of goods earns a return many more times in the course of a year, even if each individual return is slightly lower than in the corner grocery store, where the goods turn over fewer times a year. Low-income ethnic neighborhoods typically have relatively more small grocery stores and relatively fewer major supermarkets. Even if each item sold for the same price in ethnic neighborhood grocery stores as in other grocery stores, and the same price in ethnic neighborhood supermarkets as in other supermarkets, the average price paid in the ethnic neighborhoods would still be higher than elsewhere, simply because the mixture of grocery stores and supermarkets is different in such neighborhoods.

There are reasons why low-income communities have a different mixture of small and large stores. Major supermarket chains have lower costs of delivering goods to the customer because of a higher volume of business for each hour that a store is open—that is, for each hour that they are paying salaries to their employees. The more hours they stay open, the harder it is for them to have as high a volume of business per hour and per employee. Ghetto supermarkets are usually not open as many hours per day as the local grocery stores. Obviously they eliminate those hours which bring in the least revenue in proportion to cost. Evening hours are especially costly because of overtime pay or night differential pay for supermarket employees, or because the store may operate less efficiently after the manager has gone home, or because of the higher cost of getting a good manager who is willing to stay in the store extra long hours. Evening hours are also more costly in terms of an increased probability of getting robbed at night. Supermarkets therefore tend to do a high volume of business per hour during the day and then close—especially in high crime areas.

While there is a demand for supermarket services in low-income ethnic neighborhoods, there are more people in such neighborhoods who cannot rely wholly on supermarkets. People who arrive home in the evening after a day of work—especially at manual labor—may lack the time or energy to get to the supermarket before it closes. A smaller proportion of the families have wives who are at home during the day to do supermarket shopping. A smaller proportion have automobiles, so that the distance to the store is more of a factor. Because of sporadic unemployment and other financial problems, a certain proportion of the residents of low-income ethnic communities use credit in buying grocery items. Supermarkets do a cash business, eliminating the time and paperwork of credit transactions, the cost of collection agencies, and the losses from unpaid debts. Such credit arrangements are left to the small grocery store, or at least to some of them. In short, although the supermarket may deliver the same physical package as the small grocery store, it does not deliver it at the same time, or as close to home, or under the same arrangements, so that the total service sold may be very different and have different costs, which are passed on to the consumer. Even when the service is no different, the fact that the goods on the shelf turn over at different rates means that different prices are required to cover operating costs, which are based on time (rent, salaries, electricity, etc.). If a supermarket sells twenty refrigerators full of beer in the same time it takes a local grocery store to sell 10 refrigerators full of beer, then it has cost the local grocery store twice as much to refrigerate each can of beer. The same principle applies to operating costs in general.

In addition to different kinds of stores that are represented in low-income ethnic neighborhoods, there are generally different costs for any given kind of store.

Insofar as such neighborhoods are less attractive to potential employees or managers (justifiably or not does not matter in cause-and-effect terms), the cost of operating and managing stores tends to rise. Theoretically, this could take the form of paying higher salaries to get the same quality of personnel in the ethnic community stores as in other stores. However, since companies tend to maintain standard salaries, it is more likely to take the form of attracting less efficient employees and managers for the same pay. In either case, the net result is a higher cost of operation.

Insurance costs vary greatly with neighborhoods. Where there are higher rates of pilferage, robbery, arson, and civil disorder, insurance companies raise premiums accordingly, and/or reduce the coverage for a given premium, increase the "deductible" level, or otherwise make the policy less valuable. They may require additional security measures by the store as a condition of issuing a policy. Beyond some level of risk, they refuse to issue a policy at all, forcing the individual store to protect itself in various ways: self-insurance if it is part of a chain or tying up money in a contingency fund if it is not; using more locks, screens, burglar alarms, or guards; or laying out the goods in ways designed to minimize theft, even if these designs are less efficient from other points of view. These costs, whatever form they take, are ultimately paid by the customer in the price of the product. In recent years, a new cost has been added in some ethnic communities—"voluntary" contributions to local "causes," collected by tough young men or by others who speak with the actual or apparent backing of tough young men. Such collections were also common in nineteenth-century ethnic communities, with the collectors being either graft-seeking policemen or gangs of toughs. What is new is the protective covering of ideology. From an economic point of view, it is simply one more additional cost of doing business in some low-income ethnic communities; its net effect is to reduce the number of individuals and institutions willing to work there, and to raise the prices to the consumers.

There is no principle of justice which causes consumers to pay the costs associated with the neighborhood. The bulk of the population, even in crime-ridden areas, are law-abiding people. It is not equity but economics which forces up the prices they pay. The differences in prices between ethnic ghettoes and middle-class suburbs cannot be explained by stores charging "all that the traffic will bear" in one case and not in the other. Stores charge all that the traffic will bear in *both* cases. The traffic will just not bear as much in the middle-class suburb—and the *reason* for this is that there are so many more *competing* stores. Those businesses are *able* to operate at lower costs because they can more readily attract efficient workers, management, capital, and low-cost insurance. They are *forced* to operate at lower cost because there are so many firms competing with one another.

For the low-income ghetto workingman who has to pay more for the same can of beer chilled to the same temperature as the beer bought by a middle-class suburbanite, it may seem like pointless hair-splitting whether the situation is explained economically or is simply called "exploitation." And if he has to pay more money for a lower quality beer than the suburbanite pays for premium beer, then he may be even more likely to prefer the latter label. The fact is, if he were not black, or Mexican, or Puerto Rican, etc., he would not have to pay as much for what he buys. Economic analysis is not philosophic justification, nor is that its purpose. What economics can do is help predict the consequences of various possible ways of dealing with the problem. While the term "exploitation" has a variety of shifting meanings, the central idea is that prices exceed cost by some unusual amount (or wages fall short of the worker's contribution to output by some unusual amount). This in turn implies an unusually high rate of profit being made by the businessmen involved. Such opportunities to make profit invariably attract more businessmen and more capital. Yet low-income ethnic communities are avoided like the plague by many chains of supermarkets, drug stores, restaurants, as well as by the mass of individual businessmen. Many corporations with branches in such neighborhoods are pulling out. If the assumption of unusually high profits were correct, there would also be great opportunities for new businesses run by members of the local ethnic community. Yet such businesses have had a very high rate of failure. Sometimes these failures are blamed on management, sometimes on inadequate financing by the banks, sometimes on red tape, or a variety of other factors. However, the fact that highly successful supermarket chains, with well-trained and experienced management, and with millions of dollars of their own capital available, have also had to pull out, suggests that the situation itself makes success very difficult to achieve. Far from being a situation of unusually high profits, it is a situation where it is hard to break even—even when charging higher prices.

Chapter 7

Race
and the Government

There are a great variety of ways in which the government can have an economic impact on people, including ethnic minorities. The government is an employer, provides various services (free or for a price), collects taxes, has the power of confiscating income or property (including demolishing homes), dispenses wealth in money or in kind, and may even take individual services via the military draft. In addition to engaging in massive economic activities of its own, the government regulates the economic activities of others—landlords and tenants, creditors and debtors, employees and employers, etc.—and establishes the legal framework within which all economic activity takes place. The particular manner in which the government chooses to exercise its vast powers is of major importance to all, but perhaps more so to vulnerable groups such as ethnic minorities. The U.S. government is officially nonracial in its structure and laws, and the Constitution limits the extent to which federal, state, or local governments may explicitly follow policies based on race as such. Clearly the whole history of the country would have been different if these de jure provisions had been in full force de facto. In determining the impact of government on ethnic minorities, or on race relations generally, it must be recognized that such impact does not depend upon whether government policy is explicitly racial, or even racial in intention, but only on whether its *effects* are different for different ethnic groups. For example, public utility regulation has an effect on racial hiring policies, as already noticed, even though the purpose of public utility regulation is wholly nonracial.

Rather than attempt to cover the whole range of government's economic impact, the discussion here will concentrate on the legal framework, government employment, the provision of public services, and various subsidy activities. Despite a tendency in many quarters to think of the government as "the public interest" personified (with some allowance for individual opportunists), government officials have their own career interests in maintaining and increasing their appropriations, staff, and scope of action. In some cases, these institutions are strongly linked in long-run relationships with nongovernment organizations —the Labor Department with unions, the Commerce Department with corporations, the Department of Transportation with the construction industry, the Defense Department with military products industries, and many regulatory agencies with the industries they regulate. Only within this framework is it rational to talk about "the government" and ethnic minorities.

However the government may be conceived of in its ideal role, the government as a living reality must maximize the votes it can attract by its programs and minimize the votes it will lose by the costs of these programs. One of the lowest-cost ways to "do something" about social problems is to create "rights." The cost of creating "rights" is little more than the cost of paper and ink. Rights have therefore abounded throughout the political history of the United States. Agitation about the hideous conditions in the slums in the nineteenth century led to laws creating the right to live under different conditions as specified in various housing codes. The right to decent housing is much cheaper than decent housing itself. The net result was that people continued to live in slums, new housing cost more to build because of the codes, and building inspectors earned supplementary income in the form of bribes.[1] The cold fact that better housing cost more than the slum dwellers were prepared to pay was never faced. It was only obliquely recognized by *not* closing down buildings that violated the tenants' right to decent housing—which is a right that would have left a substantial portion of the population with no place to live.

One of the symptoms of poverty in the nineteenth century was child labor. This symptom was particularly offensive to middle-class social reformers and was therefore outlawed. To eliminate the poverty that caused child labor would have meant spending astronomical sums of money compared to the modest outlay required to print copies of the law and hire enough inspectors to keep the violations from becoming a public scandal.

Rights enforceable on the initiative of the individual concerned are even cheaper, for then the government need not hire inspectors or maintain any elaborate enforcement machinery. For example, the widespread cheating of the poor has been met by establishing small claims courts where no lawyers are required or allowed, where the procedures are informal, and decisions swift. It was a social reformer's dream, and it was politically ideal, for it conferred rights on everyone at very low cost to anyone. Here the democratic ideal was also affirmed, as the businessman and the low-income (often minority) individual met in "no-holds-barred, man-to-man" intellectual combat—the businessman, familiar with this and other courts, often having multiple suits in the same court at the same time, having a staff to maintain his records and documents, versus his low-income, frequently undereducated opponent for whom this is likely to be his first unnerving experience in an unfamiliar setting, with ground rules that were neither self-explanatory nor explained to him at any length (the average trial in such courts lasts from five to fifteen minutes).[2] The net effect was to make it easier for merchants and other businessmen to sue the poor and to use the court as a cheap collection agency. The poor are usually *defendants* in such courts, and over 90 percent of the defendants lose.[3] But, as in other cases, no one cares much about net results after the law is passed. Social reformers have publicly declared themselves on the side of the angels. The politicians have done what will get them votes at the next election. And minorities have been given some "rights." Those who get caught in this legal trap know how little those rights mean, but they hardly have enough votes or enough other weight to bring about change. It is only by looking at end results—not principles, not intentions—that it is possible to make even a general estimate of the impact of government.

Government Employment

The government, as an employer, is in a nonprofit-making situation. This means, among other things, that racial discrimination is free, except for political repercussions. It is not surprising, therefore, that government employment has tended to follow a pattern very similar to that found in profit-regulated public utilities and in nonprofit organizations. The government as an employer was far more discriminatory than private industry, until this became politically impossible, at which point it made extremely rapid increases in minority employment, leading eventually to a higher proportion of minority employment than in private industry. In 1930, Negroes constituted only 1 percent of public service workers outside the Post Office.[4] During Reconstruction in the South after the Civil War there had been many Negro officeholders in local government, but these were all driven out with the passing of Reconstruction. During the 1910–30 period, when Negroes were making at least some occupational advances in private industry, the federal government was reducing the number of Negro employees, especially among the few at the higher level (Negro postmasters declined from 153 in 1910 to 78 in 1930), and segregation was introduced into Washington government offices "where it has scarcely occurred before."[5] This retrogression in the federal government was in keeping with the political trends of the time, including the increase in racial animosity by whites as blacks moved into previously all-white jobs in private industry and into previously all-white neighborhoods. Objective hiring by civil service test results was also amended during this period to allow the government hiring official concerned to choose among the top *three* applicants available—and a photograph was also made mandatory.[6] In the military, there were simply no Negroes at all in the Marine Corps during World War II. The navy, which had had large numbers of Negroes during the Civil War, and substantial numbers even in earlier wars, eliminated the remaining 1 percent of Negroes in its ranks at the end of World War I, and accepted no more until 1932, when it began accepting Negroes only for kitchen jobs.[7] The army had only two black combat officers in 1940.[8] For both the navy and the army, these were major retrogressions from earlier periods. It would be difficult to find private employers in unregulated nationwide industries who moved backward to such a degree during the same period.

As in the case of public-utility hiring, the rise in minority employment followed lines of political development. The number of black postal workers in northern cities tripled during the same 1910–30 period, when the national trend in government employment was the other way[9]—but when the number of black voters in northern cities was growing by leaps and bounds. In these northern states, Negroes were overrepresented in the postal service. In New York City, the number of black municipal employees increased from 247 in 1917 to 2,275 in 1929.[10] Other minorities have also been overrepresented in government jobs after acquiring political strength. About half the schoolteachers of New York City are Jews.[11] The Irish have long been overrepresented in municipal government jobs after building political power in the nineteenth century.[12]

After civil rights became a great political issue in the 1950s and 1960s, the federal hiring policy underwent a great reversal. In the military, Negroes were slightly overrepresented. In the civilian federal agencies, Negroes gained 20 percent of all new employment in a five-year period following the establishment of the equal-employ-ment program, with almost a doubling of blacks in the top six grades during this period,[13] and blacks often received fancier perquisites than their white counterparts as well.[14]

In short, despite an officially nonracial hiring policy and despite the "merit" principle embodied in civil service systems, government hiring policies have been highly discriminatory, in one direction or the other. Like other nonprofit organizations, the government's discrimination has been unconstrained by economic considerations and has varied widely according to public opinion.

Price Regulation

The impact of the government on the economy depends not only on its own transactions but also on its power to regulate the terms and conditions of transactions between other parties—for example, the wages of labor, the interest charged on loans, the rent paid for apartments, and the prices paid for various goods and services. All these powers are not exercised continuously, nor by the same level of government, nor does price regulation imply the actual setting of a single price by the government. Often the government simply restricts the possible range of prices by declaring it illegal to pay wages below a certain level, to charge interest above a certain level, or to raise rent more than a certain percentage above the rents existing at some specified time.

Most laws controlling the terms on which various kinds of transactions may take place do *not* require that the transaction take place at all. A transaction requires that the terms be mutually agreeable to the parties involved, in the light of their respective alternatives. Restricting the terms without changing the alternatives generally means that one side is less likely to engage in the transaction at all or to the same extent. And since a transaction requires two parties, this often means that the transaction takes place less often. There may therefore be fewer workers hired, fewer loans made, the development of a housing shortage, etc.—and these reductions in transactions are likely to be disproportionately at the expense of low-income ethnic minorities.

In the labor market where many employers compete with each other for workers and many workers compete with each other for jobs, the wage rate tends to be at such a level that there are few qualified workers without jobs and few employers who cannot find workers by offering the same wage rates and working conditions as other employers. If there were either a persistent shortage of workers or a persistent surplus, that would of course tend to raise or lower the wage rate. When a minimum-wage rate is imposed in such a market, it is typically set above the level that would have occurred by uncontrolled economic forces. Otherwise there would be no point in such a law. A higher wage rate simultaneously attracts more job applicants and reduces the number of persons whom it is profitable to hire. There are many ways of getting a job done with fewer employees, and as the cost of employees rises, more of these ways are used. The net result is that the number of jobs decreases as the number of applicants increases. One consequence of this is that ethnic discrimination becomes less costly—perhaps free— to the employer, even in a profit-seeking business. Since he now has a chronic surplus of job applicants, he can pass up whatever race, religion, or nationality he does not like while still getting all the qualified workers he can actually use. Without the legal restriction on wages, his alternative would be to offer somewhat lower wages, have somewhat fewer job applicants as a result, and fill the jobs by hiring a larger percentage of the qualified applicants. The opportunity to make more profit in this way is one of the economic factors tending to erode ethnic barriers to employment. Even in the Union of South Africa, in the early twentieth century, before government regulation, ethnic barriers to employment eroded along an advancing frontier as black workers began acquiring the skills and experience to replace European workers in a number of occupations.

Some indication of the strength of this trend is that the white supremacist government had to threaten many firms and industries with various reprisals if they did not maintain a certain quota of European employees.[15] Only when minimum-wage laws were passed and extended to the black workers was the South African government able to reverse this trend. Employers who had not given in to government pressure now gave in to the economics of the situation, and black workers lost many jobs which they previously had been holding in South African labor markets.[16]

In most countries, minimum-wage laws are not passed for the purpose of racial exclusion, but the actual economic effects do not depend upon the intentions of those who establish a given institutional situation. The net effect of any institutional arrangement which sets the rate of pay above that required to attract the number of qualified workers needed is to make it cheaper to discriminate in deciding who *not* to hire. In this way, the same principle is extended to profit-seeking businessmen as applies to nonprofit-seeking organizations, or to businesses whose profits are limited by regulation. The major difference is that the nonprofit or politically regulated enterprises are subject to some constraint by public opinion, whereas ordinary profit-seeking businesses are less constrained by public opinion, especially the large mass of businesses that are not big enough to be singled out for public scrutiny.

Principles similar to those in the labor market apply in loan markets and in housing markets. The rate of interest between borrowers and lenders depends upon how many people want to borrow how much money and how many lenders have how much money to lend. When banks, finance companies, credit unions, etc. have much money on hand (which they must lend out to make a profit), they may either lower the interest rate charged or extend credit to those with lower credit ratings than they would lend to at other times. By the same token, if the lending organizations have relatively little money on hand that is not out earning a return, and there are many borrowers wanting money, then they may either raise the interest rate or lend only to those with the highest credit ratings. When the government sets an upper limit on the interest rate, the lender still retains the right to determine how much they will lend and to whom. If the rate that the government sets is well below what the economics of the situation would otherwise produce, then there will be many more applicants for loans than will be profitable to lend to. Since interest rates are forbidden to be raised, credit rating requirements will be raised instead. People who are 90 percent sure to repay in a specified time will be refused loans in favor of people who are 95 percent sure to repay in a specified time. People with reasonably steady jobs at good pay will be passed over in favor of people whose jobs are protected by seniority or annual contract and/or who have unusually high rates of pay. Ethnic minorities lose in two ways. First, they are more likely to be in those categories with no better than average credit ratings. Secondly, ethnic discrimination now becomes cheap (or free) to the banker or other official, and any such officials may indulge whatever prejudices he has at little or no cost.

Rent control has a similar effect in the housing market. Ethnic discrimination and exclusion is very old in housing markets, and it has probably applied to every ethnic minority in America, at some time or other. But even the strongest barriers, and those easiest to police— those involving physical color differences—have been fighting a constant retreating action for more than a century. In short, though the housing market is far from perfect, it is also one in which it has been virtually impossible to maintain a permanent ethnic boundary. The reason is simple: there are profits to be made by landlords or realtors who erode that boundary. In some cases, high vacancy rates force the opening of buildings, blocks, or whole neighborhoods to previously excluded groups. Small parts of Harlem were first opened to Negroes for this reason.[17] In short, the existence of a shortage or a surplus determines whether ethnic discrimination is more profitable, less profitable, or disastrously costly to those who deal in housing. Rent control creates a price lower than that which would have developed spontaneously in the market, given the existing supply and demand. Otherwise there would be no point in imposing rent control. At the lower price there tends to be more housing demanded (larger dwellings for a given family, more single individuals wanting their own place, etc.) and a greater reluctance to supply the same quantity and quality of housing. There is a housing shortage—at the imposed price. Despite a tendency to think of shortage as meaning fewer goods relative to people, the crucial fact is that *at a given price* more is demanded than supplied. At different prices, with the same number of people and goods, there could be a surplus. The worst housing shortage in U.S. history occurred during World War II, at a time when the civilian population had *declined* while the number of housing units had increased slightly. At the low rents imposed by law at that time, many people got their own apartments who normally would have lived with others, many got larger apartments than they could have afforded before, and many who no longer needed large apartments (couples with their children already grown) had little economic incentive to give up their current apartments in order to save rent.

The housing shortage allowed the landlord to reduce the quantity of auxiliary services supplied—cleaning, painting, maintenance, repair, heat, hot water, lighting—because he had an excessive number of applicants over vacancies at the legally imposed rent level. Reductions in such services, of course, speed the decay process which turns buildings into slums. Low-income minorities were more likely to be living in buildings requiring considerable upkeep to hold off complete deterioration. More directly, however, a housing shortage drastically reduced any incentive for landlords or realtors to erode the ethnic boundary lines. The net result is that rent control reduces the cost of discrimination in housing, and enables ethnic boundaries to be maintained longer than otherwise.[18]

Public Services

Government services, ranging from local police to a variety of federal projects, not only affect ethnic minorities but affect them in ways different from their effect on the general population. The different incidence of government power need not be so blatant as the internment of the Japanese-Americans or the enslavement of the Negroes, and need not be explicitly racial at all in order to have serious racial impacts.

One public service that is formally nonracial in character is the police force. Yet both nineteenth- and twentieth-century disadvantaged minorities have been victims of biased law enforcement, graft, and police violence. Jews, Orientals, and Negroes have all been victims, at one time or another, of the police practice of arresting the victim and letting his attackers go free. Graft has been particularly common in ethnic neighborhoods. The Irish "Tenderloin" district of New York City in the nineteenth century got its name from the widespread belief that policemen assigned there dined on tenderloin paid for by the graft they collected in this vice-ridden section of town. One of the severe punishments for policemen in this district was to be transferred out, away from the rich sources of revenue.[19] A classic twentieth-century study of an Italian-American slum in Boston found the same pattern of corruption, and the same pattern of punishment for policemen who "rocked the boat." [20] The grafting activities of the police have likewise, at various times, aroused the suspicions and hostility of people living in Jewish, Negro, Mexican-American, and other minority communities.[21] Indeed, the plainly biased application of the law—not occasionally, but as a common practice—has been true not only with ethnic minorities in the United States, but also with low-income groups here and in other countries in various periods of history. Moreover, even in aspects of police work having nothing to do with race, policemen found guilty of crimes have often received nothing more than "wrist-slap" punishment, even for serious offenses for which the ordinary citizen would receive stiff jail sentences.[22] In short, impartial law enforcement has been a goal rather than a reality, and it is only in relatively recent times that important organizations and influential public figures have challenged the conduct of policemen. The hostility between police and ethnic minorities is not a recent one, however. A study of the 1920–32 period showed that of all blacks killed by whites in the United States, more than one-half were killed by policemen, and of all whites killed by blacks during that period, 37 percent were policemen.[23]

The problem is not one solely—or primarily—of police behavior toward minority members accused or suspected of breaking the law. The bitterest complaints from black communities concern the lack of police protection, both in terms of the small number of policemen assigned to their neighborhoods and the slowness and apparent unconcern with which they respond to emergency calls. Independent studies in different cities confirm both these charges.[24] Courts also tend to give lighter sentences where the victims of crimes are black.[25]

The police, though, are only one aspect of the law. Legislative enactments, court decisions and procedures, and the administrative actions of government agencies all affect ethnic minorities, as they affect other citizens, but not always in the same way. Legislation created Jim Crow in the South, despite later defenses of these laws which claimed that stateways cannot change folkways. Public education is unequally supplied in a great number of ways. In the elementary and secondary schools of the United States as a whole, the money spent per pupil in minority neighborhoods is typically less than that spent per pupil in other areas, in some cases only half as much as in middle-class suburban neighborhoods. There is also less mental testing done in Negro and Puerto Rican schools, so that students in such schools are less familiar with such tests.[26] There is also a less adequate supply of textbooks in black schools,[27] less enforcement of attendance laws,[28] and less of either remedial or accelerated schoolwork.[29] The teachers of minority children in general tend to have lesser educational qualifications whether measured by test scores, experience, quality of college, or family educational background.[30] Perhaps more important than these quantifiable magnitudes are the qualitative differences in *attitudes* of teachers and administrators toward minority-group children. For example, surveys show that most teachers, black or white, do not wish to teach black children.[31] In Italian-American neighborhoods of a generation ago, the "disdain, even contempt of many teachers and administrators for the children" was common.[32] A pioneering study done thirty years ago in a small white community found the teachers and administrators discriminating in their treatment of children by ethnic and social-class origins.[33] The treatment of immigrant children in the nineteenth century showed similar patterns:

> From the desk the teacher looked down, a challenge they dared not meet. It was foolhardy of course to question her rightness. What an arsenal was at her command to destroy them! The steel-edged ruler across the knuckles was the least of her weapons. Casually she could twist the knife of ridicule in the soreness of their sensibilities; there was so much in their accent, appearance and manner that was open to mockery. Without effort she could make them doubt themselves; the contrast of positions was too great. As she snapped shut the closet upon the symbols of her ladyhood within—the white gloves, the rolled-up umbrella, and the sedate hat—she indicated at once the superiority of her own status. There was visible evidence of her correctness in her speech and in her bearing, in her dress, and in the frequent intimations of the quality of her upbringing.

> Perhaps a few were touched with sympathy at the condition of their charges. But what these offered was pity, nobler than contempt, but to the children no more acceptable. It was rare indeed to find the dedicated

woman whose understanding of her students brought a touch of love into her work. After all it was not of this they had dreamed in normal school when they had surrendered a part of their girlhood to acquire a profession, that they would devote the rest of their lives to a surveillance of a pack of unwashed ruffians. Mostly the teachers kept their distance, kept flickering the hope that a transfer might take them to a nicer district with nicer pupils from nicer homes. When that hope died, bitterness was born; and there was thereafter more savagery than love in their instruction.[34]

It would be hard to imagine a profit-making enterprise that could treat the users of its services in this way. The point here is not that there happened to have been abuses in the public school system but rather that the institutional structure of the school system is one in which such abuses can flourish. A public school has a monopoly within its assigned district (where those in the district are not prosperous enough to afford private schools), and in fact a monopoly in which the customers are forced to take the service for as long as the law specifies, whether they are satisfied with it or not. Government-supplied education of ethnic minorities tends to be not only quantitatively substandard, but even more substandard qualitatively. Significantly, outstanding teachers tend to raise the performance level of disadvantaged minority children even more than they raise the performance level of children in the population at large,[35] so apparently the problem is not all in the children or in the home. Minority children from ethnic groups which greatly stress the value of education—Jews, Orientals, West Indians—survive and develop despite the inadequacies of the school or its personnel. Those groups without such a tradition—American Negroes, Italian-Americans, Puerto Ricans, or Mexican-Americans—do not tend to develop in a hostile setting.

Inequalities in government-provided education do not stop at the public school level, but extend on to state universities and even to "private" universities heavily subsidized by the federal government. Again it is necessary to distinguish intention from effect. A state university is supposed to help equalize opportunities for the poor, including disadvantaged ethnic minorities. However, "free" tuition, without provision for living expenses, amounts to a *matching grant*—a subsidy available only to those who can raise substantial amounts of money on their own to make up the difference between the subsidy and the total cost. For example, where tuition cost would be about $2,000 in a similar private college, and living expenses about the same, the state school in effect offers $8,000 for a four-year education to anyone who can come up with another $8,000 for living expenses over the same period. Not surprisingly, few poor people can take them up on such an offer. Moreover, poor people do not have the option of taking the $8,000 in the form of fully paid education for two years rather than half-paid education for four years. It is not surprising that study after study shows state colleges and universities populated primarily by students from families of above-average income.

With colleges and universities, differences in the quantity and quality of education become even more important than on the public school level. Investment per year in a junior college student is likely to be only a fraction of the investment per year in a doctoral candidate at the state university. The junior college student is likely to be taught in large classes by a faculty member with modest credentials and modest salary, while the doctoral candidate is more likely to be taught in small seminars, and his dissertation directed personally by a leading authority in his field, who earns double or triple the salary of a junior college instructor. Because of poorer academic preparation, low-income students, including those from ethnic minorities, constitute an ever-smaller proportion of the student body as you progress from the poorer-quality junior colleges up through the better state colleges and universities, or as you proceed from the freshman year to the Ph.D. level. In addition, since low-income minority students have lesser public school preparation, they are also more concentrated in easier and less remunerative fields such as sociology, education, etc., rather than in the more demanding fields such as mathematics, engineering, medicine, and law, which require far better educational background and which constitute more expensive education in terms of both equipment needs and higher-salaried faculty.

Each of these inequalities in cost and quality compounds the previous inequalities. The government pours highly unequal amounts into different kinds of colleges and universities. This applies not only to state institutions but to private institutions as well, most of whom are heavily dependent upon a great variety of federal subsidies. These federal subsidies go disproportionately to schools such as Harvard, MIT, Cornell, and other prominent or high-level institutions. These kinds of institutions have long been beyond the financial or scholastic reach of most disadvantaged ethnic minorities, and even when they have recruited students from such minorities in recent years, it is highly questionable whether such students have really been educated in the manner of the other students or simply housed on campus and provided with substandard courses under inspiring labels.[36]

The inequalities in the provision of government services to disadvantaged ethnic minorities extend well beyond law and education—though these are the most basic—to garbage collection, recreational facilities, and innumerable other municipal, state, and federal services. This is not always, perhaps not usually, the result of a direct intention to discriminate by race. The government, as mentioned earlier, is not simply the public interest personified. It is an institution with its own needs as an organization, and it is run by individuals with their own interests and needs as people pursuing a career. Like every other institution or individual in society, government agencies have inadequate resources to do all that they would like to do or all that is demanded of them. Government agencies quickly learn that there are some people you can deny more easily than others.

Inadequate schools, libraries, garbage collection, police protection, or traffic lights in a middle-class neighborhood are going to bring a storm of protests by mail, phone, and in person, supplemented perhaps by lawsuits, newspaper publicity, and pressures through local political leaders. If nothing is done, political heads are likely to roll at the next election, and administrative agency heads shortly thereafter. Therefore majority, and particularly middle-class, interests must be at least appeased even if this means that less will be left to take care of other citizens using the same public services. Minorities, by definition, have fewer votes, and most disadvantaged minorities do not vote as high a percentage of the time as the middle class. They also typically lack the knowledge, experience, and access to use other forms of political pressure effectively. Given these circumstances, inequalities in the provision of government services are virtually inevitable. That is, it is futile to single out particular individual villains as the "cause" of the problem, even though some individuals may be particularly obnoxious, for the basic inequalities will persist as long as the other conditions remain.

Subsidies

In addition to being an employer, regulating economic transactions, and providing public services, the government also subsidizes the economic activities of a wide variety of other organizations and individuals. Perhaps the government subsidy most often identified in the public mind with ethnic minorities is welfare, including Aid to Dependent Children. Despite the public image of a typical welfare recipient as a Negro mother with a large brood, most welfare recipients are neither Negro, Puerto Rican, nor Mexican-American. It is also worth noting that while government figures show that $11.4 billion would raise all the poor above the officially defined poverty level,[37] in fact more than $30 billion are spent on programs to get people out of poverty, and there still are more than 5 million families below the poverty level.[38] Clearly most of the money spent on the poor does not directly reach the poor, but is absorbed by the salaries of officials, staffs, consultants, and by other expenses of antipoverty organizations.

Since government subsidies are paid for by taxes, the degree to which a particular group is subsidized depends upon their share of the subsidies compared to their share of the taxes which pay for them. Neither set of data is collected by ethnic group, but other data that are available provide some clues and insights. Contrary to popular belief, the actual taxes collected—local, state and national—are not collected in any such progressive tax pattern as that suggested by the federal income tax schedule. Many of the earnings of the high-income classes are not legally defined as "income" at all, but as "capital gains" (taxed at a lower rate) or as perquisites (not taxed at all). Moreover, a variety of state and local taxes are regressive—that is, they take a higher percentage of low incomes than of high incomes. Sales taxes are an obvious example: they tax only that proportion of income which is spent, which is a higher proportion in low-income brackets than in higher-income brackets, where more is saved.

One study of the actual payment of taxes—state, local, and national together—found that the highest rate of taxation was on those earning less than $2,000. Such individuals pay 44 percent of their incomes in taxes to the various levels of government, while those in higher brackets pay between a quarter and a third of their incomes.[39] The receipt of subsidies tends also to be biased against low-income groups, both in the amount received and in the manner in which it is received. It has already been noted that the public school systems tend to give disadvantaged minorities less expenditures per pupil and to provide the education in a more hostile atmosphere. Similar patterns exist in other subsidies.

Prosperous farmers and large corporation farms receive billions of dollars of agricultural subsidies each year with much less personal disclosure and none of the other indignities and humiliations (night-time "raids" to check on the possibility of "a man in the house") which welfare recipients face. The federal income tax laws allow home buyers (mostly middle class) exemptions on mortgage interest, which amount to rent supplements of 20 to 30 percent of their monthly housing costs—again, without any of the means tests, etc. which the poor must submit to in order to get much smaller rent supplements. Indeed, many of the various massive subsidies to the middle- and upper-income groups are neither labeled nor commonly thought of as subsidies. Billions of dollars of federal subsidies to the maritime industry or to the aviation industry are usually depicted as aids to "national" interests, even though the people who actually receive these subsidies are stockholders, management, and employees, most of whom are well above the national average in income—as are airline passengers, private plane owners, boat owners, and people who take ocean voyages. Another recent study indicates that government subsidies received by the typical high-income family are many times more than government subsidies received by the typical low-income family.[40]

For the disadvantaged ethnic minorities, it seems highly unlikely that subsidies are—on net balance—giving them more than their taxes are taking away. Even in specifically poverty-oriented programs, it is clear that the bulk of the money does not actually reach the poor but rather is paid to the predominantly middle-class suppliers of professional services designed to "fight poverty."

In housing, the subsidies involved in the massive Urban Renewal programs are predominantly subsidies to the businesses and middle- and upper-income tenants who constitute the bulk of those housed in the modern structures built after "slum clearance" has driven out the small businesses and low-income families who must "relocate." Here ethnic data are available. In the first ten years of urban renewal, more than two-thirds of those displaced were either Negroes or Puerto Ricans,[41] though such "redevelopment" has also hit low-income, Italian, Irish, and Mexican-American neighborhoods as well.[42] The total number of housing units destroyed by the Urban Renewal program (predominantly low-income housing in ethnic neighborhoods) greatly exceeds the total number of housing units created by the Urban Renewal programs—or by all government housing programs put together. Once again, the manner in which the subsidies are dispensed to different groups is as contrasting as the amounts. Those who decide to rent office or store space in the "redeveloped" area, or to rent some of the luxury apartments typically included, face no humiliating personal investigations, much less the petty regulation of their day-to-day lives common in public housing projects.

None of this is necessarily the result of deep plots, and some of it is done with the best of intentions. The general, overall results are almost inevitable in the circumstances, however. Democratic, political, and bureaucratic processes are by nature most responsive to the best-organized, most articulate, most prestigious, and best-financed interests. Such special interests can of course be readily defeated by a majority of the voters whenever it is clear to the voters that (1) special interests are benefiting at the expense of the public interests, or that (2) a serious injustice is being done by those special interests to some other group or groups. This is much easier to determine in the case of a simple law or policy which the voter can accept or reject on a once-and-for-all basis. It becomes progressively more difficult, and approaches impossibility, when the problem is one of monitoring the day-to-day decisions of an intricate administrative agency, analyzing statistical data and other information requiring professional expertise to understand, or tracing out widely varying effects on millions of separate individuals who gain and lose in a wide variety of ways from the actual working-out of the program. Where part of the harm is in intangible form, the disruption of millions of lives of already vulnerable individuals, the destruction of neighborhood ties, the loss of customer relations built up by many small businesses—it is almost certain to be overlooked entirely.

Where a program is sufficiently massive and complex, it creates a formidable army of defenders in those who administer it. Moreover, they are necessarily those most familiar with its intricacies, and therefore best able to discredit outside criticism, conceal damaging evidence, and develop direct lines to sources of financial or political power. And as a major employer of "independent" experts and consultants, they can often marshal support from other quarters, or at least make some of these experts reluctant to get into their bad graces by saying "the wrong thing." Even the press is often dependent upon such agencies for much of their information about particular programs. The easiest way for a reporter to collect "news" in time for his newspaper's deadline is to go to the agency concerned and simply write up what they say. To get the contrary view and to dig up enough facts from independent sources to be able to make informed personal judgments is a job requiring several times as much work and one which may dry up official sources of official news even if it pays off in an immediate exposé.

Government programs, like all other forms of human activity, have their benefits and their disadvantages. Those best able to maximize the benefits and minimize the disadvantages are those already well off, financially and socially, and those most likely to end up with the smallest benefits and the largest losses are the poor, the less educated, the less organized, and the less prestigious. Disadvantaged minorities are clearly in the latter categories.

The defenses used by ethnic minorities take a variety of forms, of varying degrees of effectiveness. One defense has been simply to minimize contact with the hostile outside world and/or to minimize personal emotional involvement in such contacts. Italian-American immigrants were (and to some extent are) a striking example of this approach, but most American minorities have followed similar patterns at some point or other in their development in the United States. While this approach minimizes the pain felt by each setback, it increases the total number of setbacks that are likely, since it reduces the knowledge and understanding of the outside world necessary to ward off many avoidable problems. This is particularly true in a political system based on votes and pressure groups.

In addition to their own defenses, ethnic minorities have also at various times had helpers and defenders from the outside world itself—social workers, reporters, doctors, lawyers, etc. Where such outside people simply make information or a service available for the voluntary use of minority individuals, they are clearly enlarging the set of options available to the ethnic group, and it is reasonable to expect that the group will in general end up better off when choosing from a larger array of possibilities rather than a smaller number of options. Where the activities of such outsiders have negative as well as positive effects, members of the ethnic community have the option to use or not use the services offered, or to use them in ways that minimize the negative results while maximizing the positive benefits. However, not all outside help or would-be help takes this particular form. Some of the outside concern is directed toward governmental programs and policies. The benefits contemplated by the social reformers may not be voluntary at all, so that (1) the intended beneficiaries no longer have the option whether to accept or reject on the basis of their own values and more intimate knowledge of their situation, and (2) the chances of reversing a policy or assumption is far less than in voluntary activities. Social reformers—as distinguished from suppliers of voluntary services—acquire both institutional governmental power and administrative and political allies, and all these acquire a vested interest in a certain approach and are threatened with public humiliation if that approach is publicly admitted to be wrong, directly or by its cancellation.

Social Reformers

Social reformers have long been a factor in the life of

the poor in general and ethnic minorities in particular. Sometimes they have served the needy and defended the vulnerable, but at other times their own misconceptions and arrogance have brought additional pain and suffering to those already heavily burdened. There is no need here to attempt to judge the past balance. What is far more important is to understand how the current position of social reformers has changed and is changing, and what this implies for minorities and for society as a whole.

Ethnic minorities have never seen social reformers as these reformers have seen themselves. In both the nineteenth and twentieth centuries, ethnic minorities have often rejected the outside missionaries as dilettantes, slummers, ideologues, moral imperialists, or hopelessly uncomprehending human beings. They have nevertheless *selectively* used the services provided by these missionaries. This means that whatever the mixture of motives among social reformers, and whatever the mixtures of possible effects of their various programs, campaigns, and institutions, the ethnic minorities had the opportunity to maximize the benefits and minimize the losses through their free choice of when and how to participate. It is precisely this free choice which is now progressively disappearing. Social reformers are increasingly armed with the power of government, backed up by foundation and tax money, indoctrinated with institutionalized ideologies, and at least passively accepted by a public awed by "experts."

Ethnic minorities do not *choose* to "participate" in such grand designs as Urban Renewal. Federal laws, court orders, police, wrecking crews, and bulldozers simply move them out. They do not choose whether to accept the social reformers' judgment on the optimal number of years in school or its applicability to their particular circumstances. Judges and jails ensure that youth will spend certain hours of the day in certain buildings for certain years of their lives, though of course such devices cannot ensure that they will be educated. Rates of pay or rates of interest which offend the sensibilities of social reformers will be forbidden by the power of the government, whether or not those happen to be the best rates that a particular man can get. While the power of the government is virtually absolute when it comes to forbidding certain visible actions in an institutional setting, it is far more limited, or even completely ineffective, for producing results that depend upon intangible, individualized responses and creativity. The net result is that the government can easily *remove* options but cannot equally easily add options. At very low cost it can take away an option of a low-skill worker to accept a job at a correspondingly low rate of pay, but it would cost a hundred or a thousand times as much to create an alternative job at the rate of pay authorized by the government. This is not anyone's "fault." It is inherent in the situation and in the nature of the institution of government. What can be questioned is the extent and manner in which such an institution is placed at the disposal of social reformers.

Social reformers are like all other human beings in having their own individual preconceptions and overall vision of the world. Most people find their views subjected to continuous modification in the face of experience—especially experience that is costly, either in money or in personal consequences. Social reformers usually do not pay for their mistakes in either sense. If they are wrong about slum clearance, the cost is paid by those millions of families uprooted from their neighborhoods, by those in the other neighborhoods which now become overcrowded as they move in, and by the taxpayers. If they are wrong about the best number of consecutive years to force people to attend school, the cost is paid by those young people for whom school becomes a daily drag or humiliation, by the teachers driven to distraction (or to other occupations) by the rebellious members of their captive audience, by those children who want to learn but cannot because of disinterested or disruptive classmates, and again by the taxpayers. The constraints and enforced self-correction in most other decision-making situations are either lacking entirely or very weak in the case of social reformers with government power behind them. The worst that is likely to happen to the person who makes disastrous decisions is that a particular program is discontinued, while he moves easily into other programs because of his expertise and experience. Far from being sobered or made cautious by the great powers entrusted to them, social reformers are more likely to regard such grants of power as a confirmation of their own broader vision and deeper insights, and therefore as a mandate to force people to do what is "really" best for them.

In addition to social reformers, as such, social reform attracts and supports an army of "experts," consultants, statisticians, and miscellaneous processors of paper. Admissions of errors or concern over results are even less likely from this group, which may be several times as large as the pure social reformers. To say that these people are concerned about their jobs and their prestige is only to say that they are human. It does mean, however, that listening uncritically to their statements is extremely naive. Everyone understands that when a representative of a soup company tells us that his product makes the best lunch, a healthy skepticism is in order. But when a housing "expert" unveils the latest plan to "save the cities," or a member of the education lobby asks for expanded "opportunities" for youth to consume his product at taxpayer expense, there is a tendency to regard them as wise men promoting the public interest.

Social reform itself is as much needed now as it ever was in the past. It is just too important to be left to social reformers. Whenever possible, social reform programs, especially those dispensing money, should be so structured as to increase the number of options available at the discretion of the individual beneficiary. This is not to claim that there is anything mystically all-wise or all-good about "the people." The one difference between individual decision makers and social reformers is that the former pays a price for being wrong. Even when it is the taxpayer who pays the financial cost, it is the individual involved who wastes his time, sees his hopes dashed, and has to tell his family and friends that he failed. Nevertheless, some individuals will make decisions that are not merely wrong but catastrophic. The relevant comparison, however, is not between their decisions and perfection but between one decision-making process and another decision-making process. The disasters in the social reforms of recent years alone are all too apparent and painful. One need only mention Urban Renewal, public housing projects, welfare, or inner city schools to realize that the "experts" have produced more than their share of disasters.

Chapter 8

Looking Back

Discussions of ethnic minorities tend to drift toward the *problems* of ethnic minorities, or the problems that ethnic minorities cause other people. Both kinds of problems deserve serious attention. However, the history of American ethnic minorities is not exclusively a history of problems. The *contributions* of American ethnic minorities are too numerous to elaborate, whether considering the special achievements of outstanding individuals—the discoverer of blood plasma (American Negro), the first man-controlled atomic reaction (Italian-American), the basic theory of modern physics (Jewish-American)—or the mass contributions of whole groups in particular occupations, in American popular culture, or in enriching the language food, or way of life of Americans in general. It would be hard to think of any leading American singer of the past one hundred years who was not either Irish, Negro, or Italian (the few exceptions being Jewish in most cases). Jews and Orientals are prominent in a number of professional and intellectual fields. Even such small ethnic minorities as the West Indians have had award-winning entertainers, as well as a solid record of middle-class success among the group at large. Even relatively late arriving groups from Latin America have produced a number of individuals whose names are household words.

Perhaps most important, *all* American ethnic minorities show unmistakable signs of economic progress, and those minorities commonly thought of as "disadvantaged" or "problem" minorities have advanced not only absolutely but relative to the American population as a whole. This is especially likely to be overlooked in a country such as the United States, where progress is taken for granted, and where only exceptional relative progress is noticed. Yet none of this progress occurred "automatically" and much of it was the result of painful uphill struggles. In a world where many people still live much as their ancestors lived generations or even centuries ago, there is nothing automatic about such advancement. Virtually every American ethnic group—majority or minority—has a higher standard of living than that prevailing today in their group homeland. This is all the more remarkable considering that most immigrants to America were *not* from the more fortunate classes in their homeland, and were often forced to emigrate because of economic distress.

The progress of American ethnic minorities has not been the result of great racial tolerance. On the contrary, racial and religious animosities have been high throughout much of American history, and American color prejudice has been among the strongest anywhere in the world. Although America has long been a haven for oppressed and persecuted groups, many of these groups did *not* come here with the idea of creating a tolerant (much less a democratic) society, but rather with the idea of establishing themselves, their institutions, and their ideas as dominant—and persecuting anyone within their jurisdiction who disagreed.[1] Early America became a pluralistic society, not in any melting-pot sense or any rights-of-the-individual sense, but in the sense that a great variety of groups had their own territory within which they were dominant—and usually intolerant. People could therefore sort themselves out and live where the institutions and customs best suited them, but there were by no means any general "self-evident" or "inalienable" rights of dissent or even individuality. There was simply a choice among conformities—which was much more than many other countries had at the same time.

Such concepts of tolerance, acceptance, rights, cooperation, etc. as developed in the United States were not the realization of ideals or an initiating force in the economic advance of groups or the nation as a whole. Rather, the original ideals of establishing The Truth—religious, political, or social—had to be abandoned as each group discovered itself not strong enough to wipe out "error," establish its own brand of "justice" or keep "lower" groups in their "place." In short, the rise of pluralism and tolerance represented the *abandonment* or erosion of ideals in the face of hard facts and economic self-interest. The great material wealth of the United States—and especially the individual opportunities to become *more* materially wealthy—provided incentives for a variety of different peoples to advance themselves by creating wealth rather than concentrating on fighting others over the division of existing wealth, or over philosophic and political differences. Very often the opportunities for material advancement required tolerance of, or even cooperation with, other ethnic groups. In the United States, as in other countries, tolerance developed—first in practice and later in theory—in the centers of commercial activity involving a variety of peoples, especially in port cities where people from other lands regularly came and went.

These basic historical facts need emphasis because of a belief in some quarters that the economic advancement of minorities is the result of tolerance, which is the result of ideals promoted in missionary fashion. While this may be true in some individual instances, in many other cases the economic advancement of ethnic groups came first, toleration in practice next, and acceptance of the principle of tolerance or equality last, if at all. Jews were tolerated in Europe in the religiously intolerant Middle Ages not because it was believed that they deserved toleration or that toleration was a good thing, but because they were useful to important people. Blacks have been tolerated more in other parts of the Western Hemisphere than in the United States, not because these other countries were initially any less white supremacist in philosophy, but because they have long been more dependent upon black or "colored" artisans and professionals than the United States, which has long had a large European-origin working class due to the British institution of indentureship and empty space on returning cargo vessels. As Frederick Douglass observed in 1853: "Men are not valued in this country, or in any country, for what they *are;* they are valued for what they can *do.*" [2] Appeals to principles of brotherhood have been far less effective than the unplanned effects of mutual economic advantage. Economic incentives destroyed slavery throughout much of the Western Hemisphere, just as economic incentives destroyed serfdom in Europe. Where governmental and ideological power protected slavery, as in the United States, then other governmental power was necessary to destroy it.

Some ethnic minorities came already prepared to do the work needed in a modern industrial and commercial economy. Others had to painfully adjust to a whole new world. It was not merely that certain specific job skills were lacking, for most of the specific skills could be learned in much less time than one generation. What could not be done in one generation was to change whole patterns of behavior formed under vastly different conditions, or to master a mass of information about how the surrounding world functioned. It is difficult to explain the magnitude of this task to those for whom it is no task at all. Perhaps the most convincing evidence that it is a major transformation is the number of generations it has taken most minorities to be able to function in the American economy and society when they have come from different cultures and different economic systems. Even the concept of "cultural deprivation" is misleading. Every ethnic group and social class in American society has had a highly complex cultural pattern, and however much some elements of that pattern might prove to be handicaps in a particular economic context, it was never a question of creating a cultural element to fill a void but of *transplanting* an element from an alien culture. Since the elements of a culture do not exist in isolation, but are part of an elaborate web of social and psychological relationships, the problem is not the simple one of transmitting specific information but the much more complex and frustrating problem of trying to change a whole mass of attitudes. Pain and rejection are as much part of social transplants as of biological transplants. This is not to claim that it cannot be done. It already has been done, to some degree, with every ethnic group in the United States, whether the initiative in the process was taken by outsiders or by members of the group itself in seeking a better life for themselves. It is necessary, however, to understand the nature of the process and how that affects the rate and the trauma of the process.

Often the outstanding success of some ethnic minority (such as the Jews) or of some individual from a less successful minority (such as Ralph Bunche) will be cited as a prelude to asking, "Why can't the *others* do it too?" The history of American ethnic minorities in general suggests that the others not only *can* do it but *are* doing it—but history also suggests that it takes a very long time, much longer than the lifetime of one man. The antebellum "free persons of color" moved from poverty to middle-class status in about three generations, and their descendants supplied a disproportionate number of the outstanding Negroes who were used as examples by those who asked, "Why can't the *others* do it?" The others were simply back where the antebellum "free persons of color" had been while still struggling to survive and find themselves. Similarly, the urbanization of Jews and their commercial and intellectual activity is far older than that of most minorities, or of the Protestant Anglo-Saxon majority. The special case of the Jews is not one of more rapid adaptation so much as one of much earlier beginning. Their adaptation to the American economy and society, and their acquisition of the specific skills needed in this setting, was indeed more rapid than that of most other immigrant groups, but this was only a special case of their more general advanced stage of development before arriving on American shores. Among all American immigrant minorities, the great differences between the first two generations, and the continuing changes among subsequent generations, further emphasizes the time required for adaptation.

Theory and Research

More important than any particular theory of ethnic minority progress is the testing of all theories against facts. Obvious as this may seem, it has been widely disregarded in practice. Ideas about ethnic groups have been accepted or rejected on the basis of plausibility, of how well they fit in with a preexisting scheme of philosophy or vision of the social process, or even the emotional needs of minorities or those interested in minorities.

The often repeated assertion that American Negro family patterns are a direct result of slavery has gone unchallenged for generations, simply because it was not subjected to even the simplest empirical test of comparing this family pattern with the family patterns of other formerly enslaved groups (West Indian immigrants) and of groups not enslaved (Irish-Americans). Emotionally powerful but logically vague and shifting charges of "exploitation" of various low-income minorities have likewise escaped empirical tests, even of the simplest sort, such as seeing whether those who employ or sell to such groups make an unusually high rate of profit—such as would attract others into ethnic neighborhoods or make indigenous ethnic businesses highly profitable. Even scholarly works often take as axiomatic the view that the history of ethnic minorities is decisively shaped by their political power or "rights," and sometimes treat the history of such minorities as the history of their political and legal status. Evidence could be marshaled on either side of the question of the relative importance of political factors in the economic and social development of American minorities, but such evidence seldom is in fact marshaled, for it is seldom treated as a question.

Perhaps most revealing of all, the social pathology of ethnic minorities has been researched and elaborated in massive volume and minute detail, while the advancement of ethnic minorities has either been of-coursed aside or treated as something for which the group or the society should be congratulated—but not as a serious subject for *cause and effect* analysis. Sometimes what purports to be the history of an ethnic group is in reality a history of other people's sins against this group,[3] as if the group had no existence or significance except as the object of such sins. This approach leaves unanswered—indeed, unasked—the question of how ethnic groups advanced, the differences in the rates of advance and the reasons for these differences, and why some groups advance through entirely different channels from others.

The consideration of ethnic minorities as symbolic objects with which to indict the larger society leads not only to intellectual preoccupation with social pathology but to policies that focus on society's sins rather than on whatever will advance the disadvantaged people fastest. The moral failings of slum landlords, drug pushers, racists, and unscrupulous operators of various sorts provide an inexhaustible source of evils to condemn. It is by no means clear that they are the major causes of social problems or that campaigns directed against them will benefit ethnic minorities more than alternative uses of the same resources in ways more directly designed to advance the disadvantaged. Certainly those minorities who have advanced the fastest have not put their main energies into fighting evil individuals or institutions. It would be an incredible coincidence if those actions that are most effective are at the same time the most emotionally satisfying, either to reformers or to minorities themselves. Because it has become axiomatic in some quarters that making an "issue" is the only way to get "progress," it may be worth noting that housing and welfare have been issues in municipal politics for more than a century, whereas cleanliness and superstition have not. The most casual study of social history shows great progress in the latter two areas over the past century, whereas serious questions have been raised whether any progress has come out of the many programs designed to cope with the slums and with welfare dependency.

The study of ethnic minorities has important implications not only for such groups but also for understanding the factors involved in human development generally. The similar social pathology among groups whose men have been regarded and treated as "boys"—the Irish and the Negroes—may have implications for the growing tendency in society at large to artificially prolong adolescence with increasing educational "requirements." The recognized value of strong family ties may need to be tempered somewhat in the light of the experience of the Italian-Americans and Japanese-Americans, which suggest, in both cases though in different ways, that such ties can be *too* strong to permit the individual to achieve all that he is capable of. The success of black West Indians in the United States may suggest that even such adversity as the brutalities and degradations of slavery may be less damaging in the long run than the destruction of self-reliance.

It may be unsettling to American ideology to believe that a man's current performance in a factory or classroom is related to how his ancestors lived thousands of miles from here and hundreds of years ago. Yet the extent to which this is true, and the manner in which it is true, is ultimately an empirical question, and not a question of philosophy or politics. The American ideal has always emphasized—in concept at least—letting each individual start the race from the same starting line, but once economic progress is seen as an intergenerational *relay* race, then it is not clear at all that any fairness to individuals is likely to lead to the results expected. Whether the methods or the goals should be modified is a separate question.

Intellectual Ability

Differences among American ethnic minorities have been considered thus far in terms of their historical and cultural background, and how well this background prepared them for the American economy and society. The possibility of innate genetic differences in intellectual ability among races has not been explored, largely because the broad outlines of the various groups' economic progress seemed highly related to such factors as (1) length of time in the United States in general or in American cities in particular, (2) median ages of the respective groups, (3) current educational level and past intellectual traditions, (4) family size and family ties, and (5) special factors tending to promote or reduce self-reliance. It was not clear that any very major differences among ethnic groups was left to be explained by innate biological differences. It was even more doubtful that what is currently known about genetics and mental ability could explain very much, even if genetic differences among races were in fact substantial.

Genetic or racial explanations of ethnic differences have been axiomatic among some conservative elements, just as some liberal and radical elements regard color prejudice as an overwhelming barrier. Yet the fact that American Negroes long earned more than Puerto Ricans in the United States undermines both these theories, for most Puerto Ricans in the United States are white, and Puerto Ricans as a group score higher than Negroes as a group on the mental tests which the genetic intelligence theorists rely on.[4] These economic results would be virtually impossible if both assumptions were correct, and highly improbable if either assumption were correct. None of this touches the more general controversy over heredity versus environment, which has raged for centuries with no sign of being settled. It is possible for individual mental differences to be highly related to heredity, and yet for racial groups to differ very little in mental ability, when each race contains a very wide range of inherited abilities.

Significantly, most leading environmentalists recognize the powerful effect of heredity, and most leading proponents of the hereditary intelligence theory recognize the powerful effects of environment.[5] The question is not even which one is more important than the other, in any absolute sense (that is like asking whether food or air is more important for sustaining human life), but which explains most variation for most people under existing environmental conditions with the existing pool of genes. There need not be one answer even to this question. The answer may be different for subgroups whose environments—including their history and cultural traditions—are very different from those of the majority. Every American ethnic group studied has had individuals who range from the mentally retarded to far above the average mental level of *any* group. The variations within each ethnic group are many times greater than the variations between ethnic groups.

It would be much easier to assess the relative importance of heredity and environment if there were (1) some ethnic group whose traditions emphasized intellectual work but who were not very good at it, or (2) an ethnic group whose traditions gave no special place to intellectualism, but who were outstanding at what intellectual work they did. It is easy enough to find *individuals* who meet these descriptions, but not groups. That fact may be significant in itself.

None of this denies that there have been major differences in intellectual *end results* from one ethnic group to another. Only the causes of these differences in end results are unclear. It is worthwhile to explore the history of groups with outstanding records of intellectual accomplishments. The Jews are perhaps the most obvious example, though the history of the Scots is perhaps more revealing. Both are well worth considering.

Jews have not only been overrepresented in intellectual occupations, in a variety of countries and ages, but they have been particularly overrepresented among the outstanding intellectual figures who have revolutionized the whole way of thinking in various fields—Freud,

Einstein, and Marx being obvious examples. Twenty-seven percent of the Americans who received Nobel Prizes from 1901 to 1965 were Jewish, though Jews are only 3 percent of the American population.[6] Many explanations have been offered for the intellectual achievements of Jews, although Jews have also not escaped the accusation made against virtually every ethnic minority, at one time or other that they are innately inferior mentally.[7] The problem in sorting out the different explanations for the Jews' intellectual success is that they—like other intellectually outstanding groups—have had a *combination* of favorable factors at work simultaneously, so that it is difficult to assign weights to different factors. For example, Jews tend to have small families. Among people in general, the firstborn and the only child are overrepresented among individuals of high intellectual achievement. Obviously a group whose members include an unusually high proportion of the firstborn and the only child would tend to be unusually well represented in intellectual achievement from this factor alone. The Jewish tradition of honoring learned men is centuries old, and has at least two important consequences: (1) the obvious encouragement of individual Jews with any intellectual ability at all to develop it, and (2) the selection of the brightest Jews—in past centuries—as rabbis meant that the leading intellects were also the most eligible bachelors, married younger, and had more children.[8] In short, this tradition had both environmental and genetic benefits. Among various other ethnic groups, the movement of the most intellectual members into the Catholic priesthood during the same centuries would tend to create a similar environmental effect but the opposite genetic effect, since Catholic priests cannot marry.

Another feature of Jewish life and tradition would not be consistent with their intellectual achievements compared to those of other groups, but would help explain some of the *internal* differences in intellectual achievement among various subgroups of Jews. For lack of a better term, this factor may be called "alienation." The Jews have been not only an oppressed minority down through the centuries, but also a *small* alien minority. The present concentration of Jews in and around New York City is the greatest concentration of Jews anywhere for thousands of years.[9] The "wandering Jew" had no secure "place" in most societies. He was a marginal outsider. Moreover, many leading Jewish intellectuals have been *doubly* marginal, lacking a Jewish identity as well as lacking full acceptance in the outside world. Karl Marx was a prime example, for he was baptized and raised as a Christian, in a Christian country, though the townspeople all knew that he was descended from rabbis on both sides of his family. Similar double-marginal status existed for the philosopher Spinoza, for the classical economist David Ricardo, for statesman Benjamin Disraeli, and to a greater or lesser extent for Freud, Einstein, and other outstanding Jewish intellectuals. If the relatively small Jewish population is overrepresented among the leading intellectuals, the *very* tiny doubly marginal Jews—the "renegade Jews" in Veblen's words[10]—are fantastically overrepresented.

If one considers those subgroups of Jews who have become more "accepted" and/or assimilated by the society around them—who would therefore be *less* marginal or less alienated—they are also less intellectually prominent. The Sephardic Jews, who lived for centuries along the fringe of North Africa, were not as persecuted by the Moslems as their European counterparts were by the Christians, and were much more acculturated and assimilated. They never produced the intellectual leaders other Jewish groups have produced, nor have their populations as a whole experienced the progress of other Jewish populations. They are today an economically depressed minority in Israel.[11] In the United States, the descendants of these Jews, even when middle class in income and social status, do not score as high on IQ tests as other Jews.[12] Another group of Jews who have shed the "marginal" role are those in Bohemian communities in New York City. Although such communities are in themselves somewhat marginal to the larger society, the Jews in such communities are less alienated from family and childhood associations than the non-Jews in such communities. In such settings, the *non*-Jews have tended to be the more intellectually creative element.[13]

Clearly alienation or marginality alone is not sufficient to produce outstanding intellectuals, or more small minorities would produce the same results as the Jews. What has been rare, however, especially in past ages, has been an oppressed minority with a quantity and quality of education comparable to that of the dominant majority. This requirement alone would eliminate most other minorities. The Jews are not unique, however, in the combination of marginality and high educational standards. The Scots had better schools and a higher rate of literacy than the English in the eighteenth and nineteenth centuries.[14] During this period, British intellectual life was as much dominated by the Scots as European or American intellectual life have ever been dominated by Jews. A list of the leading British intellectuals from 1750 to 1850 would be full of men of Scottish ancestry: David Hume, Adam Smith, T. R. Malthus, James Mill, John Stuart Mill, Sir Walter Scott, Thomas Carlyle, etc. (Two other outstanding British intellectuals of this period were also marginal men: Edmund Burke, an Irish convert from Catholicism, and Benjamin Disraeli, a convert from Judaism.) What makes the Scottish dominance even more remarkable than the intellectual eminence of the Jews is that just one century earlier the Scots were *wholly unrepresented* among the leading European intellectuals,[15] and the mass of the Scottish people were illiterate and so lacking in culture as to be regarded by many as hopelessly primitive savages.[16] What happened in between was a series of religious, political, and economic revolutions which transformed Scotland from a country where even the nobility were illiterate to a country where even the ordinary farmer respected education and made sacrifices to get it for his children, even if he did not have it himself.[17]

Most of the great Scottish intellectuals of this period made their mark not in Scotland but in England—i.e., as aliens or marginal men. They were a minority not only in a numerical sense but in the sense of not being fully accepted. Adam Smith experienced discrimination as a student at Oxford, and in later life complained to the Oxford administration about continuing discrimination against Scottish students.[18] He warned his fellow Scotsman David Hume to avoid a certain controversy because "the whole wise English nation . . . will love to mortify a Scotchman." [19] James Mill went to elaborate pains to shed all traces of Scottish identity in England, and would not even talk about his youth in Scotland in the presence of his children.[20]

Precisely because the Scots did not have a long intellectual tradition like the Jews, nor centuries of making their ablest intellects the most eligible bachelors, their rise to intellectual eminence suggests something of the effect of the combination of marginality and solid education. Many of today's American ethnic minorities have only the first of these, because their public school education is typically substandard and there are many substandard colleges, and substandard programs even in good colleges, where they need never make a commitment to intellectual discipline in order to survive.[21] One of the few exceptions was an all-Negro high school in Washington, D.C., which for a period of eighty-five years (1870–1955) sent many students to the leading colleges in the United States, where they were a marginal minority. That one high school produced the first black Cabinet member, the first black general, the first black federal judge, the discoverer of blood plasma, and the first black senator since Reconstruction, as well as a number of leading black intellectuals of the period.[22] The example of this one high school suggests what might have been possible if there were other such schools for Negroes throughout the country.

The role of marginality in intellectual achievement, like many other features of ethnic minority experience, has implications for the society at large. It suggests that the well-rounded, well-integrated, poised, and assured personality—which many project as an ideal—may be far less creative than the man without real "roots" or "identity," who does not really "know who he is." It also suggests—as Veblen (a very marginal man) noted long ago—a painful choice between personal happiness and intellectual creativity.[23]

Chapter 9

Looking Forward

There is no shortage of programs, projects, demands, or philosophies for advancing ethnic minorities, or of individuals, groups, and organizations claiming to serve that end. Merely to enumerate them would be a major task, and to analyze them all would require many volumes. However, a useful survey can be kept to manageable proportions by broadly grouping these many approaches into militant, reform, and conservative categories.

The Militant Approach

The militant vision of ethnic minority advancement typically involves social cohesiveness, cultural conformity, and ideological solidarity within the ethnic community. This approach does not favor integration, assimilation, acculturation, or any other tendency that would mean a dispersion or a weakening of group political strength or the group's emergency potential for armed struggle. For similar reasons, militants oppose population control as subtle "genocide" or at the very least a tendency that would undermine political strength and/or effective armed resistance.

Within this framework of ideas, the advancement of individual ethnic group members in the larger society is viewed ambivalently at best. Social mobility is feared as a process whereby the best brains and potential leaders of the ethnic community are coopted by the dominant establishment of the larger society. In some cases, it is felt that such people openly or unconsciously "sell out" and become "traitors" who ought to be "dealt with." Counter-measures include early indoctrination of minority children, politicization of minority college students, and activities designed to create such racial polarization as to make the position of "moderates" untenable.

The militant vision has adherents not only among disadvantaged minorities such as Negroes, Mexican-Americans, and Puerto Ricans, but even among more successful minorities, such as Orientals, though much more of a fringe in the latter case. The fact that even members of groups who have advanced substantially by entirely different means would be attracted by the militant vision is one measure of its emotional appeal. Another measure is the extent to which many who do not accept all its conclusions either applaud its approach or are sufficiently sympathetic to excuse tactics which they would otherwise oppose. Whatever the varied subtleties and complexities of its tactics, the militant vision is basically a simple vision of the social process, as well as an emotionally appealing one. It stresses its *newness,* and implicitly therefore its exemption from the usual intellectual or ethical standards by which other ideas and movements are judged. However, this tactic is itself a very old one, as are many of the individual elements of the militant vision and the manner in which they are combined.

The community solidarity, ideological orthodoxy, and cultural conformity necessary for either political or armed struggles were not only espoused but achieved by Irish-Americans in the mid-nineteenth century. Some of their approaches and tactics had been perfected in centuries of underground activity in Ireland itself, before the Irish immigration to America. They were politically the most successful of American ethnic minorities, creating powerful and enduring political machines in cities across the country. In guerrilla activities, the Molly Maguires were peerless, creating "a reign of terror without parallel in American history." [1] Irish-American youngsters learned at their mother's knee to revere and emulate their leaders, heroes, and martyrs, past and present.[2] The thoroughgoing success of the early Irish-Americans in achieving the tactical goals now proposed by other minority militants only reveals the essential weakness of this approach. For the Irish remained the most discriminated-against, despised, and slowest rising of any major white ethnic minority in the United States. They were passed economically not only by such well-prepared ethnic groups as the Jews, but also by later arrivals from similar peasant backgrounds, such as the Italians and the Poles. Moreover, the real rise of the Irish-Americans came *after* they had abandoned the tactics which had been so successful in themselves, though largely futile as a means of advancing the group as a whole.

One of the pitfalls in pressure tactics—violent or moderate—is that such tactics often produce some immediate tangible "results" without producing the basic long-run changes actually needed. Since pressure tactics always seem to work in the short run, they tend to attract great amounts of energy and ingenuity in order to get small, quick, payoffs, to the neglect of the kind of long-range investment of talent necessary to change the underlying situation. Pressure can get contributions or jobs from outside merchants located in an ethnic ghetto—by tactics which repel other enterprise, outside or indigenous. Pressure can create "issues," "victories," and "achivements" by "leaders" without doing very much for the average individual in the group, and perhaps distracting him from the efforts necessary for his own individual development and advancement. Pressure can produce many symbolic victories which have little effect on the everyday economic life of millions of people. Even where the pressure creates something as tangible as government jobs, such jobs can themselves be a trap. One reason cited for the slow rise of the Irish was their great success in getting jobs in municipal government, in cities where the Irish political machine was in control.[3] Such jobs do not usually provide opportunities for great individual development or for passing along a skill, a business, or a profession to the next generation. The best that they do is provide steady income to the current generation—at the price of suppressed initiative. The preoccupation with recurrent campaigns to get such jobs prolongs the role of *recipient* rather than *creator* for the group as a whole. For groups rising from poverty these "small potatoes of political success"[4] may be valuable as a transitional development. However, it is significant that more successful groups such as Jews and Japanese-Americans are *declining* in government employment as they rise in more promising areas.

The Reform Approach

The reform approach to ethnic problems often proceeds in a manner directly opposite to that of the militants. It promotes integration in education, housing, and jobs, sometimes favors quotas (under a variety of names) for minority representation, and tries to bring disadvantaged ethnic minorities "into the mainstream" of American life. However, it is very much like the militant approach in trying to implement a grand design, largely through political efforts, and largely to be imposed from above. Because reformers are more often outsiders, they are in some ways less realistic than militants from within the ethnic group. The outside reformer may in fact be focusing on other outsiders more so than on the ethnic community itself. For example, ethnic minority educational policies may be conceived in terms of forcing racists to mend their ways and accept integration, rather than as a policy of maximizing minority education with given resources.

Reforms sometimes expand options, sometimes reduce options, and sometimes vary in their effects according to an unending series of day-to-day, case-to-case decisions by the institution that administers them. Where benefits are made directly available to the individual according to well-known standard rules—as with education under the GI Bill—the reformers and the voting public can make an informed decision, and the potential beneficiaries can choose to accept or reject the benefit in the light of their individual circumstances, and can continue or not continue, according to whatever their actual experience with the program may happen to be. In short, an informed decision can be made beforehand and modified afterward in the light of actual experience. When options are simply taken away—as with minimum wage laws, school attendance laws, or Urban Renewal—then only the reformers and the voters decide, once and for all, what is good for a third party, whose feeling beforehand and experiences afterward have little or no effect. Where the reform sets up institutions to make continuing day-to-day decisions at the institution's own initiative or discretion, then the reformers, the voting public, and the ostensible beneficiaries all lose power and initiative to functionaries who have their own objectives and interests. Moreover, the monitoring of an unending series of day-to-day decisions is far more readily accomplished by some other well-staffed and permanent institution than by unorganized lay citizens. The net result is that governmental institutions are particularly prone to fall under the influence of businesses, unions, political and other organizations equipped to follow what they are doing.

The bias in reform efforts has been toward creating "caretaker" institutions which make day-to-day decisions for those who are its intended beneficiaries. Welfare departments are perhaps a classic example of this approach, though schools, public housing projects, and many other governmental agencies also follow this pattern. Even if all the caretaker institution's decisions were superior to the decisions its clients would have made for themselves, the disadvantages of undermining the individual's right of choice and his experience at decision making would open this approach to serious question. It is, however, highly unlikely that the caretaker institution's decisions will be better in most cases, for those who make the decisions are free to indulge their illusions, vanity, caprice, and narrow institutional self-interest without suffering any repercussions.

Reforms that enlarge options and allow the individual to decide are a great threat to a wide variety of organized special interests. Social workers become superfluous if the government "just gives money" to the poor. Public schoolteachers and administrators are endangered by voucher systems that allow parents and children their choice of where to attend school. Moral crusaders would lose the power to shape other people's lives according to "higher" principles.

Reforms can be enacted in a democracy only insofar as they are formulated as politically acceptable doctrines and issues. For example, "job retraining" is politically acceptable, but telling people that they have to shed certain cultural habits which have handicapped their ethnic group for generations is not. What is politically possible and what is economically necessary need not always coincide. A social problem may therefore be politically "insoluble," even though a solution may be known, cheaper, and faster than many other approaches that are being pursued zealously. Political reforms are also biased toward short-run "results," if only because elections take place in the short run. Any reform that would raise taxes today in order to drastically reduce welfare dependency in ten years is unlikely to be seriously considered by politicians who are elected every two, four, or six years.

The Conservative Approach

Conservatives are often thought of as people who want no changes, or who would restrict their changes to repealing various liberal reforms. Nevertheless, American conservatives have a general vision of society, even as revolutionaries and reformers do. In the conservative American vision, the individual is supreme, not only in the sense that the system is conceived of as maximizing individual opportunity, but also in the sense that pluralistic *group* factors and interests are an uneasy and awkward appendage to the American Dream. Group phenomena of all sorts—discrimination, quotas, bloc voting—are likely to be either denied or deplored.

Individualism as a philosophic value cannot change the historical fact of group discrimination and group conditioning, both of which severely limit the opportunities facing any particular individual in a disadvantaged group. Moreover, the fact that dominant social groups impose *their* group cultural patterns and mores as preconditions for success within both private and public institutions cannot be overlooked in any attempt to understand American pluralism and its problems. The massive institutional favoritism enjoyed by the "haves" is at least comparable to the social charities given the "have nots," though many a subsidized businessman or a doctor whose income is greatly increased by the restrictive practices of the American Medical Association may feel sincerely indignant at "welfare chiselers" and others who want "special treatment." Moreover, conservatives are particularly likely to overlook the fact that one of the most important ways in which discrimination takes place is precisely through the *selective* application of fundamentally sound principles.

Often the life experience of a conservative is simply different, and his generalizations from that experience to the experience of others distorts, sometimes beyond recognition. The friendly policeman known to middle and upper income Americans is not the same policeman experienced by the poor, the black, and by disadvantaged immigrants—either because different kinds of policemen are assigned to different areas or because the same policeman changes his manner in dealing with groups who can and groups who cannot retaliate. The *principle* of "law and order" may be the same for everyone but the living reality is not. Asking the poor to respect law and order is asking them to respect something very different from what the middle- or upper-income person has known. The institutional distortion of the law to favor the affluent—

from tax loopholes to zoning—also poses a difficult problem to the disadvantaged when asked to respect the law.

Conservatives who demand stricter and sterner applications of the law to criminals often overlook the fact that the very reason for the reluctance of juries, judges, or legislators to go all out in applying the principles of the law is precisely the "gut" feeling that it is a biased law—that capital punishment really means capital punishment of blacks and the poor only, that "support your local police" really means letting them vent their anger and frustrations with a nightstick on whatever groups they dislike, that tough jail sentences mean the dehumanization of those who cannot afford good lawyers.

Moreover, the ability to punish the "have nots" effectively is severely restricted by the small difference between their ordinary life as free men and the degree of punishment permitted by Constitutional prohibitions against "cruel and unusual punishment." In a sense, higher standards of living—and particularly greater economic opportunities for advancement—would do much to widen that difference and make a given punishment more "severe" or effective within the limits of the Constitution. In short, what makes punishment so ineffective now is that many feel that they have *nothing to lose.* Many of the social policies to enlarge opportunities, which some conservatives oppose, are among the most effective ways of making punishment meaningful. To someone with many opportunities to advance himself economically and develop his individual potential, even a misdemeanor conviction with suspended sentence is a serious blot on his record, while to someone going nowhere even a felony conviction and incarceration may not make enough difference to deter him. For its own protection, no society can afford to have a significant proportion of its population feel that they have nothing to lose.

Conservatives, like reformers and militants, have something to contribute to an understanding of the world, but in all three cases their positive contributions are often buried under a multitude of illusions and unexamined assumptions. The point here is not simply that particular groups are politically self-defeating but that the vital insights each could offer, from different perspectives, are lost to the society at large.

The Future

A common charge against reformers and revolutionaries for at least two hundred years has been that they seem more interested in punishing evildoers than in helping those who need help. Indeed, other people's sins have held a powerful fascination, not only for reformers and revolutionaries, but for conservatives, moderates, and the apolitical as well. Perhaps the first thing that needs to be done in dealing with the problems of disadvantaged ethnic minorities is to recognize that their problems are sufficiently painful and urgent that solutions cannot be restricted to those which enable third parties to feel noble in attacking villains, or which require the services of miscellaneous caretakers, the principles of moral crusaders, or the vote-getting tactics of politicians. If these third parties happen to benefit from efforts to aid the disadvantaged, fine. But if they do not happen to benefit, also fine.

Education The segregation of children from ethnic minorities, and the provision of inferior educational facilities for them, is a very old pattern brought under serious fire only in relatively recent times. The pressure against these practices as a moral evil has been relentless, and yet from the point of view of actually advancing the education of minority children, it is an open empirical question whether changes in racial distribution and increasing expenditures in minority school districts produce more or less benefit than other things which could be achieved with similar expenditures of effort and money. The point here is not to insist on one conclusion rather than another, but rather to emphasize that the moral crusade has superseded this practical question to the point of wholly obscuring it.

Oriental children in the United States score at least as well as white children on most mental tests, despite the de facto segregation (imposed or voluntary) of "Chinatowns" and "Little Tokyos" in various American cities, and the corresponding segregation of public schools. The same has been true of Jewish children in Jewish neighborhoods. It is apparently not the segregation, as such, which is educationally handicapping, but the segregation of children from groups whose cultural norms do not emphasize education or the behavior patterns required for intellectual development. Although public interest has centered on Negro children, similar patterns are found in other ethnic groups that do not emphasize education, such as Italian-Americans, Mexican-Americans, and Puerto Ricans. In fact, such patterns are found in Protestant Anglo-Saxons from low socioeconomic backgrounds.

What gains may occur in educational performance among children from such groups are not the result of putting them in school districts with higher per pupil expenditures, for where equally high (or higher) expenditures have been made in segregated schools in these children's own neighborhoods, there has been little, if any, educational impact, and they do not reach the levels achieved in other neighborhoods, even when the disadvantaged children have *more* money spent on them.[5] This has sometimes been attributed to genetic lack of mental capacity, but when such children are transferred to a different cultural environment, even one with the same or even lower per pupil expenditure, their educational performances improve significantly.[6] Moreover, the educational performances of the other children (from an environment that does emphasize education) has not been found to be significantly affected by the presence of the disadvantaged students, as long as the proportion of these latter students remains below some level, usually about 30 percent. Apparently the dominant culture in the school attracts disadvantaged children toward higher educational achievements, without an offsetting attraction of educationally oriented children toward antieducational patterns, as long as it remains the substantially dominant culture. Under special conditions, such cultures or atmospheres have existed in schools made up entirely of students from a disadvantaged minority, and normal or even outstanding educational results have been achieved. All-Negro Dunbar High School in Washington, D.C., was one such school during the 1870–1955 period, as indicated by above-normal IQ scores and distinguished career achievements by its alumni.[7] In short, the major problem with low-performance schools whose children are from noneducationally oriented groups is *not* the more emotionally laden factors of segregation, discrimination in expenditures, or genetic capacity.

The atmosphere in low-performance schools attended by children from disadvantaged groups (native white as well as ethnic minorities) is often one where behavior problems take up as much as half of the class time,[8] and where the interruptions and mental stress undoubtedly reduce the effectiveness of the school work done in the other half. Comparisons of school performances by children in such schools with that of other children with the "same" amount of education elsewhere are substantively misleading, however formally accurate in terms of years of school attendance. The attributes and behavior of the disadvantaged children may range from apathy through restlessness, disruption, sporadic violence, to calculated terrorism. However serious or even devastating their educational consequences may be, they are unlikely to attract as much public attention as other factors which may be much less important in affecting the educational outcomes. Such behavior provides no basis for either a moral crusade or for vote-getting political issues. The students whose behavior makes good education difficult or impossible are themselves victims of circumstances as well as victimizers of others, so that moral condemnation would be on shaky ground, particularly if it came from persons from more fortunate backgrounds. Politically there are no votes to be won by telling people that their own children make good education impossible, and doing so might well be the first step toward oblivion for either a politician or a school administrator.

The demonstrated educational improvements from putting disadvantaged students in a different atmosphere have serious implications for ethnically segregated college programs. Some of these programs strive consciously to insulate their students from the cultural patterns of the other students and to shield their academic performances and standards from outside scrutiny. Stirring and defiant rhetoric has often accompanied this retreat under fire. Alternatives here are very painful. Students who have had twelve years of inferior education cannot compete successfully with other students without efforts by themselves and by others which far exceed what most human beings are prepared to do. Most students from such backgrounds must either (1) continue to receive inferior education, under a variety of "experimental," "relevant," or "innovative" labels, or (2) have inferior performance in intellectually solid and demanding educational programs. The path of least resistance for all is to continue the automatic-passing, automatic promotions practices of the public school system into college.

The education of ethnic minorities cannot be entirely separated from the problems of American education in general. The widespread use of high school diplomas and college degrees as employment screening devices by employers has led to a belief that increasing education will increase opportunities, and/or that the reason for escalating educational "requirements" is a corresponding increase in the knowledge necessary to perform a given job. The well-organized education lobbies exploit these beliefs to the fullest. In fact, however, educational "requirements" are often used by employers who are wholly unconcerned about the specific content of the education, but who regard a diploma or degree as an indication of the job applicant's willingness to persevere and his grades as a rough index of his mental capability. The educational requirements are a hurdle which eliminates enough job applicants to narrow the employer's choice down to manageable proportions. By making it possible for more young people to go over a given hurdle, society also makes it necessary for employers to raise the hurdle in order to weed out the same proportion of applicants. The result has been an upward spiral of credentials and requirements, with more and more young people being forced to endure more and more years of education that they do not want in order to qualify for jobs where the education is not needed. As more and more jobs have been put beyond the reach of those without the necessary credentials, whether or not such individuals can do the work itself, those ethnic minorities who are not traditionally oriented toward formal education are particularly hard hit.

Education has been seen as an "opportunity," particularly by those who have achieved success by this route. But *any* hurdle is a path to success for those who have succeeded. It has eliminated rivals and left the survivors with a clear field. This is true *regardless* of the nature of the hurdle or its intrinsic merits. At different places and times the hurdle had been membership in the Catholic church or the Communist party, a British upper-class accent and life style, or being more adroit with a sword or faster with a gun. It may be very rational for the individual to cultivate the ability to surmount whatever hurdles society puts in his way, but it is not therefore rational for the society to insist on a particular hurdle, much less to constantly raise that hurdle, at great expense to everyone.

Even where society provides subsidized or "free" education, this still leaves to the individual the heaviest investment of all to make—years of his life and what is often a stultifying experience for the spirit. This is not to say that colleges and universities are not "relevant" or are doing their jobs wrong. Their job is not to be universally popular and enjoyable, but to perform an important *specialized* service, just as airports, hospitals, and shoe repair shops perform specialized services. It is no condemnation, either of the institution or of any particular individual, if the needs and desires of the two do not happen to mesh. If the individual is a member of an ethnic minority that has not had a tradition that would lead him to want what a college or university has to offer, refusing him an opportunity in life if he does not submit to its demands may mean that a change in such institutions to meet his desires will become one of his demands. The compromises, distortions, and general charade may become mutual, but hardly more justified.

As long as the larger society makes long years of formal training a hurdle for young people in general, it is futile to hope that ethnic minorities will be exempted. A reconsideration of beliefs and practices may benefit everyone, and especially those who most need opportunity.

Income The respective incomes of American ethnic minorities reflect many factors, such as the degree of discrimination encountered, the level of job capability achieved by the group, and the level of public subsidies received. All these are matters of intense public interest and controversy—which is *not* to say that their actual effect is greater than the effect of other variables that receive much less attention. The median ages and regional distribution of American ethnic groups—never subjects of heated discussion—accounts for a substantial part of the differences in income among minorities, and between minority and majority. They also account for a substantial part of the differences in unemployment rates. That is, differences in income and employment among individuals of the same age from different ethnic backgrounds are only a fraction of the differences between ethnic groups as a whole. Income is also highly correlated with the amount of time that an ethnic group has spent in the American urban economy. Even such major and blatant factors as color and slavery did not prevent American Negroes (who entered the urban economy in the 1920s) from earning higher incomes than the Puerto Ricans (who entered after World War II). Similarly, in the closing years of the nineteenth century, the northern urban blacks, largely descended from the antebellum "free persons of color," were economically somewhat in advance of the white immigrants of the same period.[9]

In a world of complex and reciprocal cause and effect, no factor ever stands in splendid isolation as either cause or effect. The median age of an ethnic minority is a given fact of life during the current time period, but it is very much a function of social variables at work in previous time periods, including such variables as income and employment. The Malthusian theory of population argues that efforts to raise the standard of living of the poor are doomed by their tendency to increase population in proportion to any additional income they receive, driving the income per capita back to where it was before.[10] Anti-Malthusians have argued that the large families of the poor are an effect of their hopeless situation, in which such virtues as foresight and self-restraint show little prospect of making a difference.[11] If the anti-Malthusians are correct, then those poor people suffering extra handicaps as minority poor would be expected to have even more children than other equally poor people. This is in fact the case with Mexican-Americans, Puerto Ricans, and American Negroes. Moreover, such groups would be expected to shed such patterns as their prospects brighten—as among higher-paid and better-educated individuals from these groups. Again, it is the *anti*-Malthusian theory that fits the facts, for all three groups have *fewer* children than their Anglo-Saxon counterparts, once they rise above some income or educational level. From a moral point of view, it cannot be said that the larger society is not responsible for differences in income due to differences in median age (due in turn to differences in the ratio of children to adults), for these differences are results of past conditions, often conditions very much controlled by the majority. However, for a cause-and-effect analysis of the current functioning of the economy, it is useful to understand how much of current income differences reflect current discrimination, and for this it is necessary to understand how much of the earnings and employment differences among ethnic groups really reflect differences in society's current treatment of comparable individuals from different ethnic backgrounds—that is, how much discrimination there still is, and how important it is in creating other differences.

The word "discrimination" has often been used to cover such widely differing situations that it is of little help in specifying causes, effects, or corrective policies. If *all* differences between the earnings, occupations, employment, etc. of different ethnic groups are simply *defined* as "discrimination," [12] then it is circular reasoning to say that discrimination *causes* these differences, and compounded meaninglessness to quantify the effects of discrimination in dollars and cents.[13] Yet this is the approach of a leading "study" of poverty and discrimination.

With both "exploitation" and "discrimination" the point is not to select the philosophically best label, but to understand the actual mechanisms and relationships involved, so as to specify actions that lead to other results. Consider an individual whose native ability is sufficient to enable him to enter an occupation where the average income is $20,000 a year. If he is a member of a disadvantaged ethnic minority, then he may never be able to realize his potential because of discrimination in education and/or employment and/or the counterproductive behavior patterns he picks up from his environment. If he ends up making $4,000 a year as a dishwasher, he may not be "exploited," at all, even though he may be greatly victimized by circumstances beyond his control. If the actual value of his current services to his current employer are not significantly misstated by the $4,000 salary, any attempt to force his wages up by fiat to end "exploitation" —by minimum-wage laws, union pay scale, pressures of one sort or another—are likely to lead to the use of more dishwashing machines and therefore higher unemployment rates among dishwashers. It is not just a matter of words but of consequences.

Labor is of course only one source of income. Increasingly business is promoted as a source of higher incomes, as well as a source of "success models" to inspire the younger generation among disadvantaged ethnic minorities. Both these goals imply that the businesses formed are going to be successful—contrary to a massive body of evidence that most small businesses end in failure, whether run by members of a minority or the majority. Most small businesses fail within a few years of being established, and yet thousands of people set up new businesses with their life savings each year, partly because they believe that there is nothing complicated about it. In a sense, they are right; a small business may have no single aspect that is intellectually complicated, and yet dozens of small pieces of knowledge that must be acquired by experience—often disastrous experience—and the firm's assets may be gone before the owner learns why he should deal with one kind of supplier rather than another, prefer one location rather than another, have one kind of employee rather than another, etc. If it were simply an intellectual process, it could be taught in schools, so that a new businessman would know what to do from the outset, but much of the knowledge is the kind which can be acquired only by actual experience, including knowledge of particular people in a given trade or locality. The process of producing a whole class of experienced businessmen is necessarily a gradual one, whether one believes in gradualism as a principle or not. Driving existing merchants out of an ethnic community is easy, but replacing them with indigenous businessmen is much harder, and people have to eat in the meantime. Given the high odds against the survival of a new small business, the American Dream of business success can easily turn into a nightmare of still fewer stores in ethnic ghettoes, still poorer service, still higher prices, and still more minority members losing their painfully acquired life savings in such ventures. This is not to say that nothing should be done. What must be recognized is that expectations must be geared to a painfully slow trial-and-error process rather than to an inspired formula for social salvation.

One idea underlying many schemes for community-based enterprises is that prosperity will be increased if money is kept in the ethnic community instead of being siphoned off by outside business interests. Wealth, however, does not consist of money but of goods (including services), so that maximizing real income means maximizing the flow of goods through the community per unit of time. This is not simply a matter of different words but of policies with completely opposite implications. To keep money from leaving the community implies efforts at economic self-sufficiency, while maximizing the flow of goods implies spending the money wherever it will buy the most. Money flows *through* minority communities, just as it flows through all communities, and the very process that would reduce the flow *out*—increasing self-sufficiency— would also reduce the flow *in,* as fewer minority-group members earn incomes in the outside world. The real difference in economic well-being would be measured by the difference between the flow of goods under internal production compared to the flow of goods attainable by buying wherever the best price is available. To the extent that locally produced goods are cheaper or better, no *policy* would be necessary to get local people to buy them.

Another meaning of "keeping money in the community" is that community savings should be invested in community businesses instead of being used to finance business ventures elsewhere. But just as community residents are not going to be made more prosperous by buying inside the community at higher prices than those outside the community, or by working at lower wages inside the community than outside, so local savers are not going to prosper by having their savings invested at a lower rate of return inside the community than those outside the community. The physical location of jobs, investment, or income sources makes little difference economically to a given community; what matters is the size of the flow of real goods to the people located in the community, regardless of where the flow originates. Capital is the most fluid of all resources. It goes wherever the rate of profit is highest, allowing for risk. If the ghetto, barrio, or other ethnic community were a high-profit location, nothing is more certain than that capital would be flowing into it instead of avoiding it.

Some of the more sophisticated proponents of indigenous business enterprise, or community controlled economic life generally, point out that the classical economic refutations of mercantilistic keep-the-money-at-home arguments overlook the possibility of changing the terms of trade between societies and/or utilizing otherwise idle resources to produce goods that would otherwise be imported. These abstract possibilities seem very remote in practice, given that the ethnic minority economies are so small compared to the huge American economy with which it is trading, and that all the ethnic minority resources are available also in the larger economy, while the reverse is not true.

Perhaps the greatest dilemma in attempts to raise ethnic minority income is that those methods which have historically proved successful—self-reliance, work skills, education, business experience—are all slow developing, while those methods which are more direct and immediate—job quotas, charity, subsidies, preferential treatment —tend to undermine self-reliance and pride of achievement in the long run. If the history of American ethnic groups shows anything, it is how large a role has been played by attitudes—and particularly attitudes of self-reliance. The success of the antebellum "free persons of color" compared to the later black migrants to the North, the advancement of the Italian-Americans beyond the Irish-Americans who had many other advantages, the resilience of the Japanese-American despite numerous campaigns of persecution, all emphasize the importance of this factor, however mundane and unfashionable it may be.

Notes

Chapter 1

1. Clement Eaton, *The Freedom of Thought Struggle in the Old South* (New York: Harper & Row, 1964), chaps. 5, 7, 8, 9; J. E. Cairnes, *The Slave Power* (New York: Harper & Row, 1969), pp. 176, 177, 178*n*.
2. Kenneth M. Stampp, *The Peculiar Institution* (New York: Vintage Books, 1956), pp. 30, 31; see also Lewis C. Gray, *History of Agriculture in the Southern United States* (Washington, D.C.: Carnegie Institution of Washington, 1933), 1:481, 482.
3. Eaton, *Freedom of Thought Struggle in the Old South*, p. 87; Frederick Law Olmsted, *The Cotton Kingdom* (New York: Modern Library, 1969), p. 66; Cairnes, *The Slave Power*, p. 170*n*.
4. See Stanley M. Elkins, *Slavery* (Chicago: University of Chicago, 1969); Herbert S. Klein, *Slavery in the Americas* (Chicago: Quadrangle Books, 1961).
5. Elkins, *Slavery*, p. 60; Eaton, *Freedom of Thought Struggle in the Old South*, pp. 114, 122, 123; Ulrich B. Phillips, *Life and Labor in the Old South* (Boston: Little, Brown, 1964), p. 163; Cairnes, *Slave Power*, pp. 45–46.
6. William L. Westerman, *The Slave Systems of Greek and Roman Antiquity* (Philadelphia: American Philosophical Society, 1955), pp. 13, 92, 102, 114–15.
7. Olmsted, *Cotton Kingdom*, pp. 28, 32, 42, 78, 100, 101, 140, 219, 254, 303, 306, 367; Ulrich B. Phillips, *American Negro*

Slavery (Baton Rouge: Louisiana State University Press, 1969), p. 287; Eugene D. Genovese, *The Political Economy of Slavery* (New York: Vintage Books, 1967), p. 55.

8. Cairnes, *Slave Power*, p. 56n.
9. Ibid., p. 180.
10. Ibid., pp. 228–38.
11. Olmsted, *Cotton Kingdom*, pp. 439–42.
12. Ibid., p. 438; Phillips, *Life and Labor in the Old South*, p. 326; Klein, *Slavery in the Americas*, p. 179.
13. Olmsted, *Cotton Kingdom*, pp. 440–41; Phillips, *American Negro Slavery*, pp. 280–81.
14. Olmsted, *Cotton Kingdom*, pp. 440–41.
15. Alec Nove, "Soviet Agriculture Marks Time," *Foreign Affairs* Vol. 40, no. 4 (July 1962): 590.
16. Alfred H. Conrad and John R. Meyer, "The Economics of Slavery in the Antebellum South," *Journal of Political Economy* (April 1958): 95–130: Robert W. Fogel and Stanley L. Engerman, *Time on the Cross* (Boston: Little, Brown, 1974), pp. 59–106, 174, 184–90.
17. Cairnes, *Slave Power*, p. 81.
18. Olmsted, *Cotton Kingdom*, p. 19.
19. Ibid., p. 103.
20. Cairnes, *Slave Power*, pp. 81–82, 143, 144; Olmsted, *Cotton Kingdom*, pp. 64, 85, 87, 88, 90, 147, 257, 290, 327, 390, 391, 397, 421, 448, 527.
21. Alexis de Tocqueville, *Democracy in America* (New York: Alfred A. Knopf, 1945), 1:362–63.
22. Olmsted, *Cotton Kingdom*, p. 12.
23. Ibid., p. 305.
24. Ibid., p. 86.
25. Ibid., pp. 29, 38, 43, 44, 126, 152, 158, 168, 177, 186, 212, 214, 220, 232, 258–59, 294, 307, 317–18, 330, 374, 423, 425, 427.
26. Ibid., p. 72.
27. Eaton, *Freedom of Thought Struggle in the Old South*, chaps. 5, 9.
28. Ibid., pp. 127, 212.
29. Ibid., pp. 220, 222, 228–29.
30. Ibid., pp. 229, 231–32.
31. Ibid., p. 216.

32. Ibid.
33. Ibid., pp. 219–20.
34. Ibid., p. 220.
35. Ibid., pp. 178, 180, 182, 190.
36. Ibid., p. 67.
37. Olmsted, *Cotton Kingdom*, pp. 114–15.
38. Ibid., p. 116.
39. Ibid., p. 119.
40. Ibid.
41. Ibid., p. 120.
42. Klein, *Slavery in the Americas*, p. 188; see also Frederick Law Olmsted, *A Journey in the Seaboard Slave States* (New York: New American Library, 1969), p. 127.
43. Phillips, *American Negro Slavery*, p. 411.
44. Ibid.
45. Phillips, *Life and Labor in the Old South*, p. 216.
46. Richard C. Wade, *Slavery in the Cities* (London: Oxford University Press, 1967), p. 110.
47. John Hope Franklin, *From Slavery to Freedom* (New York: Vintage Books, 1969), pp. 218–20; Phillips, *American Negro Slavery*, p. 448; Benjamin Brawley, *Social History of the American Negro* (London: Collier Macmillan, 1970), p. 31; John H. Russell, *The Free Negro in Virginia, 1619–1865* (New York: Dover Publications, 1969), pp. 52, 66, 69–72, 106–7, 143; John Hope Franklin, *The Free Negro in North Carolina, 1790–1860* (New York: W. W. Norton, 1971), pp. 10, 42, 76, 81, 82, 83, 84, 131, 193.
48. Stampp, *Peculiar Institution*, pp. 141, 222; Elkins, *Slavery*, pp. 56–57.
49. Olmsted, *Cotton Kingdom*, p. 75; Stampp, *Peculiar Institution*, pp. 113, 114.
50. Stampp, *Peculiar Institution*, p. 128; Phillips, *Life and Labor in the Old South*, pp. 194–95.
51. Stampp, *Peculiar Institution*, p. 128; Phillips, *American Negro Slavery*, p. 305; idem, *Life and Labor in the Old South*, pp. 194–95.
52. Stampp, *Peculiar Institution*, pp. 127–28.
53. Phillips, *American Negro Slavery*, p. 458.
54. Ibid., pp. 456–58.
55. Wade, *Slavery in the Cities*, pp. 214, 215, 216.
56. Ibid., p. 219.

57. Stampp, *Peculiar Institution*, p. 115.
58. Phillips, *American Negro Slavery*, p. 305.
59. Stampp, *Peculiar Institution*, p. 110.
60. Phillips, *American Negro Slavery*, pp. 433–34; Brawley, *Social History of the American Negro*, pp. 243–45.
61. Wade, *Slavery in the Cities*, pp. 84–90, 157.
62. Ibid., pp. 173–77.
63. Ibid., p. 174.
64. Ibid., p. 235.
65. Phillips, *Life and Labor in the Old South*, p. 170; idem, *American Negro Slavery*, pp. 99–100.
66. Stampp, *Peculiar Institution*, p. 234.
67. Ibid., p. 194.
68. Ibid., p. 234.
69. W. J. Cash, *The Mind of the South* (New York: Vintage Books, 1967), p. viii.
70. Phillips, *American Negro Slavery*, p. 425.
71. Franklin, *From Slavery to Freedom*, pp. 138–40.
72. Phillips, *American Negro Slavery*, p. 124.
73. Stampp, *Peculiar Institution*, pp. 218–20.
74. Phillips, *American Negro Slavery*, pp. 122–24; idem, *Life and Labor in the Old South*, p. 250.
75. Franklin, *From Slavery to Freedom*, p. 140.
76. Eaton, *Freedom of Thought Struggle in the Old South*, p. 19.
77. Phillips, *American Negro Slavery*, p. 122.
78. Elkins, *Slavery*, pp. 51n., 78; Phillips, *American Negro Slavery*, p. 52; Gray, *History of Agriculture in the Southern United States*, 2:519; Carter G. Woodson, *The Negro in Our History* (Washington, D.C.: Associated Publishers, 1945), p. 71.
79. Elkins, *Slavery*, pp. 84, 85.
80. Phillips, *American Negro Slavery*, p. 172.
81. Phillips, *Life and Labor in the Old South*, p. 125.
82. Ibid., p. 126.
83. Ibid., p. 127.
84. Olmsted, *Cotton Kingdom*, pp. 505–6; Gray, *History of Agriculture in the Southern United States*, pp. 479–80.
85. Phillips, *Life and Labor in the Old South*, pp. 127–28.
86. Ibid., p. 126.
87. Eaton, *Freedom of Thought Struggle in the Old South*, p. 130; Stampp, *Peculiar Institution*, p. 206.

88. Eaton, *Freedom of Thought Struggle in the Old South*, p. 129.
89. Ibid., p. 131.
90. Stampp, *Peculiar Institution*, p. 210.
91. Ibid., pp. 232–33.
92. Gray, *History of Agriculture in the Southern United States*, 1:519, 520.
93. Eaton, *Freedom of Thought Struggle in the Old South*, p. 33.
94. Phillips, *Life and Labor in the Old South*, p. 339.
95. Ibid., p. 9.
96. Ibid., p. 10.
97. Ibid., p. 11.
98. Eaton, *Freedom of Thought Struggle in the Old South*, p. 239.
99. Ibid., pp. 86, 87.
100. Ibid., pp. 129, 178.
101. Ibid., pp. 166.
102. Ibid., pp. 178, 190.
103. Ibid., pp. 180, 182–83.
104. Olmsted, *Journey in the Seaboard Slave States*, p. 367.
105. Tocqueville, *Democracy in America*, 1:367.
106. Olmsted, *Cotton Kingdom*, pp. 258–59; Phillips, *American Negro Slavery*, p. 126.
107. Tocqueville, *Democracy in America*, p. 379.
108. Herbert S. Klein, *Slavery in the Americas*, pp. 205–11, 225–26.
109. Stanley M. Elkins, *Slavery*, p. 62n.
110. Ibid., p. 64.
111. Ibid., p. 62n.
112. Klein, *Slavery in the Americas*, pp. 2–22.
113. Ibid., pp. 22–36.
114. Adam Smith, *The Wealth of Nations* (New York: Modern Library, 1937).
115. Klein, *Slavery in the Americas*, pp. 150–52.
116. Ibid., pp. 150–51.
117. Ibid., pp. 144, 145.
118. Ibid., pp. 146.
119. Ibid., pp. 202, 236.
120. Frank Tannenbaum, *Slave and Citizen* (New York: Alfred A. Knopf, 1947), pp. 53–54, 61.
121. Ibid., pp. 58, 59, 61.

122. Klein, *Slavery in the Americas*, pp. 143–44.
123. Ibid., pp. 205–10.
124. Tannenbaum, *Slave and Citizen*, p. 92.
125. Klein, *Slavery in the Americas*, p. 211.
126. Lewis C. Gray, *History of Agriculture in the Southern United States* (Washington, D.C.: Carnegie Institution of Washington, 1933), 1:535.
127. John Hope Franklin, *The Free Negro in North Carolina, 1790–1860* (New York: W. W. Norton, 1971), pp. 113–14.
128. John Melish, *A Geographical Description of the United States* (Philadelphia: 1822), p. 314.
129. Eaton, *Freedom of Thought Struggle in the Old South*, p. 87.
130. Klein, *Slavery in the Americas*, p. 258.
131. Tannenbaum, *Slave and Citizen*, p. 100.
132. Ibid., p. 64.
133. Ibid., pp. 75, 82.
134. Klein, *Slavery in the Americas*, p. 97.
135. Tannenbaum, *Slave and Citizen*, pp. 65–69.
136. Ibid., p. 97.
137. Ibid., pp. 86–87.
138. Benjamin Brawley, *Social History of the American Negro* (London: Collier Macmillan, 1970), pp. 244–45.
139. Tannenbaum, *Slave and Citizen*, p. 90.
140. Ibid., p. 106.
141. Klein, *Slavery in the Americas*, p. 206.
142. Stampp, *Peculiar Institution*, p. 356.
143. Ibid., p. 357.
144. Roi Ottley, *New World A-Coming: Inside Black America* (New York: Arno Press, 1968), p. 36; Ira De A. Reid, *The Negro Immigrant* (New York: Columbia University Press, 1939), pp. 220, 227.

Chapter 2

1. Benjamin Brawley, *Social History of the American Negro* (London: Collier Macmillan, 1970), p. 238.
2. E. Franklin Frazier, *The Negro Family in the United States* (Chicago: University of Chicago Press, 1969), pp. 319–20; E. Franklin Frazier, *Black Bourgeoisie* (New York: Collier Books, 1962), pp. 23–24, 92, 98.

3. Maldwyn Allen Jones, *American Immigration* (Chicago: University of Chicago Press, 1970), pp. 13, 32.
4. Frazier, *Black Bourgeoisie*, p. 17.
5. Ulrich B. Phillips, *Life and Labor in the Old South* (Boston: Little, Brown, 1964), p. 205; G. Franklin Edwards, ed., *Frazier on Race Relations* (Chicago: University of Chicago Press, 1968), p. 92; August Meier and Elliot Rudwick, eds., *The Making of Black America* (New York: Atheneum, 1969), 1:208; Harold J. Laski, *The American Democracy* (New York: Viking Press, 1948), p. 696.
6. Richard C. Wade, *Slavery in the Cities* (London: Oxford University Press, 1967), p. 124; see also Ulrich B. Phillips, *American Negro Slavery* (Baton Rouge: Louisiana State University Press, 1969), pp. 437, 439.
7. Carter G. Woodson, *Free Negro Heads of Families in the U.S. in 1830* (Washington, D.C.: Association for the Study of Negro Life and History, 1935), pp. xviii–xx.
8. Herbert S. Klein, *Slavery in the Americas* (Chicago: Quadrangle Books, 1961), pp. 228–29.
9. John Hope Franklin, *From Slavery to Freedom* (New York: Vintage Books, 1969), p. 217.
10. Ibid., pp. 156–58.
11. Ibid., pp. 157–58.
12. Klein, *Slavery in the Americas*, pp. 230–32.
13. Ibid., pp. 41, 51, 230–32.
14. Woodson, *Free Negro Heads of Families in the U.S. in 1830*, pp. xxi–xxii.
15. Clement Eaton, *The Growth of Southern Civilization* (New York: Harper & Row, 1961), p. 93; Lorenzo J. Greene and Carter G. Woodson, *The Negro Wage Earner* (New York: Columbia University Press, 1930), p. 16; John H. Russell, *The Free Negro in Virginia, 1619–1865* (New York: Dover Publications, 1969), p. 104; John Hope Franklin, *Free Negro in North Carolina, 1790–1860* (New York: W. W. Norton, 1971), pp. 68, 76, 84, 131, 168.
16. Woodson, *Free Negro Heads of Families in the U.S. in 1830*, p. xviii.
17. Ibid., p. xx.
18. Ibid., pp. xxvi–xxvii; Franklin, *From Slavery to Freedom*, pp. 234–36; Woodson, *Education of the Negro Prior to 1861* (New York: Arno Press, 1968), p. 171.

19. Woodson, *Education of the Negro Prior to 1861*, chap. 9.
20. Frederick Law Olmsted, *Cotton Kingdom* (New York: Modern Library, 1969), p. 30.
21. Franklin, *From Slavery to Freedom*, p. 229.
22. Ibid., p. 230.
23. Woodson, *Free Negro Heads of Families in the U.S. in 1830*, pp. li–lii; idem, *Education of the Negro Prior to 1861*, chap. 13.
24. Brawley, *Social History of the American Negro*, p. 247.
25. Franklin, *From Slavery to Freedom*, pp. 224–25.
26. Franklin, *Free Negro in North Carolina, 1790–1860* pp. 228–29.
27. Franklin, *From Slavery to Freedom*, pp. 223–24.
28. Brawley, *Social History of the American Negro*, pp. 244–45.
29. Franklin, *From Slavery to Freedom*, p. 224.
30. Phillips, *American Negro Slavery*, p. 433.
31. Frazier, *Black Bourgeoisie*, p. 35.
32. Meier and Rudwick, *Making of Black America*, 1:202.
33. Olmsted, *Cotton Kingdom*, p. 30; Brawley, *Social History of the American Negro*, p. 243.
34. Meier and Rudwick, *Making of Black America*, 1:210.
35. E. Franklin Frazier, *The Negro in the United States* (New York: Macmillan, 1949), pp. 387–88; Abram L. Harris, *The Negro as Capitalist* (Philadelphia: American Academy of Political and Social Science, 1936), pp. 9, 10, 11.
36. Edwards, *Frazier on Race Relations*, p. 54.
37. Frazier, *Black Bourgeoisie*, p. 74.
38. Ibid., pp. 74–75, 110, 165–68.
39. Ibid., p. 74.
40. James Bryce, *The American Commonwealth* (London: Macmillan, 1900), 2:499.
41. Asa H. Gordon, *Sketches of Negro Life and History in South Carolina* (Columbia: University of South Carolina Press, 1971), pp. 76–77; see also Franklin, *From Slavery to Freedom*, p. 382.
42. Edwards, *Frazier on Race Relations*, pp. 211–12.
43. Nathan Glazer and Daniel Patrick Moynihan, *Beyond the Melting Pot* (Cambridge, Mass.: MIT Press, 1963), p. 187.
44. Brawley, *Social History of the American Negro*, p. 299.
45. Ibid., p. 330.
46. Greene and Woodson, *Negro Wage Earner*, p. 22.

47. Ibid., p. 23; Woodson, *Education of the Negro Prior to 1861*, p. 388.
48. Greene and Woodson, *Negro Wage Earner*, p. 24.
49. Ibid., pp. 24–26.
50. Ibid., p. 29.
51. Ibid., pp. 34–35.
52. Ibid., p. 37.
53. Ibid., p. 37.
54. *The Negro Handbook* (Chicago: Johnson Publishing, 1960), p. 289.
55. Brawley, *Social History of the American Negro*, p. 342.
56. *Negro Handbook*, p. 289.
57. Brawley, *Social History of the American Negro*, p. 347.
58. Ibid., p. 361.
59. Reynolds Farley, "The Urbanization of Negroes in the United States," *Journal of Social History* 1, no. 3 (Spring 1968): 251.
60. Ibid.
61. U.S. Bureau of the Census, *Changing Characteristics of the Negro Population* (Washington, D.C.: U.S. Government Printing Office), p. 11.
62. Farley, "The Urbanization of Negroes in the United States," p. 255.
63. Philip M. Hauser, "Demographic Factors in the Integration of the Negro," *Daedalus* 94, no. 4 (Fall 1965): 859.
64. Louis R. Harlan, "Booker T. Washington in Biographical Perspective," *American Historical Review* 75, no. 6 (October 1970): 1585.
65. Thomas Sowell, *Economics: Analysis and Issues* (Glenview, Ill.: Scott, Foresman, 1971), p. 155.
66. Edward C. Banfield, *The Unheavenly City* (Boston: Little, Brown, 1970), p. 84.

Chapter 3

1. Foster Rhea Dulles, *Labor in America* (New York: Thomas Y. Crowell, 1955), p. 13.
2. J. C. Furnas: *The Americans* (New York: G. P. Putnam's Sons, 1969), p. 63.
3. Maldwyn Allen Jones, *American Immigration* (Chicago:

University of Chicago Press, 1970), p. 9; Herbert S. Klein, *Slavery in the Americas* (Chicago: Quadrangle Books), p. 168; Ulrich B. Phillips, *Life and Labor in the Old South* (Boston: Little, Brown, 1964), p. 23; Dulles, *Labor in America*, p. 3.

4. Kenneth M. Stampp, *The Peculiar Institution* (New York: Vintage Books, 1956), pp. 18, 22.

5. Klein, *Slavery in the Americas*, p. 227; Jones, *American Immigration*, pp. 13, 32.

6. Ulrich B. Phillips, *American Negro Slavery* (Baton Rouge: Louisiana State University Press, 1969), p. 3; Dulles, *Labor in America*, p. 6; Warren B. Smith, *White Servitude in Colonial South Carolina* (Columbia: University of South Carolina Press, 1970), pp. 42, 43; Furnas: *Americans*, pp. 104–5; Klein, *Slavery in the Americas*, p. 170.

7. Dulles, *Labor in America*, p. 7.

8. Ibid., pp. 7, 8.

9. Ibid., p. 9; Smith, *White Servitude in Colonial South Carolina*, pp. 88–93; Furnas: *Americans*, p. 101.

10. Phillips, *American Negro Slavery*, pp. 464–65.

11. Smith, *White Servitude in Colonial South Carolina*, p. 70.

12. Klein, *Slavery in the Americas*, p. 179.

13. Ibid., p. 172.

14. Oscar Handlin, *The Uprooted* (New York: Grosset & Dunlap, 1951), p. 3; see also Jones, *American Immigration*, pp. 133, 155.

15. Handlin, *Uprooted*, p. 4.

16. Jones, *American Immigration*, p. 133.

17. Handlin, *Uprooted*, pp. 147, 148, 149; Oscar Handlin, *The Newcomers* (Garden City, N.Y.: Doubleday Anchor Books, 1962), pp. 14, 16.

18. Handlin, *Uprooted*, pp. 151, 152, 153.

19. Handlin, *Newcomers*, pp. 32, 37.

20. Handlin, *Uprooted*, p. 156.

21. Ibid., p. 157.

22. Edward C. Banfield, *The Unheavenly City* (Boston: Little, Brown, 1970), p. 72.

23. Handlin, *The Uprooted*, pp. 101, 102; idem, *Newcomers*, p. 17.

24. Handlin, *The Uprooted*, p. 163; Moses Rischin, *The Promised City* (Cambridge, Mass.: Harvard University Press, 1967), pp. 89–90.

25. Furnas, *Americans*, pp. 698–99.
26. Ibid., pp. 522, 527; Jones, *American Immigration*, pp. 150, 151.
27. Furnas, *Americans*, p. 524.
28. Ibid., p. 839.
29. Ibid., p. 842.
30. Ibid., p. 840.
31. Ibid., p. 700; Jones, *American Immigration*, pp. 133, 152.
32. Furnas, *Americans*, pp. 842–43.
33. Handlin, *Uprooted*, p. 159.
34. Furnas, *Americans*, pp. 702, 703.
35. Jones, *American Immigration*, p. 94.
36. Ibid., pp. 118, 119.
37. Ibid., p. 120.
38. Ibid.
39. Jones, *American Immigration*, p. 185.
40. Ibid., p. 179.
41. Ibid., p. 184.
42. U.S. Bureau of the Census, *Historical Statistics of the United States* (Washington, D.C.: U.S. Government Printing Office, 1960), pp. 56–57.
43. Ibid.
44. Jones, *American Immigration*, p. 179.
45. Ibid., p. 187.
46. Ibid.
47. Ernest van den Haag, *The Jewish Mystique* (New York: Stein & Day, 1969), p. 167.
48. Rischin, *Promised City*, p. 51.
49. Furnas, *Americans*, p. 393.
50. Nathan Glazer and Daniel Patrick Moynihan, *Beyond the Melting Pot* (Cambridge, Mass.: MIT Press, 1963), p. 139.
51. Furnas, *Americans*, pp. 392–94.
52. Rischin, *Promised City*, p. 67.
53. F. J. Brown and J. S. Roucek, *Our Racial and National Minorities* (New York: Prentice-Hall, 1937), p. 411.
54. Rischin, *Promised City*, p. 69.
55. Ibid., p. 70.
56. Ibid., pp. 68–73.
57. Ibid., p. 82.
58. Ibid., pp. 80, 84.
59. Ibid., p. 84.
60. Ibid., pp. 86–87.

61. Ibid., p. 88.
62. Ibid., p. 89.
63. Ibid., p. 93.
64. Ibid., p. 97.
65. Ibid., p. 98.
66. Ibid., pp. 98–99.
67. Ibid., pp. 102, 104.
68. Ibid., p. 105.
69. Brown and Roucek, *Our Racial and National Minorities*, pp. 417–18.
70. Rischin, *Promised City*, pp. 110–11.
71. Ibid., p. 53.
72. van den Haag, *Jewish Mystique*, pp. 19–20.
73. *Newsweek*, 1 March 1971, p. 63.
74. Furnas, *Americans*, p. 393.
75. Rischin, *Promised City*, pp. 261, 262.
76. Erik Lundberg, *The Rich and Super Rich* (New York: Lyle Stuart, 1968), p. 292.
77. Glazer and Moynihan, *Beyond the Melting Pot*, p. 256.
78. Handlin, *Newcomers*, p. 26.
79. Glazer and Moynihan, *Beyond the Melting Pot*, p. 232.
80. John Rae, *Life of Adam Smith* (London: Macmillan, 1895), pp. 57–58.
81. Glazer and Moynihan, *Beyond the Melting Pot*, p. 224; Carl Wittke, *The Irish in America* (Baton Rouge: Louisiana State University Press, 1956), p. 125.
82. Wittke, *Irish in America*, p. 6.
83. Frederick Law Olmsted, *The Cotton Kingdom* (New York: Modern Library, 1969), p. 215; see also Furnas, *Americans*, p. 394; Phillips, *American Negro Slavery*, pp. 301–2; idem, *Life and Labor in the Old South*, p. 186; Lewis C. Gray, *History of Agriculture in the Southern United States* (Washington, D.C.: Carnegie Institution of Washington, 1933), 2:520.
84. Olmsted, *Cotton Kingdom*, p. 215.
85. Wittke, *Irish in America*, p. 32; Jones, *American Immigration*, pp. 130–31.
86. Furnas: *Americans*, p. 704.
87. Wittke, *Irish in America*, p. 34.
88. Ibid., p. 32.
89. Ibid., p. 35.
90. Ibid., pp. 34–35.

91. Ibid., pp. 43–45.
92. Ibid., p. 34.
93. Ibid., pp. 34, 37.
94. Ibid., p. 37.
95. Glazer and Moynihan, *Beyond the Melting Pot*, p. 240; Furnas, *Americans*, pp. 386, 705.
96. August Meier and Elliot Rudwick, eds., *The Making of Black America* (New York: Atheneum, 1969), 1:255.
97. Wittke, *Irish in America*, pp. 44–46; Brown and Roucek, *Our Racial and National Minorities*, pp. 99–100.
98. Wittke, *Irish in America*, p. 45.
99. Jones, *American Immigration*, p. 133.
100. Wittke, *Irish in America*, pp. 45, 120.
101. Ibid., pp. 119–20; Jones, *American Immigration*, p. 150.
102. Lorenzo J. Greene and Carter G. Woodson, *The Negro Wage Earner* (New York: Columbia University Press, 1930), p. 348.
103. Wittke, *Irish in America*, pp. 125–26.
104. Furnas, *Americans*, p. 700.
105. Olmsted, *Cotton Kingdom*, p. 231.
106. Wittke, *Irish in America*, pp. 125–26; Furnas, *Americans*, pp. 520–21.
107. Gilbert Osofsky, *Harlem: The Making of a Ghetto* (New York: Harper & Row, 1966), p. 13.
108. Furnas, *Americans*, p. 700; Ivan H. Light, *Ethnic Enterprise in America* (Berkeley: University of California Press, 1972), p. 6.
109. Glazer and Moynihan, *Beyond the Melting Pot*, p. 240.
110. Wittke, *Irish in America*, p. 143.
111. Ibid., pp. 125, 132, 147.
112. Ibid., pp. 130–31.
113. Furnas, *The Americans*, p. 702; see also William L. Stone, *History of New York* (New York: Charles Scribner's Sons, 1892), chap. 11.
114. *Report of the National Advisory Committee on Civil Disorders* [*United States Riot Commission Report*] (New York: Bantam Books, 1968), p. 115.
115. William L. Stone, *History of New York* (New York: Virtue & Yorston, 1872), p. 559.
116. Glazer and Moynihan, *Beyond the Melting Pot*, p. 233.
117. Furnas, *Americans*, p. 704.
118. Glazer and Moynihan, *Beyond the Melting Pot*, p. 242.

119. Ibid., p. 243.
120. Furnas, *Americans*, p. 704.
121. Wittke, *Irish in America*, pp. 41–43, 48–50, 96.
122. Furnas, *Americans*, p. 702; Wittke, *Irish in America*, pp. 100, 101.
123. Wittke, *Irish in America*, p. 89.
124. Ibid., p. 101.
125. Ibid., pp. 128–29.
126. Ibid., pp. 137, 146.
127. Ibid., p. 51.
128. Ibid., p. 23.
129. Ibid., p. 42.
130. Glazer and Moynihan, *Beyond the Melting Pot*, p. 240.
131. Jones, *American Immigration*, p. 22.
132. Ibid., p. 24.
133. James G. Leyburn, *The Scotch-Irish* (Chapel Hill: University of North Carolina Press, 1962), chap. 14; Jones, *American Immigration*, pp. 25, 49; Furnas, *Americans*, p. 92; Gray, *History of Agriculture in the Southern United States*, p. 124.
134. Jones, *American Immigration*, p. 118.
135. Leyburn, *Scotch-Irish*, pp. 43–44, 72–74, 319–21.
136. Carter G. Woodson, *The Education of the Negro Prior to 1861* (New York: Arno Press, 1968), pp. 182, 223.
137. Furnas, *Americans*, p. 91.
138. Jones, *American Immigration*, p. 118.
139. Ibid., p. 84.
140. Furnas, *Americans*, pp. 93–94; Leyburn, *Scotch-Irish*, p. 191.
141. Jones, *American Immigration*, p. 78; Leyburn, *Scotch-Irish*, pp. 331–32.
142. Jones, *American Immigration*, pp. 108–9.
143. U.S. Bureau of the Census, *Historical Statistics of the United States*, pp. 56–57.
144. Leyburn, *Scotch-Irish*, pp. 317–18.
145. Gray, *History of Agriculture in the Southern United States*, 1:124.
146. Wittke, *Irish in America*, pp. 260, 262.
147. Glazer and Moynihan, *Beyond the Melting Pot*, pp. 252–53.
148. Ibid., pp. 252, 254.
149. Ibid., pp. 168, 272.
150. Ibid., pp. 258, 259–60.

151. Ibid., p. 200.
152. Ibid., p. 261.
153. Grazia Dore, "Some Social and Historical Aspects of Italian Emigration to America," *Journal of Social History* 2, no. 2, (Winter 1968): 95–97.
154. Herbert F. Gans, *The Urban Villagers* (New York: Free Press, 1965), pp. 200, 210, 212; Robert F. Foerster, *The Italian Emigration of Our Times* (New York: Arno Press, 1969), pp. 83–85, 87.
155. Gans, *Urban Villagers*, p. 207; Foerster, *Italian Emigration of Our Times*, p. 85.
156. Dore, "Italian Emigration to America," p. 103.
157. Ibid., pp. 117–18.
158. WPA Writers' Project, *The Italians of New York* (New York: Random House, 1938), p. 2.
159. Ibid., p. 3.
160. Ibid., p. 2; Foerster, *Italian Emigration of Our Times*, p. 325.
161. WPA Writers' Project, *Italians of New York*, p. 2; see also Foerster, *Italian Emigration of Our Times*, p. 325; William F. Whyte, *Street Corner Society* (Chicago: University of Chicago Press, 1969), pp. xvii–xviii.
162. Dore, "Italian Emigration to America," p. 110.
163. Ibid., p. 120; Whyte, *Street Corner Society*, pp. xvi, xvii.
164. Jacob Riis, *How the Other Half Lives* (New York: Charles Scribner's Sons, 1892), pp. 48–50; Foerster, *Italian Emigration of Our Times*, pp. 326, 327, 391–92.
165. WPA Writers' Project, *Italians of New York*, p. 15.
166. Riis, *How the Other Half Lives*, p. 37.
167. Ibid., pp. 23–24.
168. Ibid., p. 25, 150.
169. WPA Writers' Project, *Italians of New York*, p. 202.
170. Ibid., p. 61; Foerster, *Italian Emigration of Our Times*, pp. 357–59.
171. WPA Writers' Project, *Italians of New York*, p. 62.
172. Ibid., chap. 5.
173. Ibid., p. 64.
174. Ibid., chaps. 9, 10, 11.
175. Glazer and Moynihan, *Beyond the Melting Pot*, p. 194.
176. Rudolph J. Vecoli, "Prelates and Peasants: Italian Immigration and the Catholic Church," *Journal of Social History* 2, no. 3 (Spring 1969): 221–22.

177. Ibid., p. 222.
178. Ibid., p. 229; Gans, *Urban Villagers*, p. 111.
179. Vecoli, "Prelates and Peasants," pp. 230–35; see also Gans, *Urban Villagers*, pp. 111–13.
180. Vecoli, "Prelates and Peasants," p. 235.
181. Ibid., p. 238.
182. U.S. Bureau of the Census, *Historical Statistics of the United States*, pp. 56–57.
183. Samuel L. Bailey, "The Italians and the Development of Organized Labor in Argentina, Brazil, and the United States, 1890–1914," *Journal of Social History* 3, no. 2 (Winter 1969–70): 124–26.
184. Glazer and Moynihan, *Beyond the Melting Pot*, p. 184.
185. Bailey, "Italians and Organized Labor," p. 124.
186. Ibid., pp. 124–25.
187. Glazer and Moynihan, *Beyond the Melting Pot*, p. 185.
188. Ibid., p. 201.
189. Ibid., p. 210.
190. WPA Writers' Project, *Italians of New York*, pp. 50–51.
191. Ibid., p. 54.
192. Glazer and Moynihan, *Beyond the Melting Pot*, pp. 206–7.
193. Ibid., pp. 205–6; see also U.S. Bureau of the Census, "Characteristics of the Population by Ethnic Origin, November 1969," *Current Population Report*, Series P-20, No. 221 (Washington, D.C.: U.S. Government Printing Office, 1971), p. 23.
194. Glazer and Moynihan, *Beyond the Melting Pot*, p. 198; Gans, *Urban Villagers*, p. 219; Richard Gambino, "Twenty Million Italian-Americans Can't Be Wrong," *New York Times Magazine*, 30 April 1972, p. 26.
195. Gans, *Urban Villagers*, pp. 130–32; Gambino, "Twenty Million Italian-Americans," p. 40; Glazer and Moynihan, *Beyond the Melting Pot*, p. 202.
196. U.S. Bureau of the Census, "Population Characteristics, November 1969," p. 22.
197. Ibid., p. 23.
198. Ibid., p. 22.
199. Ibid., p. 19.
200. Foerster, *Italian Emigration of Our Times*, p. 406.
201. Wittke, *Irish in America*, p. 45.
202. Ibid., p. 85.

203. Conrad M. Arensberg and Solon T. Kimball, *Family and Community in Ireland* (Cambridge, Mass.: Harvard University Press, 1968), pp. 50, 55, 56.
204. Ibid., p. 54.
205. Glazer and Moynihan, *Beyond the Melting Pot*, pp. 257–58.
206. Robert L. Goodwin, ed., *A Nation of Cities* (Chicago: Rand McNally, 1968), p. 54.

Chapter 4

1. U.S. Bureau of the Census, *Historical Statistics of the United States* (Washington, D.C.: U.S. Government Printing Office, 1960), pp. 56–57.
2. Ibid., p. 58; immigration from Germany reached brief peaks of more than 100,000 in 1950 and 1957 (ibid., p. 56).
3. Harry H. L. Kitano, *Japanese Americans* (Englewood Cliffs, N.J.: Prentice-Hall, 1969), pp. 1, 2, 47–48; William Peterson, "Success Story, Japanese-American Style," *New York Times Magazine*, 9 January 1966, p. 40.
4. F. J. Brown and J. S. Roucek, *Our Racial and National Minorities* (New York: Prentice-Hall, Inc., 1937), p. 470; U.S. Bureau of the Census, *Historical Statistics of the United States*, p. 58.
5. Peterson, "Success Story," p. 21; Ivan H. Light, *Ethnic Enterprise in America* (Berkeley: University of California Press, 1972), p. 9; Maldwyn Allen Jones, *American Immigration* (Chicago: University of Chicago Press, 1970), p. 265.
6. Brown and Roucek, *Our Racial and National Minorities*, p. 482; Peterson, "Success Story," p. 21.
7. Brown and Roucek, *Our Racial and National Minorities*, p. 476; Kitano, *Japanese Americans*, p. 176.
8. Peterson, "Success Story," p. 33.
9. Ibid., p. 33.
10. Ibid.
11. Ibid., p. 36.
12. Ibid., pp. 33, 36.
13. Kitano, *Japanese Americans*, p. 35.
14. Ibid., p. 42.
15. Ibid., p. 47.
16. Ibid.

17. Ibid., p. 175.
18. Nathan Glazer and Daniel Patrick Moynihan, *Beyond the Melting Pot* (Cambridge, Mass.: MIT Press, 1963), p. 35.
19. Ibid.
20. Ira De A. Reid, *The Negro Immigrant* (New York: Columbia University Press, 1939), p. 227; David Rosenthal, "Race and Color in the West Indies," *Daedalus* 96, no. 2 (Spring 1967): 610–11.
21. Ira De A. Reid, *Negro Immigrant*, pp. 168–69.
22. Gilbert Osofsky, *Harlem: The Making of a Ghetto* (New York: Harper & Row, 1966), pp. 134–35; Harold Cruse, *The Crisis of the Negro Intellectual* (New York: William Morrow, 1967), pp. 44–47.
23. Osofsky, *Harlem*, pp. 134–35; Reid, *Negro Immigrant*, pp. 138–39.
24. Ibid., pp. 168–69, 222–24; Lennox Raphael, "West Indians and Afro-Americans," *Freedomways* (Summer 1964): 438–45.
25. John J. Spurling, "Social Relations Between American Negroes and British West Indians in Long Island City" (Ph.D. dissertation, New York University, 1962), p. 88.
26. Phillip D. Curtin, *Two Jamaicas* (New York: Atheneum, 1970), pp. 14, 15.
27. Rosenthal, "Race and Color in West Indies," p. 587; Ulrich B. Phillips, *American Negro Slavery* (Baton Rouge: Louisiana State University Press, 1969).
28. Curtin, *Two Jamaicas*, p. 18.
29. Ibid., p. 38.
30. Ibid., p. 19.
31. Ibid.
32. John Hope Franklin, *From Slavery to Freedom* (New York: Vintage Books, 1969); Curtin, *Two Jamaicas*, pp. 10, 81–98.
33. Phillips, *American Negro Slavery*, p. 464.
34. Curtin, *Two Jamaicas*, pp. 42–46.
35. Ibid., p. 61.
36. Ibid., chap. 4.
37. Ibid., pp. 84–85.
38. Ibid., pp. 107–9.
39. Ibid., p. 127.
40. See Franklin, *From Slavery to Freedom*, pp. 66–67, 118–19, 122.

41. Phillips, *American Negro Slavery*, p. 464.
42. Oscar Handlin, *The Newcomers* (Garden City, N.Y.: Doubleday Anchor Books, 1962), p. 60.
43. Glazer and Moynihan, *Beyond the Melting Pot*, p. 116.
44. Ibid.
45. Ibid., p. 119.
46. Ibid., pp. 116–17.
47. Ibid., p. 118.
48. Handlin, *Newcomers*, p. 57.
49. Ibid.
50. Glazer and Moynihan, *Beyond the Melting Pot*, p. 93; Handlin, *Newcomers*, p. 52.
51. Glazer and Moynihan, *Beyond the Melting Pot*, p. 103.
52. Ibid., p. 104.
53. Ibid., p. 114.
54. Ibid., p. 115; see also p. 47.
55. For example, ibid., p. 115.
56. Gerald D. Suttles, *The Social Order of the Slum* (Chicago: University of Chicago, 1968), pp. 150–51; Glazer and Moynihan, *Beyond the Melting Pot*, pp. 128–29.
57. Ibid., p. 117.
58. Ibid., pp. 98–99.
59. Ibid.
60. Ibid., p. 98.
61. Ibid., pp. 117–18.
62. Ibid., p. 112.
63. Ibid., pp. 113–15.
64. Ibid., pp. 113–14.
65. Ibid., p. 116.
66. Ibid., p. 115.
67. Elena Padilla, *Up from Puerto Rico* (New York: Columbia University Press, 1958), pp. 91–92; Glazer and Moynihan, *Beyond the Melting Pot*, p. 102.
68. Dan Waketido, *Island in the City* (Boston: Houghton-Mifflin, 1959), pp. 128–29.
69. U.S. Bureau of the Census, "Persons of Spanish Origin in the United States: November 1969," *Current Population Reports*, Series P-20, No. 213 (Washington, D.C.: U.S. Government Printing Office, 1971), p. 10.
70. Fred H. Schmidt, *Spanish Surnamed Americans—Employ-*

ment in the Southwest (Washington, D.C.: U.S. Government Printing Office, n.d.), p. 4.

71. U.S. Bureau of the Census, "Persons of Spanish Origin," p. 7.

72. Schmidt, Spanish Surnamed Americans, p. 53; Joan W. Moore and Alfredo Cuellar, Mexican Americans (Englewood Cliffs, N.J.: Prentice-Hall, 1970), p. 60.

73. U.S. Bureau of the Census, "Persons of Spanish Origin," p. 4.

74. Ibid., p. 10.

75. Ibid.

76. Moore and Cuellar, Mexican Americans, p. 49.

77. Glazer and Moynihan, Beyond the Melting Pot, p. 134.

78. U.S. Bureau of the Census, "Selected Characteristics of Persons and Families of Mexican, Puerto Rican and Other Spanish Origins, March 1971," Current Population Reports, Series P-20, No. 224 (Washington, D.C.: U.S. Government Printing Office, 1971), p. 6.

79. Moore and Cuellar, Mexican Americans, p. 75; U.S. Department of Labor, The Negro Family [Moynihan Report], March 1965, chap. 2.

80. Edward C. Banfield, The Unheavenly City (Boston: Little, Brown, 1970), p. 72.

81. Moore and Cuellar, Mexican Americans, p. 75.

82. Manuel P. Servin, The Mexican-Americans: An Awakening Minority (Glencoe, Ill.: Free Press, 1970), pp. 152–53.

83. Moore and Cuellar, Mexican Americans, p. 65; see also Servin, Mexican-Americans, p. 154.

84. Moore and Cuellar, Mexican Americans, p. 65.

85. Ibid., p. 69.

86. Ibid., p. 95.

87. Ibid., p. 71.

88. Ibid., p. 73.

89. Ibid., chap. 5.

90. Ibid., p. 43.

91. Ibid., pp. 14–20.

92. Servin, Mexican-Americans, p. 155.

93. Ibid.

94. Ibid., p. 156.

95. Moore and Cuellar, Mexican Americans, p. 39.

Chapter 5

1. Maldwyn Allen Jones, *American Immigration* (Chicago: University of Chicago Press, 1970), pp. 212–13. The success of agriculture in Israel is an entirely different phenomenon for (1) their competition is with the primitive agriculture of the region and (2) the emotional climate associated with the creation of Israel is quite different from that surrounding ordinary economic ventures.
2. Elliot M. Rudwick, *W. E. B. DuBois* (New York: Atheneum, 1969), pp. 59–64.
3. Ira De A. Reid, *The Negro Immigrant* (New York: Columbia University Press, 1939), p. 133; David Lowenthal, "Race and Color in the West Indies," *Daedalus* 96, no. 2 (Spring 1967): 603–604.
4. Carl Wittke, *The Irish in America* (Baton Rouge: Louisiana State University Press, 1956), pp. 262–63.
5. Nathan Glazer and Daniel Patrick Moynihan, *Beyond the Melting Pot* (Cambridge, Mass.: MIT Press, 1963), pp. 252–53.
6. Ibid., p. 62.
7. Claude McKay, *Harlem: Negro Metropolis* (New York: Harcourt Brace Jovanovich, 1968); Allen H. Spear, *Black Chicago* (Chicago: University of Chicago Press, 1970), pp. 168–69; see also James Weldon Johnson, *Black Manhattan* (New York: Atheneum, 1968), p. 73.
8. G. Franklin Edwards, ed., *Frazier on Race Relations* (Chicago: University of Chicago Press, 1968), p. 173.
9. E. Franklin Frazier, *The Negro in the United States* (New York: Macmillan, 1949), p. 370.
10. Abram L. Harris, *The Negro as Capitalist* (Philadelphia: American Academy of Political and Social Science, 1936), p. 6.
11. Frazier, *Negro in the United States*, pp. 368–70.
12. Ibid.
13. Benjamin Brawley, *Social History of the American Negro* (London: Collier Macmillan, 1970), p. 243; Carter G. Woodson, *The Education of the Negro Prior to 1861* (New York: Arno Press, 1968), pp. 129, 131, 132, 135, 141, 143, 145, 148; Leon F. Litwack, *North of Slavery* (Chicago: University of Chicago Press, 1961), pp. 17–18.
14. Harris, *Negro as Capitalist*, p. 44.

15. Glazer and Moynihan, *Beyond the Melting Pot*, p. 247.
16. Ibid., p. 251.
17. Betty Lee Sung, *The Story of the Chinese in America* (New York: Collier Books, 1967), p. 103.
18. U.S. Bureau of the Census, "Characteristics of the Population by Ethnic Origin, November 1969," *Current Population Reports*, Series P-20, No. 221 (Washington, D.C.: U.S. Government Printing Office, 1971), p. 7.
19. Ibid.
20. Glazer and Moynihan, *Beyond the Melting Pot*, p. 197.
21. Ibid., pp. 123–24.
22. Ibid., p. 192.
23. Herbert F. Gans, *The Urban Villagers* (New York: The Free Press, 1965), pp. 23, 136.
24. Ibid., p. 186; William F. Whyte, *Street Corner Society* (Chicago: University of Chicago Press, 1969), p. xix.
25. Glazer and Moynihan, *Beyond the Melting Pot*, p. 194.
26. Ibid., p. 213.
27. Ibid., pp. 196, 210, 258.
28. Ibid., pp. 206–7.
29. Ibid., p. 199; see also p. 184.
30. Ibid., p. 202.
31. W. E. B. DuBois, *The Negro American Family* (New York: New American Library, p. 1969); U.S. Department of Labor, *The Negro Family* [Moynihan Report], pp. 6–10.
32. Gunnar Myrdal, *An American Dilemma* (New York: McGraw-Hill, 1964), p. 931.
33. Eric Williams, *The Negro in the Caribbean* (Westport: Negro Universities Press, 1971) p. 57; see also Rosenthal, "Race and Color in the West Indies," p. 588.
34. Daniel Patrick Moynihan, "Employment, Income, and the Ordeal of the Negro Family," *Daedalus* 94, no. 4 (Fall 1965): 767–68.
35. Ibid., pp. 755, 757.
36. Edward C. Banfield, *The Unheavenly City* (Boston: Little, Brown, 1970), p. 72.
37. August Meier and Elliot Rudwick, eds., *The Making of Black America* (New York: Atheneum, 1969), 2:467.
38. Herbert F. Gans, *The Urban Villagers* (New York: Free Press, 1965), pp. 238–39.
39. Moynihan, "Ordeal of Negro Family," p. 759.

40. U.S. Bureau of the Census, "Negro Population: March 1966," *Current Population Reports*, Series P-20, No. 168 (Washington, D.C.: U.S. Government Printing Office), p. 5.
41. E. Franklin Frazier, *The Negro Family in the United States* (Chicago: University of Chicago Press, 1969), pp. 330–31.
42. Andrew F. Brimmer and Henry S. Terrell, "The Economic Potential of Black Capitalism," *The Black Politician* (April 1971): 21 ff.
43. Arthur R. Jensen, "How Much Can We Boost IQ and Scholastic Achievement?" *Harvard Educational Review* (Winter 1969): 95.
44. U.S. Bureau of the Census, "Fertility Variations by Ethnic Origin: November 1969," *Current Population Reports*, Series P-20, No. 226 (Washington, D.C.: U.S. Government Printing Office), p. 19.
45. Brawley, *Social History of the American Negro*, p. 15; see also John Hope Franklin, *From Slavery to Freedom* (New York: Vintage Books, 1969), p. 83.
46. Ray Marshall, *The Negro Worker* (New York: Random House, 1967), p. 8; see also Woodson, *The Education of the Negro Prior to 1861*, p. 284; Lorenzo J. Green and Carter G. Woodson, *The Negro Wage Earner* (New York: Columbia University Press, 1930), p. 22.
47. Moses Rischin, *The Promised City* (Cambridge, Mass.: Harvard University Press, 1967), p. 79; Maurice Hindus, *The Old East Side* (Philadelphia: Jewish Publication Society of America, 1969), p. 123.
48. Robert L. Goodwin, ed., *A Nation of Cities* (Chicago: Rand McNally, 1968), p. 55.
49. Rischin, *Promised City*, p. 83.
50. Rischin, *Promised City*, pp. 82–83; Oscar Handlin, *The Uprooted* (New York: Grosset & Dunlap, 1951), pp. 152, 153.
51. Lawrence Friedman, *Government and Slum Housing* (Chicago: Rand McNally, 1968), p. 30.
52. Handlin, *Uprooted*, p. 155.
53. Rischin, *Promised City*, p. 83.
54. Ibid., p. 222; Handlin, *Uprooted*, pp. 204–5, 214.
55. Ibid., pp. 177–78, 247–48.

56. Banfield, *Unheavenly City*, pp. 56–57.
57. Ibid., p. 57.
58. Glazer and Moynihan, *Beyond the Melting Pot*, pp. 261–62.
59. Ibid., p. 258.
60. U.S. Bureau of the Census, "Persons of Spanish Origin," p. 6.
61. Ibid., p. 34.
62. U.S. Bureau of the Census, "Persons of Spanish Origin in the United States: November 1969," *Current Population Reports*, Series P-20, No. 213 (Washington, D.C.: U.S. Government Printing Office), p. 34; U.S. Bureau of the Census, "Characteristics of the Population by Ethnic Origin, November 1969," *Current Population Reports*, Series P-20, No. 221 (Washington, D.C.: U.S. Government Printing Office), p. 22; U.S. Bureau of the Census, "Income in 1970 of Families and Persons in the United States," *Current Population Reports*, Series P-60, No. 80 (Washington, D.C.: U.S. Government Printing Office, October 1971), p. 22.
63. Ibid.
64. U.S. Government, *Manpower Report of the President* (Washington, D.C.: U.S. Government Printing Office, 1971), p. 221.
65. U.S. Bureau of the Census, "Persons of Spanish Origin," p. 34; U.S. Bureau of the Census, "Differences Between Incomes of White and Negro Families by Work Experience of Wife and Region, 1970, 1969, and 1959," *Current Population Reports*, Series P-23, No. 39 (Washington, D.C.: U.S. Government Printing Office), pp. 6–7 (average computed by combining 25–34 and 35–44 age brackets).
66. Ibid., pp. 8, 9 (average computed by combining 25–34 and 35–44 age brackets).
67. Ibid., p. 8; U.S. Bureau of the Census, "Selected Characteristics of Persons and Families of Mexican, Puerto Rican and Other Spanish Origin, March 1971," *Current Population Reports*, Series P-20, No. 224 (Washington, D.C.: U.S. Government Printing Office).
68. Ibid., p. 6.
69. U.S. Bureau of the Census, "Characteristics of the Low-

Income Population, 1970," *Current Population Reports*, Series P-60, No. 81 (Washington, D.C.: U.S. Government Printing Office, 1971), p. 2.

70. Herbert Northrup, *Organized Labor and the Negro* (New York: Kraus Reprint Corp., 1971) p. 22.
71. Daniel Patrick Moynihan, "The Schism in Black America," *The Public Interest*, no. 27 (Spring 1972): 8.
72. U.S. Bureau of the Census, "Differences Between Income of White and Negro Families by Work Experience of Wife and Region, 1970, 1969 and 1959," *Current Population Reports*, Series P-23, No. 39, pp. 7–8.
73. Moynihan, "Schism in Black America," pp. 12–13.

Chapter 6

1. Carl Wittke, *The Irish in America* (Baton Rouge: Louisiana State University Press, 1956), chap. 12, pp. 168–69; Gilbert Osofsky, *Harlem: The Making of a Ghetto* (New York: Harper & Row, 1966), pp. 45–46, 48; St. Clair Drake, *Black Metropolis*, pp. 62, 66; S. Spero and A. L. Harris, *The Black Worker* (New York: Atheneum, 1972), pp. 11–12–13, 197–198; Leon F. Litwack, *North of Slavery* (Chicago: University of Chicago Press, 1961), pp. 162, 166.
2. Wittke, *Irish in America*, p. 126.
3. Herbert F. Gans, *The Urban Villagers* (New York: Free Press, 1965), p. 167; Wittke, *Irish in America*, pp. 189, 225; William F. Whyte, *Street Corner Society* (Chicago: University of Chicago Press, 1969), p. xix; Spero and Harris, *Black Worker*, p. 199.
4. Abram L. Harris, *The Negro as Capitalist* (Philadelphia: American Academy of Political & Social Science, 1936), pp. 183–84.
5. Edward C. Banfield, *The Unheavenly City* (Boston: Little, Brown, 1970), pp. 56–57.
6. Nathan Glazer and Daniel Patrick Moynihan, *Beyond the Melting Pot* (Cambridge, Mass.: MIT Press, 1963), pp. 128, 199; Manuel P. Servin, *The Mexican-Americans* (Glencoe, Ill.: Free Press, 1970), pp. 156–57.
7. Robert Riggs, "Race, Skills and Earnings: American Immi-

grant in 1909," *Journal of Economic History* 31, no. 2 (June 1971): 424.

8. Ibid., p. 426*n*.
9. Armen Alchian and Rueben A. Kessel, "Competition, Monopoly, and the Pursuit of Money," *Aspects of Labor Economics*, National Bureau of Economic Research, pp. 157–75.
10. Herbert Northrup, *Organized Labor and the Negro* (New York: Harper & Brothers, 1944), chap. 3.
11. Carter G. Woodson, *The Education of the Negro Prior to 1861* (New York: Arno Press, 1968), p. 284; see also John Hope Franklin, *From Slavery to Freedom* (New York: Vintage Books, 1969), p. 493.
12. Bernard E. Anderson, *The Negro in the Public Utilities Industry* (Philadelphia: University of Pennsylvania Press, 1970), chap. 3.
13. Ibid., pp. 96, 102–3.
14. Ibid., p. 102.
15. Ibid., p. 150.
16. Ibid., p. 114.
17. Michael R. Winston, "Through the Back Door, Academic Racism and the Negro Scholar in Historical Perspective," *Daedalus* 100, no. 3 (Summer 1971): 695.
18. Ibid., p. 705.
19. Harold J. Laski, *The American Democracy*, p. 480.
20. Gunnar Myrdal, *An American Dilemma* (New York: McGraw-Hill, 1964), p. 323.
21. David Caplovitz, *The Poor Pay More* (New York: Free Press, 1967); U.S. Government, *U.S. Riot Commission Report* (Washington, D.C.: U.S. Government Printing Office, 1970), p. 277.
22. Warren G. Magnuson and Jean Carper, *The Dark Side of the Marketplace* (Englewood Cliffs, N.J.: Prentice-Hall, 1968), chap. 2.
23. Wittke, *Irish in America*, pp. 18–21, passim.
24. Jacob Riis, *How the Other Half Lives* (New York: Charles Scribner's Sons, 1892), pp. 48–50, 60.
25. Frederick D. Sturdivant, "Better Deal for Ghetto Shoppers," *Harvard Business Review* 46, no. 2 (March-April 1968): 133.
26. Magnuson and Carper, *Dark Side of Marketplace*, p. 34.

27. Caplovitz, *Poor Pay More*, p. 17.
28. U.S. Government, *Riot Commission Report*, p. 17.

Chapter 7

1. Lawrence M. Friedman, *Government and Slum Housing* (Chicago: Rand McNally, 1968), chap. 2.
2. Beatrice Moulton, "The Persecution and Intimidation of the Low-Income Litigant as Performed by the Small Claims Courts in California," *Stanford Law Review* 21, no. 6 (June 1969): 1658.
3. Ibid., pp. 1659–60, 1676.
4. Gunnar Myrdal, *An American Dilemma* (New York: McGraw-Hill, 1964), p. 327.
5. Ibid.
6. Ibid.
7. August Meier and Elliot Rudwick, eds., *The Making of Black America* (New York: Atheneum, 1969), 2:429–30.
8. Myrdal, *American Dilemma*, p. 420.
9. Ibid., p. 327.
10. S. Spero and A. L. Harris, *The Black Worker* (New York: Atheneum, 1972), p. 180.
11. Nathan Glazer and Daniel Patrick Moynihan, *Beyond the Melting Pot* (Cambridge, Mass.: MIT Press, 1963), p. 146.
12. Ibid., p. 260.
13. Arthur M. Ross and Herbert Hill, *Employment, Race and Poverty*, p. 348.
14. Ibid., p. 347.
15. P. D. Bradley, ed., *The Public Stake in Union Power*, p. 346.
16. Ibid., pp. 346–47.
17. Gilbert Osofsky, *Harlem: The Making of a Ghetto* (New York: Harper & Row, 1966), pp. 90–91.
18. Oscar Handlin, *The Newcomers* (Garden City, N.Y.: Doubleday Anchor Books, 1962), p. 83; Friedman, *Government and Slum Housing*, pp. 127–28; Kenneth W. Clarkson and Courtenay C. Stone, *Micro-Economics in Action* (Englewood Cliffs, N.J.: Prentice-Hall, 1971), pp. 197–204.
19. Osofsky, *Harlem*, p. 14.
20. William F. Whyte, *Street Corner Society* (Chicago: University of Chicago Press, 1969), pp. 124–125. Conversely,

transfers *into* vice-ridden areas are rewards for favored policemen; see Mike Royko, *Boss* (New York: E. P. Dutton, 1971), p. 107.

21. Moses Rischin, *The Promised City* (Cambridge, Mass.: Harvard University Press, 1967), p. 222; Myrdal, *American Dilemma*, p. 977; Leo Grebler, Joan W. Moore and Ralph C. Guzman, *The Mexican-American People* (New York: The Free Press, 1970) p. 521.

22. Mitchell Gordon, *Sick Cities* (Baltimore: Penguin Books, 1963), pp. 168–69.

23. Myrdal, *American Dilemma*, p. 542.

24. U.S. Government, *Riot Commission Report*, pp. 308–9.

25. Myrdal, *American Dilemma*, p. 551.

26. James S. Coleman et. al., *Equality of Educational Opportunity* (Washington, D.C.: U.S. Government Printing Office, 1966) p. 12.

27. Ibid., p. 76.

28. Ibid., p. 81.

29. Ibid., p. 99.

30. Ibid., pp. 16, 125, 130, 136.

31. Ibid., p. 27.

32. Glazer and Moynihan, *Beyond the Melting Pot*, p. 200.

33. August B. Hollingshead, *Elmtown's Youth*, chap. 8.

34. Oscar Handlin, *The Uprooted* (New York: Grosset & Dunlap, 1951), pp. 247–48.

35. Samuel Bowles, "Toward Equality of Educational Opportunity," *Harvard Educational Review* 38, no. 1 (Winter 1968): 93; Coleman et al., *Equality of Educational Opportunity*, pp. 516–17.

36. See Thomas Sowell, *Black Education: Myths and Tragedies* (New York: David McKay, 1972) chaps. 5, 8.

37. U.S. Bureau of the Census, "Characteristics of the Low-Income Population, 1970," *Current Population Reports*, Series P-60, No. 81 (Washington, D.C.: U.S. Government Printing Office, 1971), p. 13.

38. Daniel P. Moynihan, "The Schism in Black America," *Public Interest*, no. 27 (Spring 1972): 18.

39. Joseph A. Pechman, "The Rich, the Poor, and the Taxes They Pay," *Public Interest*, no. 17 (Fall 1969): 33.

40. Herbert J. Gans, "The New Egalitarianism," *Saturday Review*, 6 May 1972, p. 43.

41. Martin Anderson, *The Federal Bulldozer* (Cambridge, Mass.: MIT Press, 1965), pp. 64–65.
42. Mark R. Levy and Michael S. Kramer, *The Ethnic Factor* (New York: Simon & Schuster, 1972), p. 166; Herbert F. Gans, *The Urban Villagers* (New York: Free Press, 1965), chaps. 13, 14; Leo Grebler, Joan W. Moore and Ralph C. Guzman, *The Mexican-American People*, p. 254.

Chapter 8

1. John P. Roche, *Shadow and Substance* (London: Collier Books, 1969), p. 11.
2. Carter G. Woodson, *The Education of the Negro Prior to 1861* (New York: Arno Press, 1968), p. 389.
3. For example, Leon F. Litwack, *North of Slavery* (Chicago: University of Chicago Press, 1970), ostensibly a history of "The Negro in the Free States, 1790–1860," according to the subtitle, but in reality a history of white people's racial attitudes and actions.
4. James S. Coleman et al., *Equality of Educational Opportunity* (Washington: U.S. Government Printing Office, 1966), p. 20.
5. See Thomas Sowell, *Black Education: Myths and Tragedies* (New York: David McKay, 1972), chap. 11.
6. Ernest van den Haag, *The Jewish Mystique* (New York: Stein & Day, 1969), pp. 22–23.
7. Jacques Barzun, *Race: A Study in Superstition* (New York: Harper & Row, 1965), p. 106.
8. van den Haag, *Jewish Mystique*, pp. 17–18.
9. Nathan Glazer and Daniel Patrick Moynihan, *Beyond the Melting Pot* (Cambridge, Mass.: MIT Press, 1963), p. 138.
10. Thorstein Veblen, "The Intellectual Pre-eminence of Jews in Modern Europe," *The Portable Veblen* (New York: Viking Press, 1958), p. 474.
11. van den Haag, *Jewish Mystique*, p. 21.
12. Ibid., pp. 21–22.
13. Glazer and Moynihan, *Beyond the Melting Pot*, p. 173.
14. James G. Leyburn, *The Scotch-Irish* (Chapel Hill: University of North Carolina Press, 1962), pp. 73–74, 320.
15. Ibid., p. 77n.
16. Ibid., pp. 20–21.

17. Ibid., pp. 72–73.
18. John Rae, *Life of Adam Smith* (London: Macmillan, 1894), pp. 25–26.
19. Francis W. Hirst, *Adam Smith* (New York: Macmillan, 1904), p. 137.
20. Michael St. John Packe, *The Life of John Stuart Mill* (New York: Macmillan, 1954), p. 9.
21. See Thomas Sowell, *Black Education*, chaps. 5–8.
22. Ibid., pp. 283–86.
23. Veblen, "Intellectual Pre-eminence of Jews," pp. 478–79.

Chapter 9

1. Arthur Lewis, *Lament for the Molly Maguires* (New York: Pocket Books, 1964), p. 3.
2. Nathan Glazer and Daniel Patrick Moynihan, *Beyond the Melting Pot* (Cambridge, Mass.: MIT Press, 1963), pp. 241–42.
3. Ibid., p. 260.
4. Ibid.
5. Dick Hubert, "The Duluth Experience," *Saturday Review*, 27 May 1972, p. 55.
6. Ibid.
7. Thomas Sowell, *Black Education: Myths and Tragedies* (New York: David McKay, 1972), pp. 283–86.
8. Urie Bronfenbrenner, "The Psychological Costs of Quality and Equality in Education," *Child Development* 38 (1967): 912.
9. Oscar Handlin, *The Newcomers* (Garden City, N.Y.: Doubleday Anchor Books, 1962), p. 47.
10. Thomas Robert Malthus, *An Essay on the Principle of Population* (New York: E. P. Dutton, 1933), 1:chaps 1, 2.
11. Thomas Sowell, "Sismondi: A Neglected Pioneer," *History of Political Economy* (Spring 1972): 80–82.
12. Lester C. Thurow, *Poverty and Discrimination* (Washington, D.C.: Brookings Institution, 1969), p. 2.
13. Ibid., pp. 130–34.

INDEX